This book introduces an approach to mental health that dates back 3,000 years to an ancient body of Jewish spiritual wisdom. Known as the Connections Paradigm, the millennia-old method has been empirically shown to alleviate symptoms of stress, anxiety, and depression. After being passed down from generation to generation and tested in clinical settings with private clients, it is presented here for the first time to a wide audience.

The idea behind the paradigm is that human beings, at any given moment, are either "connected" or "disconnected" across three key relationships. To be "connected" means to be in a loving, harmonious, and fulfilling relationship; to be "disconnected" means, of course, the opposite. The three relationships are those between our souls and our bodies, ourselves and others, and ourselves and God.

These relationships are hierarchal; each depends on the one that precedes it. This means that we can only connect with God to the extent that we connect with others, and we cannot connect with others if we don't connect with ourselves. The author, Dr. David H. Rosmarin, devotes a section to each relationship, and describes techniques and practices to become a more connected individual. He also brings in compelling stories from his clinical practice to show the process in action.

Whether you're a clinician working with clients, or a person seeking the healing balm of wisdom; whether you're a member of the Jewish faith, or a person open to new spiritual perspectives, you will find this book sensible, practical, and timely, because, for all of us, connection leads to mental health.

David H. Rosmarin, PhD, is an assistant professor in the Department of Psychiatry at Harvard Medical School, and director of the Spirituality and Mental Health Program at McLean Hospital. A prolific researcher, Dr. Rosmarin has authored over 50 peer-reviewed scientific publications, numerous editorials/book chapters, and over 100 abstracts. His clinical work and research have received media attention from ABC, NPR, *Scientific American*, the *Boston Globe*, the *Wall Street Journal*, and the *New York Times*.

Endorsements for *The Connections Paradigm*

"A leading voice in the psychology of religion and its application to mental health problems, Dr. Rosmarin has given faith-based providers an entirely new language for how to intertwine spiritual, interpersonal, and mental health domains in the interests of clinical care. This innovative volume shows how ancient Jewish teachings on the relation of body and soul can be combined with a broad array of modern evidence-based approaches to psychological care, from exposure to experiential acceptance, from nutrition to interpersonal compassion. There is a significant body of science showing that embedding evidence-based intervention into a spiritual journey is a powerful combination for people of faith, but providers need a more general approach that stands one step above the details of particular religious commitments. Filled with clinical examples, this book radiates kindness and empathic concern, and its use of 'body and soul' could be effective with a wide range of people of faith."
—**Steven C. Hayes**, PhD, originator of Acceptance and Commitment Therapy, author of *A Liberated Mind*, and Foundation Professor of Psychology, University of Nevada, Reno

"Dr. Rosmarin has done a great mental health service for the general public. With so many today beset by anxiety and depression, and tiring of modern answers that feel superficial, *The Connections Paradigm* offers a profound, centuries-old method to relieve mental distress, enhance life's most important relationships, and achieve genuine peace of mind."
—**Harold G. Koenig**, MD, professor of psychiatry and behavioral sciences, Duke University Health Systems, and director of the Duke Center for Spirituality, Theology and Health

"*The Connections Paradigm* is not only timely, but Dr. David Rosmarin's careful attention to its rich tradition alongside its practical relevance for each of us is a gift. I am truly grateful for how well he unpacks these three critical forms of connection—*Inner Connection, Interpersonal Connection*, and *Spiritual Connection*—with such clarity alongside the relatable stories he weaves throughout this book!"
—**Holly K. Oxhandler**, PhD, LMSW, associate professor of social work and associate dean for research & faculty development, Baylor University's Diana R. Garland School of Social Work

"Infused with the warmth and wisdom of Judaism, this book offers a deeply thoughtful psychological and spiritual guide for those seeking greater connectedness within themselves, with others, and with God. Drawing on poignant stories from his own clinical practice, Rosmarin illustrates how a 'connections paradigm' can foster transformations among people facing the full range of psychological problems. This book will deepen the practice of many providers and the lives of many clients."
—**Kenneth I. Pargament**, PhD, professor emeritus, department of psychology, Bowling Green State University, author of *Spiritually Integrated Psychotherapy*

"David Rosmarin has compiled a thoughtful and relatable guide to help us reconnect with our body and soul. He shares practical instructions that are supported by theory, case studies and ancient Jewish spiritual teachings to show that we can live more fully when we are truly connected to all our parts. *The Connections Paradigm* is good for the body, mind, and soul."
—**Sharon Salzberg**, author of *Lovingkindness* and *Real Change*

"Jung famously claimed that every patient he treated over age thirty-five needed in the end to find a spiritual outlook on life. In *The Connections Paradigm*, mental and spiritual health are beautifully intertwined, and Jewish wisdom becomes a stabilizing and uplifting force in an often dark and confusing world."
—**Rabbi David Wolpe**, Max Webb Senior Rabbi, Sinai Temple

"Written in a lucid and graceful style, and full of applicable case studies, this book turns out to be an authoritative statement on the importance of spirituality in mental health. I highly recommend *The Connections Paradigm* either as a self-help guide or as a blueprint for interventions by mental health professionals. The cure for human suffering lies in healing the brokenness in a divided self, conflict in relationships, and separation from God."
—**Paul T. P. Wong**, PhD, C Psych, president of the International Network on Personal Meaning

THE
Connections
Paradigm

THE
Connections Paradigm

Ancient Jewish Wisdom
for Modern Mental Health

DAVID H. ROSMARIN

TEMPLETON PRESS

Templeton Press
300 Conshohocken State Road, Suite 500
West Conshohocken, PA 19428
www.templetonpress.org

Set in Janson Text LT Std 10.5/15.5 by Westchester Publishing Services.

This paper meets the requirements of ANSI/NISO Z39.48-1992
(Permanence of Paper).

ISBN: 978-1-59947-550-9 (paperback)
ISBN: 978-1-59947-551-6 (ebook)

Library of Congress Control Number: 2020947487

A catalogue record for this book is available from the Library of Congress.

Printed in the United States of America.

21 22 23 24 25   10 9 8 7 6 5 4 3 2 1

*In honor of my parents, Ian and Pam Rosmarin,
for investing so much in my Jewish education.*

CONTENTS

Introduction

The Context

By all standards, modern Western society is wealthier than any other society in history. The developed world enjoys unprecedented technological advancement, with broadband mobile communication, global positioning satellite navigation, lifesaving medical technologies, and many other innovations that improve and lengthen our lives. Yet, with so many blessings that previous generations never even dreamed could be possible, modern societies are experiencing unrelenting mental health decline.

According to the Harvard Medical School National Comorbidity Survey (NCS), the lifetime prevalence of mental disorders in the United States is 57.4 percent (more than one in two).[1] There were over forty-seven thousand suicides in the United States in 2017, making it the tenth-leading cause of death overall and the second-leading cause for individuals under thirty-five years of age.[2] Young Americans are much more severely affected by mental health problems than were their predecessors. The National Comorbidity Replication Survey—a study conducted by Harvard Medical School to assess the national prevalence of psychiatric disorders—recently reported that individuals aged eighteen to

---

1. "Lifetime Prevalence of DSM-IV/WMH-CIDI Disorders by Sex and Cohort," Harvard Medical School, accessed September 21, 2020, https://www.hcp.med.harvard.edu/ncs/ftpdir/NCS-R_Lifetime_Prevalence_Estimates.pdf.

2. "Suicide and Self-Inflicted Injury," Centers for Disease Control and Prevention, accessed September 21, 2020, https://www.cdc.gov/nchs/fastats/suicide.htm.

twenty-nine are more than twice as likely to have an anxiety disorder and nearly four times as likely to have a mood disorder as
individuals over sixty.[3] In March 2020 the world began suffering
from a coronavirus pandemic, and our emotional and behavioral
responses have been nothing short of extreme. Our rampant stress
and anxiety created a run on household goods due to stockpiling,
and almost toppled the financial markets after years of growth.
In short, the state of mental health in the United States today lies
somewhere between abysmal and catastrophic.

History of the *Connections Paradigm*

When I was in college, these trends in mental health decline
created two pressing questions in my mind. First, why are
Americans—the most privileged people in history—experiencing
unprecedented mental health decline? Second, what can be done
to reverse these trends and restore our society to a state of psychological well-being? These questions led me to pursue a career
in clinical psychology, and I was blessed to spend twelve years as
a student and trainee under the supervision of some of the bright-
est minds in the field. I emerged from my academic training with
substantial knowledge of mental disorders and the skills to effectively treat them, but my years of study provided neither compelling explanations for America's mental health crises nor plausible
strategies for combatting them.

Since its early years, and particularly in recent decades, mental
health science has made significant progress in distinguishing psy-

3. K. R. Merikangas, J. P. He, M. Burstein, S. A. Swanson, S. Avenevoli, L. Cui,
C. Benjet, K. Geordiades, J. Swendsen, "Lifetime Prevalence of Mental Disorders in
U.S. Adolescents: Results from the National Comorbidity Survey Replication–
Adolescent Supplement (NCS-A)," *Journal of the American Academy of Child & Ado-
lescent Psychiatry* 49 (10): 980–989. doi:10.1016/j.jaac.2010.05.017.

chological disorders and treating them, but we have learned little about the key ingredients to achieving a fulfilling life. Evidence-based therapies used by therapists across the world help countless patients recover from the dire depths of mental affliction each year, but mental health professionals mainly focus on returning their patients to a state of baseline functionality, not to a satisfying and fulfilling sense of contentment. This makes sense, because most patients come to therapy in the midst of a mental health crisis, so therapists focus on reducing the most pressing negative symptoms, such as anxiety, depression, or psychosis, rather than setting goals to help their patients achieve optimal functionality after the crisis subsides. However, after treatment, many patients are left with the same questions, which more than a few of them explicitly ask their therapists: Is *not* having a full-blown psychological disorder the best I can hope for in life? Am I missing out on a greater happiness that hovers just out of my reach?

I continued searching for solutions to modern society's mental health decline—and more broadly to the greater question of how to live a happy and fulfilling life—during my early career as a clinical psychologist. Then, a decade ago, I started to find compelling answers very close to home. As an Orthodox Jew, I've experienced the tremendous mental health benefits of a religious life since childhood. I pray every day, and I cannot imagine how significant a loss I would experience if that were to stop. Many other core obligations of my Orthodox Jewish life foster a deep sense of gratitude and fulfillment, which incidentally brings me into contact with other spiritually oriented people, who humble me and deepen my faith. Observing the Sabbath provides me with a full day each week to disconnect from daily stresses (and from technology), enabling me to refocus on what's most important in my life: my relationships with God and my family. This not only has immeasurable effects on my ability to manage stress but also gives me a weekly opportunity to reflect on my actions during the previous week and assess their impact on my family, friends, and personal and even professional goals. The emotional benefits of dedicated religious practice have always been clear to me, and as I began seeing patients as a therapist in training, it was clear to me that many of my patients who lacked religious structure in their lives nevertheless wanted to benefit from spirituality-oriented therapy. But I found few established frameworks through which spirituality could be applied in the therapeutic process.

It was during my second year of college that I initially met Rabbi Leib Kelemen, my beloved rabbinic mentor from Jerusalem. On a whim, I decided to go to Israel on a three-week summer program, and he was one of the many lecturers. However, unlike most of the other talks I attended on the trip, I remember his remarks vividly. He spoke about his personal journey from secularity to Orthodoxy when he was a young man living in Los Angeles, and how the entire purpose of life is for love and connection. I was immensely inspired by his warm and enthusiastic approach to Judaism, but even more by his core message. In fact, the concept that love is our core purpose on earth was so inspiring to me that immediately after the talk I decided to propose to my wife! Over the following years, I was fortunate to persuade Rabbi Kelemen to teach me individually, and over time I learned more and more about his worldview regarding the centrality of love and connection to human thriving. This perspective as well as Rabbi Kelemen's guidance was a major factor in my decision to become a clinical psychologist.

In 2008 I flew to Jerusalem to meet with Rabbi Kelemen in order to discuss the problems I was observing. The world was in need of a widely relatable spiritual approach to mental health that could simultaneously explain *why* our blessed society struggles so much and provide *practical solutions* to help people flourish. Without so much as batting an eyelid, Rabbi Kelemen took a small Hebrew text from the hundreds in his many bookshelves and formally introduced me to the *Connections Paradigm*. I realized right away that this was the source of the core message I learned from him years earlier. Over the following days, as we learned the Hebrew text together and my wonderful mentor patiently answered my many questions, it became clear what I had stumbled across: an ancient Jewish spiritual teaching that offered practical solutions as well as an explanatory framework to address the modern world's growing mental health problem. Over the subsequent weeks, months, and years I soaked up whatever I could in order to know and understand this paradigm and to harness its profound depth and breadth within my personal and professional life.

Rabbi Kelemen learned about the *Connections Paradigm* from his mentor Rabbi Shlomo Wolbe, who in turn had learned it from his mentor Rabbi Yerucham Levovitz, who had learned it from his mentor Rabbi Simcha Zissel Ziv, who had learned it from his mentor Rabbi Yisroel Salanter, who had inherited it from previous generations of rabbis in an unbroken chain of oral tradition stretching back to the divine transmission of the Torah on Mount Sinai over thirty-three hundred years ago. It was first formulated in modern Hebrew print by Rabbi Wolbe, in a book entitled *The World of Connection (Olam Ha'Yedidus)*, which was the book that Rabbi Kelemen had plucked from his bookshelf during our meeting in 2008. According to Rabbi Wolbe, our universe is composed of two parallel realities: the *World of Connection*, characterized by love, harmony, optimism, and compassion, and the *World of Disconnection*, characterized by fear, self-centeredness, and isolation. Depending on our behaviors and the perspectives we choose to foster, we exist in only one or the other reality at any given time. Our experience of life is entirely dependent on which reality we choose.

Over time, I have noticed many distinct features of the *Connections Paradigm* that set it apart from every other conceptualization of the human experience I've encountered in my secular training as a clinical psychologist. First, although the paradigm demonstrates significant concurrence with the most prominent schools of modern psychological discourse, it was developed wholly in the context of Jewish spiritual thought by rabbis with no formal academic training. Rabbi Wolbe and his intellectual forebears were so heavily engrossed in Torah study that they neither received any formal university education nor spent any significant amount of time outside of religious study halls. Yet, the *Connections Paradigm* possesses a profoundly deep and broad understanding of human thought, behavior, and emotion—one that is simpler yet more comprehensive than any school of clinical theory that I have studied in secular academia, and one that is now echoed by many findings within the clinical science literature that modern psychology has now identified. Furthermore, the paradigm provides a practical framework to help people not only recover from severe emotional distress but flourish and thrive as healthy people. When we are in love, not only are we protected from distress but we feel truly happy and energized and can flourish. By contrast, modern clinical psychology seeks only, as Sigmund Freud wrote, to deliver patients "from hysterical misery to common unhappiness."[4] What I found *most* compelling about the *Connections Paradigm*, though, is that it can promote thriving and contentment for all people—regardless of their religious beliefs or views.

I have now studied the *Connections Paradigm* with Rabbi Kelemen for over a decade, spanning most of my early career as a clin-

---

4. Sigmund Freud and Josef Breuer, *Studies on Hysteria* (London: Hogarth Press, 1895), 305.

ical psychologist. While my understanding of the paradigm continues to grow and evolve over time since I am very much a novice in the world of ancient Jewish spiritual wisdom, it has profoundly affected my personal perspectives on life and my approach to therapy. In addition to learning the concepts and methods of the *Connections Paradigm* from Rabbi Kelemen, I started to incorporate its teachings into my clinical methods and have been able to evaluate its effects on my patients. This sharpened my understanding of both human psychology and the paradigm itself. Then, a few years ago, I approached Rabbi Kelemen with a proposal to create a clinical treatment manual for the *Connections Paradigm* that would distill its profound perspectives into clear and easy-to-follow behavioral recommendations for my patients to implement in their day-to-day lives. Rabbi Kelemen and I had long discussed how potentially powerful the *Connections Paradigm* could be if only it were made comprehendible for readers without a background in rabbinic scholarship, so he was eager to assist with the project. And so I began organizing the paradigm into its respective parts and components in order to clarify for others how it can be used in their own lives, as well as in clinical practice. The program I created with Rabbi Kelemen's assistance was formally used with over seventy individual patients in a group format, and I have also drawn from the material with countless other patients in the courses of individual psychotherapy.

This Book

Two years ago, Susan Arellano and Angelina Horst from Templeton Press approached me with a request to author a text describing a Jewish approach to mental health. I initially hesitated, since I am not an expert in ancient Jewish wisdom by any means, but I ultimately decided to proceed since it seemed a wonderful

God-given opportunity to take the next steps in my lifelong journey to study the *Connections Paradigm*. At the same time, readers must be aware that given my nascent understanding of the paradigm, the pages that follow may contain errors and omissions. I accept full responsibility for any such issues in transmitting this knowledge to readers. Given that I am still finding my way through the deep and vast practical implications of ancient Jewish wisdom for modern mental health, the writing process was not an easy one. I therefore worked closely with my own student cum friend Sean Carp, whose support and assistance were invaluable and in fact necessary to bring this volume to fruition. Equally invaluable were input from and the careful editing of my wife, Miri Rosmarin—my life partner who has taught me more about the worlds of connection than she could ever possibly realize.

The present text culls from the treatment manual I previously created based on the *Connections Paradigm* under Rabbi Kelemen's guidance. It attempts to bring the material to life by illustrating how I have applied the paradigm's principles and practices with patients from my caseload over the past several years. In some cases, I was fortunate to consult with Rabbi Kelemen directly about clinical issues at hand, but in most cases I simply did my best based on my own limited mastery of the paradigm. All case descriptions in this book are composites of multiple cases that have been revised to protect patient confidentiality and reflect general concepts.

The ultimate goal of this book is to convey the core concepts of the *Connections Paradigm* and describe concrete skills to facilitate and maintain connection in the three domains put forth by the paradigm: *Inner Connection*, *Interpersonal Connection*, and *Spiritual Connection*. The book is divided into three sections, each of which is made up of five chapters. Each section covers one of the three domains of connection, and individual chapters focus on specific concepts and strategies to create closer relationships between body and soul, us and others, and us and God. Throughout the book, explanations of theoretical underpinnings and case study illustrations are followed by practical instructions for applying the *Connections Paradigm* in daily life, in order to improve one's outlook and well-being. Each chapter therefore concludes with an exercise specific to the chapter teaching. I fervently hope and pray that in addition to providing some inspiration, this text will serve as a practical guide for people experiencing emotional distress, and for the clinicians who help them, so all of us can inculcate and build more connection in our lives.

As we will see in the pages that follow, connection is the basis of all human fulfillment. In fact, according to the *Connections Paradigm*, connection not only is a practical tool to achieve well-being but is at the heart of every person's spiritual purpose: to connect fully with our own spirits, with other people, and with God. Perhaps for this reason, connection is inherently challenging to create and maintain. Keeping focused on the goal of connection is challenging when we are grappling with mundane daily concerns, even more so for members of a society that tends to undervalue spiritual connectedness and prioritizes productivity over relationships.

A final word before venturing forward: it is important to think of connection in all three domains (*Inner Connection*, *Interpersonal Connection*, and *Spiritual Connection*) as a lifelong project. Therefore, this book illustrates how to *begin* to use the *Connections Paradigm* to increase connection in daily life. I encourage readers to think of the process not as a way of achieving improvement in mental health or increased spirituality, but rather as a way of *embarking* on a path to living a more connected life. This path begins with small steps, but as we will find, even modest movements toward connections can yield profoundly positive effects on our emotional states.

Overview of the *Connections Paradigm*

The *Connections Paradigm* can be summarized as follows (figure 1):

1. As mentioned briefly above, each human being dwells in one of two worlds at any moment in time: the *World of Connection* or the *World of Disconnection*. Each world is characterized by one of two states; the *World of Connection*, also called the world of love, is defined by interconnectedness, compassion, generosity, and bravery, while the *World of Disconnection*, also referred to as the world of fear, is defined by separation, isolation, resentment, fear, and anxiety. Our emotional states throughout all life circumstances are entirely dependent on which world we choose to reside in.

2. Connection involves the convergence of two complementary and opposite entities, in three domains: (1) between body and soul (*Inner Connection*), (2) between individual human beings (*Interpersonal Connection*), and (3) between humans and God (*Spiritual Connection*). By contrast, disconnection involves a separation or estrangement of any of these entities.

3. These three domains are hierarchical: our relationship with God is constrained by our relationships with others, and our relationships with others are constrained by the degree to which we maintain inner connection. Healthy interpersonal connections form on a bedrock of body-soul connection, and these two domains in turn provide

FIGURE 1 Overview of the *Connections Paradigm*

This program is predicated on a spiritually based paradigm for understanding human emotion called *Worlds of Connection and Disconnection*. Here is a brief summary of the paradigm.

1. At any moment in time, human beings dwell in one of two worlds:

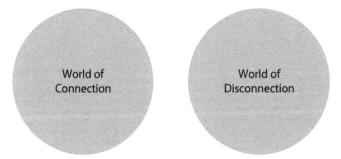

2. Connection involves the coming together of two complementary and contrasting entities. By contrast, disconnection involves their separation or estrangement. This occurs in three central domains or levels: body and soul (*Inner Connection*), us and others (*Interpersonal Connection*), and us and God (*Spiritual Connection*).

3. The three levels are hierarchical:

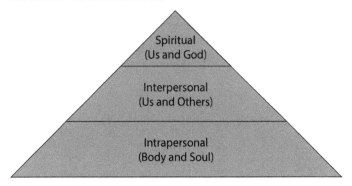

4. At each level of connection, there is a giver and a receiver. Connection occurs when one entity provides for the other, which in turn accepts its gifts.

a foundation for developing a relationship with God. By contrast, it is impossible to sustain spiritual connection without interpersonal or inner connection.

4. In each domain of connection, there is a giver and a receiver. Connection occurs when one entity provides for the other, which in turn accepts the contribution.

CHAPTER 1

Introduction to *Inner Connection:*
Body and Soul

Inner Connection involves connection between the body and
the soul. Of the three domains of connection, *Inner Connection*
is the most fundamental, yet it is the most abstract and thus the
most difficult to describe. Interpersonal dynamics are readily
observable as they occur among tangible bodies in real space, and
even those who do not engage in prayer or other acts of spiritual
reflection usually have some sense of what it means to relate to
God or an infinite spiritual existence. But *Inner Connection* is
vastly harder to grasp because it occurs in the mysterious inner
realm where souls and bodies meet. While this enigmatic setting
blurs the line between two distinct elements and leads many of us
to perceive ourselves as unified, monolithic entities, according to
the *Connections Paradigm*, we are actually made up of two complementary and distinct parts.

Rabbi Moshe Chaim Luzzato, the great eighteenth-century
Kabbalist, wrote that the division of each person into a body and
soul should not be regarded as an abstract metaphor but as a lit-
eral description of the human condition. A human being is made
up of two discrete elements. Reflecting this conception, the common Hebrew greeting *Shalom Aleichem*, which literally means
"peace unto you," is phrased in the plural even when it is used to
address an individual. In fact, there is a common custom among

scholars of Jewish mysticism to greet individuals with the double saying "Shalom, Shalom," which is an explicit double greeting of peace unto the two entities of the body and the soul. Notably, Judaism is hardly the only faith or philosophical system to recognize human duality. Various interpretations of body-soul dualism, or a similar concept termed "body-mind dualism," have been discussed by Christian theologians, Platonic philosophers, and perhaps most famously by the French Dutch philosopher Rene Descartes.

The distinction between body and soul becomes clearer when we consider the significant differences between them (figure 2). The body is composed of physical matter, which can be directly observed by the senses, and it is motivated by wants and needs that pertain to its ability to thrive in the physical world. It needs food, sleep, mental stimulation, physical activity, various kinds of social engagement, and sexuality. The body's needs are simple, but they can quickly become critical when they are not met, so it seeks to satisfy them to the greatest extent possible in the shortest amount of time. It is disinclined to forgo its needs for any amount of time even if doing so temporarily will guarantee its long-term security. It is impressed by size and numbers, and it has little regard for beauty. It cares for other people only to the extent that they can satisfy its needs.

The soul is a vastly different creature. It is nonphysical, existing in a realm beyond conscious perception, and interacting with physical reality only through its worldly counterpart, the body. Love is its highest ideal, so when it comes to connection with God and other people, it is much more eager than the body. It has little regard for the physical pleasures that the body enjoys, and even finds them repulsive, but it can learn to appreciate the body's physical beauty and the elegant simplicity of its needs. It focuses on long-term achievements that carry spiritual meaning such as

FIGURE 2 **Contrasting the Body and Soul**

Human beings are composed of two complementary entities: a body and a soul. According to the *Connections Paradigm*, body and soul thrive when they get close and stay close to each other by creating intimacy, love, and connection. To this end, body and soul have complementary and opposite qualities, and they connect in complementary and opposite ways.

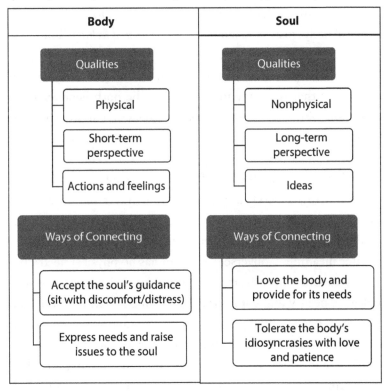

Body	Soul
Qualities	**Qualities**
Physical	Nonphysical
Short-term perspective	Long-term perspective
Actions and feelings	Ideas
Ways of Connecting	**Ways of Connecting**
Accept the soul's guidance (sit with discomfort/distress)	Love the body and provide for its needs
Express needs and raise issues to the soul	Tolerate the body's idiosyncrasies with love and patience

closeness with God and other souls. Its goals can rarely be met in a short period of time, but lacking any physical needs, it is perfectly suited to forgo gratification for as long as it takes. It is even willing to sacrifice its body's own needs, sometimes even its body's life, for the sake of another person or a higher cause. One can easily imagine why the body and the soul do not make the easiest partners.

Perhaps the most significant difference between the body and soul, however, is that they speak mutually unintelligible languages until they each develop the requisite sensibilities to understand each other. Due to its lofty spiritual perspective and noncorporeality, the soul speaks an abstract language of *ideas*, whereas the physical body speaks the language of *actions and feelings*. The soul's ideas can engage the body and become part of its own goals only after they are distilled into clear, unambiguous behavioral guidelines that the body understands to be both beneficial and achievable. Furthermore, the soul's intellectual approach needs to penetrate the heart in order to truly impact the body.

Although the soul and body have many differences, they have several significant similarities. Though spirituality is primarily the soul's domain, the body also benefits from prayer and spiritual reflection because, when it understands its role in the soul's higher goals, it can come to value itself as an important component of a greater meaning. Conversely, the soul has no physical needs, but it derives satisfaction from the physical activities that allow it to cultivate beauty and connection. Most important, the body and soul share one essential purpose: to get close and stay close to each other in a symbiotic and mutually beneficial relationship.

Whether or not we realize it, much of our daily lives involves navigating the divergent wants and needs of the body and soul. Perhaps we can understand this better when observing children. Kids are especially prone to disconnection because connection requires time, sustained effort, and wisdom, and kids are typically impatient and improvident. For instance, as we will discuss further in later chapters, a connected soul helps its body adhere to a diet that facilitates health, productivity, and clarity of thought. But kids usually prefer to eat whatever is tastiest when they are hungry, because without guidance from their souls, their bodies choose to freely eat whatever is most appealing. Children also have little regard for time and like to do what is most enjoyable at any given moment. While adults strive to develop stable, achievable career goals, the noncommittal soul of a young boy may want to be a firefighter on one day, a truck driver on the next, then an astronaut, and so on. Such imaginal play is of course an important part of childhood development, but it reflects the turbulent relationship of the child's soul with its material counterpart, its fickle body. The child's body is motivated to do what it views in the moment as important, and it does not work together with its soul in a connected relationship to achieve its goals. Consequently, most children have little hope of achieving high levels of connection until they mature. And unfortunately, the tendencies toward disconnection that characterize childhood often persist into adolescence and even adulthood, causing spiritual unfulfillment and emotional distress for years or even decades.

I first discovered the universal significance of body-soul conflict in psychological distress during my PhD studies. I was working as a therapist in training at a state-funded clinic in Bowling Green, Ohio, and studying the *Connections Paradigm* with Rabbi Kelemen over the phone whenever I had the time to do so. The clinic primarily served underprivileged communities, and many of my patients were seeking clinical professional help for the first time after enduring unremitting hardship and emotional struggles for many years. One patient was a survivor of childhood sexual assault who started coming to the clinic in his early twenties. He was struggling with drug abuse and had recently tried to take his own life. After his suicide attempt, he continued to struggle with severe depression, but he promised himself and his family that he would live and stay off drugs no matter how difficult his life continued to be. Quite literally, his body was running amok, and I had the honor of helping his body recognize the benefits of heeding his soul's guidance. There was also a woman who had such intense post-traumatic stress disorder from growing up during the Nicaraguan Contra War that she woke up screaming from nightmares almost every night. She had three teenage children at home and worked fifty hours a week to support them while pursuing a nursing degree online, all the while contending with debilitating flashbacks and exhaustion and depression due to insomnia. In her case, her soul was pushing her body to the brink, and I had to encourage taking a much softer and gentler approach of relating to herself. I had another patient who had fallen into alcoholism after being paralyzed from the waist down in a work accident. He was severely depressed because he could not imagine any worthwhile future, and he could not imagine getting through a single day without liquor to numb his physical and emotional pain. For him, the problem was twofold: his soul had not validated his body's loss or provided appropriate guidance in the wake of the accident, and his body was turning away as a result.

To be clear, all of these and many other patients presented with clear clinical diagnoses that generally gradually responded well to secular treatments that I was learning in college, and it was deeply satisfying to help them improve. In many cases, I found that secular approaches facilitated the body-soul connection, albeit without explicitly referring to the body or the soul. But in many other cases, individuals were not presenting with clinical diagnoses, and the treatments I was taught to provide were not effective. Some individuals came for help with mild anxiety or depression, but truthfully they were seeking help in sorting out, or simply discussing, which direction to take in life. These were hardworking people with immense responsibilities that they were, for the most part, handling with unbelievable finesse. They did not come to treatment to cure some crippling disorder, but rather with the hope of gaining a higher perspective on how to make life decisions. In past generations, they might have sought the guidance of their parents or even clergy instead of psychological treatment, but many of them did not have close relationships with their families or religious leaders. Furthermore, within their social circles, they wanted to appear fully competent and content, and the therapy room offered a safe place where they could confide in someone outside their social sphere that they were feeling lost in life. This was initially a difficult role for me to fill. I had spent my postsecondary education in classrooms studying diagnostic models and evidence-based approaches to treatment, with excellent professors who had taught me how to treat severe psychological distress; but in all my training I was never taught how to make greater meaning of life circumstances or provide guidance for life direction. More centrally, many of my patients simply wanted to be inspired and were seeking my advice, and all I could offer them was a sympathetic ear, which, to me, felt pathetically insufficient.

Between classes, clinical research, and therapy sessions, graduate school was perhaps the busiest time in my life, but I made time to study the *Connections Paradigm* with Rabbi Kelemen by phone. During one of our discussions he noticed that I was preoccupied, and he asked me what was on my mind. "Some of my patients are making progress," I said, "but others are seeking life direction and, to be honest, that is outside my skill set as a psychologist. My clinical supervisors keep telling me to stay the course, but I really feel like something is missing from the approach I'm being taught to use." Rabbi Kelemen is a well-rounded thinker with a general understanding of clinical psychology. We had long discussed the potential of spiritually oriented treatments to improve patient care, but I was still in the early stages of learning how to incorporate religiosity into clinical practice. He suggested that the patients I was struggling to help could benefit from spiritually oriented therapy, and specifically the *Connection Paradigm*. "So your patients don't have full-blown mental health disorders," he said, "yet they are clearly struggling. Some are looking for meaning or direction. That only happens when one's body and soul aren't getting along. Sometimes the soul struggles against the body's limitations, and other times the body doesn't accept the sage counsel of the soul." I knew that my mentor was referring to the *Connections Paradigm*, and I decided to take his advice seriously. After we spoke, I thumbed through my session notes and began to conceptualize them in terms of *Inner Connection*, trying to identify the body-soul conflicts that were contributing to my patients' distresses. Things were starting to come together.

In my second year of graduate school, I met Sharon, one of the most memorable and significant patients of my career. She was an undergraduate at Bowling Green University and was considering a career in social work, but was plagued by self-doubt and disorganization. At the beginning of our first session, I asked Sharon, as I always ask new patients, why she was seeking help. Being somewhat familiar with clinical terminology, she told me flatly, "I am not interested in being diagnosed." She said that she had had a bad experience with a psychiatrist during high school who misdiagnosed her with depression within five minutes of their first session and sent her home with a prescription. "I was never depressed, and the antidepressant didn't help me. In fact, I felt worse after I started taking them. And by the way, that session was only thirty minutes and he gave me prescription slips for a three-months' supply. At our next session, which was just fifteen minutes, I told him the meds didn't work so he just upped my dose, handed me some slips, and sent me home. I kept taking them for a while because my mom wanted me to. She said he was a doctor so I should trust him. But they never worked, and the whole thing was a complete waste of time. So, I don't want you to tell me I'm depressed or anxious or whatever. The truth is that I don't even meet clinical criteria for anything. I am just feeling lost and don't know what to do."

"I see," I responded. "Do you know why I chose you?" she asked.

"I beg your pardon?" I asked.

"The office let me choose, and there are six other therapists here. I chose you because I knew you were a rabbi," she responded.

"I'm not a rabbi," I said.

"Oh, well I knew at least that you are religious. I saw you wearing a yarmulke in your picture. I respect Judaism," Sharon said, and added, "I'm religious too, Catholic. It's very important to me, and I don't think anyone could understand my problems if they don't believe in God. It's a shame that so many psychologists and social workers are atheists nowadays. I blame Freud."

This conversation was my perfect opportunity to begin discussing the *Connections Paradigm* with Sharon. She listened enthusiastically as I explained the core concept of connection in general, and body-soul connection in particular. Her eyes welled up with tears of happiness during this session, and she smiled broadly. Her only comment was as follows: "It's a tragedy that most therapists don't bring up spirituality. My goal is to make the world better. I don't want money and I know I won't be happy until I find my calling. Right now, I am leaning towards becoming a social worker, but I can't make up my mind. I have a lot of baggage and bad habits that are holding me back. A spiritual approach is exactly what I need."

Over the next few sessions, Sharon shared that she had a difficult childhood in Youngstown, Ohio. Her father left the family when she was six, and shortly afterward her mother turned to alcohol. The family struggled to make ends meet. "I have a younger sister and brother, 13 and 16, and they're still at home. My mom is in no condition to take care of them; she can't even take care of herself. I love her and she did a lot that I'm grateful for. She took me to church and she never hit me or even yelled at me. She's very loving. But she gave me some bad habits too." Sharon shared that she started drinking in high school to cope with stress. While her drinking never got out of control as it did for her mother, it did have consequences. One night during her junior year, Sharon was so inebriated she ended up in a one-night stand with a total stranger. A few weeks later she realized she was pregnant, and she terminated the pregnancy without telling anyone. "Even at the time I was so conflicted, but I felt like I had no other option," she told me. "I didn't even tell my mom, and she still doesn't know. I had my whole future ahead of me and my mom always prayed that I would get out of poverty. But to this day, I don't know if I did the right thing. I'm not sure I'll ever get over it. That was when I went to the psychiatrist," she told me. "My mom saw I was struggling and sent me to my doctor, who made the referral. But obviously, pills were not going to alleviate my inner struggle."

In our sessions, I encouraged Sharon to facilitate conversations between her body and soul: for her body and soul to speak with each other on a regular basis. Sharon's body was encouraged to tell her soul her regrets, fears, hopes, preferences, wants, desires, and anything else on her mind. Her soul was encouraged to patiently listen, validate her feelings, and provide guidance when a clear path was evident. Sharon was encouraged to have these conversations daily for just two or three minutes.

"So, you want me to speak to myself?" Sharon asked when I introduced this idea.

"Not exactly. Remember that according to the *Connections Paradigm* your body and soul are separate entities. I'm encouraging them to speak with each other," I replied. "Part of the goal is for you to recognize each and every day that you have a soul to go to for help, and also that you have real material and emotional needs. That duality is something all human beings need to recognize about themselves."

"Am I supposed to do this in public? People are going to think that I'm crazy," Sharon said with a smile.

"That's a good point. . . . It's fine to have body-soul conversations when your body and soul are alone with each other," I responded.

"Ok. What should we speak about? And how long should these conversations be? This is a nice idea, but practically speaking what should it look like?" Sharon asked.

"Great questions. Your body and soul should speak about anything and everything. Ideally, the two of you should be like best friends. Have your body open up to your soul, and have your soul comfort your body and guide her if she has ideas that may be helpful. In any relationship, closeness is built by conversing about various topics and exchanging ideas and people recognizing that they are important to each other. This is the exact same, just inside yourself instead of with someone else. As for length of conversations, how about we aim for at least four volleys per day— each statement back and forth, from body to soul and back again, is one volley."

Sharon tried the body-soul conversations in session with me watching. At first, she blushed and smiled awkwardly, and even remarked "this feels really weird." But after a few tries she got into it, and something amazing happened. Sharon's body started talking about her abortion, how afraid she was, and how she had no one to go to. She started to cry and tell her soul how she felt so ashamed for getting drunk and "knocked up" by someone she barely knew, and that she felt so distant and alone from anything spiritual. Then she spoke about her guilt for having terminated her pregnancy, while sharing that she felt she had no other options and even to this day she feels in part that it was the right decision. Sharon cried as she spoke, and I just stood back and waited for what would happen next. After several minutes, Sharon's soul spoke back by saying she understood her body's pain, that her father's leaving the home created a situation that was just so stressful for all, and that having a mother who struggled with alcohol abuse created a risk for Sharon's drinking. Sharon's soul said that she wished she had stepped in and provided more support and guidance for her body before drinking had led to bad choices. Her soul also said that whether or not abortion was the right decision, she understood Sharon's reasons for terminating the pregnancy. Almost instantly, Sharon looked as if an enormous weight had been lifted from her shoulders. She dried her tears, gave me a big smile, and that was the end of our session.

Throughout the following weeks, I encouraged Sharon to have more body-soul conversations about various topics, including her vision to improve the world, the specifics of what she wanted to accomplish, the true extent of her monetary and other material needs (which turned out to be somewhat more than she initially thought), and her emotional "baggage," including her tendency not to trust others, her struggles with disorganization, and her relationship with God. Each week during our sessions, Sharon would share with me some highlights from what her body and soul had discussed in the previous week. It was a transformative experience for Sharon, and also for me as a therapist, since I saw the power of the *Connections Paradigm* in real-life terms. Sharon and I worked on other aspects of *Inner, Interpersonal*, and even *Spiritual Connection* together. But these aspects of the *Connections Paradigm* were still crystalizing in my mind, so body-soul conversations were the primary tool we used in therapy. On the whole, twelve weeks after her first session, Sharon had a new lease on life. She was noticeably less tense, significantly happier, and less disorganized since she did not have the day-to-day distractions of self-doubt and regret. Most of all, Sharon found the direction she was looking for: she was feeling much more confident that a career path of social work was the right one for her.

While Sharon's disconnection centered on the events of her past, the disconnection of many Americans I have counseled comes more from a pernicious disdain for their own bodies. Whereas Eastern cultures place a high emphasis on somatic mindfulness, Westerners in general tend to see biological necessities like eating and sleeping as inconvenient barriers to achievement. Most of the high achievers I have treated practice a form of misplaced asceticism in which they take pride in denying themselves healthy meals and adequate sleep for the sake of productivity. For many of them, their disconnection becomes a feedback loop: the soul becomes increasingly critical and demanding of the body as it breaks down from lack of care and struggles to do its job; and then when the body fails due to a lack of support, the soul disconnects further with criticism and sometimes even punishment or further deprivation. Perhaps this is worse in the northeastern United States where I reside and practice, but it seems to me that our society has unfortunately built untenable ideals of working excessively, "wasting" as little time as possible on meals, staying up late to work, and seldom taking vacations. All of these are self-imposed sacrifices that the body is expected to make for the sake of progress. This leads to mass inner disconnection and ironically undermines the very goals we strive for by making it harder to succeed. Indeed, by the time many of my patients come to treatment they are often in a state of total dysfunction and self-loathing over the failure of their impossible work regimens. And unfortunately, many of us are very good at concealing our dysfunction, so we give off an image of perfection; this only propagates and perpetuates the danger since others don't perceive the downsides of relentless work schedules.

This unfortunate tendency was perfectly manifested in Adam, an advertising agency executive I treated several years ago. Adam seemed wildly successful by all appearances, but privately he was falling apart because his soul was laying his body to waste. Adam worked twelve-hour days six days per week, and when I met him, he had not taken a vacation of more than two days in several years. In fact, he relished in working on statutory holidays so that he would have fewer social distractions and get a lot of things done. One year, he even went to work early on Christmas Day, which his wife never forgave him for. When he came to treatment, in the throes of an exhaustion-induced quasi-psychotic hypomanic episode, he was totally clueless to the fact that his unrelenting schedule was contributing to his rapid cognitive and emotional decline. "We're dealing with big accounts and sometimes there is urgent work to be done," he would say in his defense, but it seemed like Adam always treated his work as if it was urgent. And perhaps it was. He had a demanding and well-paying job that, up until recently, he had performed extremely well. His work ethic was admirable, but he took it too far, and by the time he came to treatment it was threatening to rob him of everything he had accomplished.

For Adam, busyness was an addiction, and he could never get enough. In fact, the hypomanic episode—a period of abnormally elevated mood and activity—that brought him to therapy had similar features to those experienced by stimulant abusers, and it had a similar cause. Adam could not get enough of productivity. In addition to his professional responsibilities, he was a board member of a nonprofit medical research organization dedicated to a rare genetic disorder that one of his nephews suffered from. The board met once a month, but there was other work to be done on a weekly basis, much of which Adam volunteered to do even though he could have delegated it to one of the nonprofit's several paid employees. Worse, Adam never took the time to enjoy his ample salary. His work schedule was simply too intense. His soul clearly appreciated the fact that he was a competent member of society who devoted his extra time to hard work and important causes. In fact, on some level his body enjoyed the stimulation of constant activity. But Adam's body was being pushed far beyond its own limits and starting to break down, since he was denying many of its most critical needs. Needless to say, Adam's family life was in disarray. He barely saw his children, who were getting older and would soon be moving on to college. His wife resented being his perpetual afterthought, and Adam feared they were on the verge of divorce, which he knew he could not withstand emotionally given his recent bout with hypomania. "I'm not really happy with Charlotte right now, but I don't want us to split up. I'm afraid that she does. I used to be able to keep her content, but I know she won't stay with me if I continue this way." Adam was especially concerned that his wife would want to separate if his symptoms ever became impossible to conceal, which seemed like a real threat. To make matters worse, Adam's aggressive schedule was making it difficult to get the help he needed. Even in the midst of a hypomanic episode, therapy had not been his priority and he rescheduled our first meeting no less than three times due to work responsibilities. Later he even told me that he almost changed his mind about coming to his first session when his symptoms briefly improved, but then he decided to come because they became worse and began affecting his work again.

"I'm concerned about you, Adam," I said during our first session. "Everything you're describing could get worse, a lot worse, if you keep working yourself to the bone. I'm concerned that your marriage could fall apart, you could lose your family, and if that happens you will lose your job."

Adam stopped in his tracks. "I could lose my job?" he asked.

"Of course. Do you expect that your work performance will continue if you cannot function emotionally?" I asked. In my mind, I kept hearing Rabbi Kelemen's voice saying, "Body-soul connection is the foundation of our relationship with others and with God. It is necessary for a person to accomplish anything in life."

"What do I need to do?" Adam asked.

I wasn't sure how to proceed. Was Adam going to understand the details of body-soul connection? Was he going to start having body-soul conversations each day? Adam was not particularly religious or spiritual. In fact, when I asked during the initial intake if he was interested in discussing spiritual matters in treatment (as I do with all patients), he said no. So, I decided to take a more subtle approach.

"Adam, what are some of your body's needs?"

"What do you mean?" he asked. Perhaps I should have seen it coming that Adam would not understand.

I rephrased the question: "All human beings have physical and emotional needs. What are some of yours?"

"Well, I need sleep, and a balanced diet, and I like nice clothing. I should probably take breaks each day. I love Charlotte and my kids, and if I didn't work so hard I would want to spend time with them. What does this have to do with me losing my job, though?" Adam responded.

"It has everything to do with your job! I would like you to make all of those a priority. I'm very concerned that you are on the edge of a cliff and if you don't back away and start taking care of yourself, you're going to plummet."

Adam seemed to get it. "Are you telling me to take a vacation?" he asked.

"That would be fantastic, actually. Is that possible?" I asked with some excitement.

"Technically it's possible. I have months of vacation time saved up," Adam responded.

"Well then yes, let's start with a family vacation. Next week!" I said.

"Are you serious? I have so much to do." Adam was starting to freak out a bit.

"You will always have a lot to do if you start enjoying life, Adam. But if you don't, I'm concerned you're going to have more time on your hands than you know what to do with."

Adam was clearly uncomfortable with the idea of taking time off, but he agreed to do so and followed through. Needless to say, Charlotte and his kids were thrilled that Adam was taking a break. Similarly, many of us have high ambitions and like to rush to complete our greatest possible achievements as quickly as we can. Our souls want to help others and change the world, and our bodies are ready to serve. And that's not a bad thing. But we must remember that *Inner Connection*—a balanced relationship between body and soul—is the crucial first stage of achieving full connection, and the foundation of everything else that we do.

As we will continue to learn in the next few chapters, *Inner Connection* can be summed up as follows: the soul is a mentor, the body is its student, and their connection is dependent on our heeding these maxims: (1) the body should accept the soul's guidance even when it is hard to do so, (2) the body should make an effort to raise issues and express its needs to the soul, (3) the soul must provide for the body's physical and emotional needs, and (4) the soul must not put inordinate pressure on the body in pursuit of its own goals.

Exercise 1: Building Body-Soul Communication

Communication is essential to any relationship, and *Inner Connection* is no different—soul and body need to communicate with each other in order to build their connection. Our first exercise, therefore, is to write a dialogue between the body and the soul. The only materials needed are a pen, a piece of paper, and a chair to sit in. The exercise can be practiced in almost any environment, such as on a commuter train or at a desk during a lunch break, but it is best performed in a quiet space without any distractions. It is important to take a minute or so to relax and detach from other concerns before initiating this exercise. It may be beneficial to close your eyes before starting the exercise. Once you are sensitive to your thoughts and feelings, it's time to start writing. There is only one rule regarding the content of the conversation: no self-criticism. Aside from that, your body and soul should communicate freely about their wishes, needs, fears, goals, and visions. This simply involves examining our bodily needs in relation to our soul's higher goals by calmly reflecting on feelings and recording them.

It can initially be difficult to distinguish the voice of the soul from that of the body, but this becomes easier with regular practice. The body's needs are generally expressed as feelings such as happiness, sadness, anxiety, or anger and also physical sensations such as tension, tiredness, hunger, and the like. Conversely, the soul's needs generally relate to long-term progress, self-improvement, spirituality, the well-being of others—in short, "bigger picture" aspects of life. For instance, the soul and the body may discuss a conflict arising from the soul's desire to work while the body is feeling bored or unrested. Or the soul may have a vision for the body that seems unattainable and creates pressure and stress. However, neither the body nor the soul should disparage its counterpart. The goal of the dialogue should be conflict resolution with mutual empathy, understanding, and love.

You can take as much or as little time as you like for the exercise, but it is best to allow both the body and the soul at least one opportunity to express its feelings to its counterpart. A good way to begin is for the soul to check with the body how it is feeling. For best results, do this exercise once per day. To keep things simple, the soul should initiate the dialogue, opening with a friendly inquiry such as "how are you?"

Here are some very basic sample conversations.

EXAMPLE #1

SOUL: How are you feeling?

BODY: Tired, hungry. Not sure I can work more.

S: I'm sorry.

B: I'm also upset because I did not get much done today.

S: We did our best and you're working hard. I should have made sure we got more sleep. We'll have sushi for dinner because I know it's your favorite, and we'll watch TV.

EXAMPLE #2

S: How are you?

B: Energized! I'm excited to go to the party.

S: I've been thinking. It's already ten o'clock. We haven't been sleeping enough and we have a big day tomorrow. It would be better if we go to sleep early.

B: Ten o'clock?! I can't fall asleep that early. I want to socialize.

S: But if we go to the party, we won't get home until one in the morning. We don't have to go to sleep right away, but we can't stay out that late.

B: Okay, but I'm going to be bored if I don't go.

S: Well, how about we play the computer chess game you like and read a little before we go to sleep?

It's worth noting that these conversations may feel a bit silly at first. But if we're in tune with our own internal conversations, we might hear ourselves say things like "I'm so clumsy!" after dropping a plate, or "I'm such an idiot" after a breakup. In other words, it's not abnormal to speak to ourselves in derogatory terms. But as noted above, the purpose of this exercise is to build *Inner Connection*, so it is critical that we do not lapse into self-criticism. Reproaching either the body or the soul for not performing to its potential is a recipe for disconnection. Always stay positive and give the body and soul adequate time to express themselves. And remember that the body's shortcomings are not its fault; it needs to be guided by a wiser soul so that it can achieve its potential.

I treat disconnection-related distress every day in my clinical practice. Recently, for instance, I met with a new patient, Brian, a twenty-year-old college student who is struggling with social anxiety that can clearly be conceptualized as a conflict between his soul's desire to interact with other people and his body's desire to play it safe and stay at home. He wants to date and make new friends, but he finds introductions so frightening that he tends to avoid them altogether. I recommended the above exercise to him, and he wrote the following dialogue:

S: How are you?

B: Embarrassed and ashamed. I want to be likable. I want a girlfriend.

S: Me too. I want to connect. I'm lonely.

B: Why do I always choke up and get nervous?

S: I don't know, but I'm trying to make it better. And I'm always here for you.

B: Thanks. At least we have each other.

As we will discuss later in regard to *Interpersonal Connection*, relationships feed the needs of both the body and the soul. And both body and soul need to cooperate to make relationships work. The soul is responsible for empathizing with and loving others, and the body's duty is to come across as confident and nonthreatening so that others feel comfortable. Brian's body instinctively avoids the kinds of situations that have caused it distress in the past, and reacts to such situations as if it is in actual danger. His soul is used to becoming frustrated with his body for failing to do its part to build relationships, and in harshly reproaching his body, his soul reinforced the body's misgivings and enhanced his social anxiety. Now that he has embraced the *Connections Paradigm* and started practicing this exercise, he is starting to realize the importance of mutual affection between the soul and the body and he is fostering connection.

As Brian's soul develops patience, it can use its ideal perspective to become his body's best teacher. Part of the reason his body reacts so strongly to anxiety-provoking social situations is that it is desperate for human contact and wants to find friends and a partner as soon as possible, but his soul is not prone to the same sense of urgency. It can reassure his body that healthy relationships will develop with time as long as the body keeps making the effort. The soul does not operate on instinct; thus, it has a more discerning memory than the body and can remind the body that past failures, especially those that occurred when both the body and the soul itself were less mature, do not make future failures inevitable. Perhaps most importantly, his soul can make a commitment to love the body no matter what happens. This will lead the body to develop a greater appreciation for the soul, then resolve to keep trying to build relationships for both of their sakes. Brian's case perfectly illustrates why *Inner Connection* is a prerequisite for *Interpersonal Connection*, which we'll discuss further in later chapters.

CHAPTER 2

Inner Connection Part I: Accepting the Soul's Guidance

Inner Connection is dependent on the body yielding to the soul's guidance, which does not come naturally. Without patient instruction, the body will not accept the soul's recommendations or even realize that it has a wiser partner in the soul. As a result, an unguided body will waste time and compromise its health in pursuit of fleeting pleasures; but a body that acts based on a well-meaning soul's recommendations can enjoy long-term and meaningful happiness. For connection to be possible, and for a human being to function optimally, the body must come to a crucial understanding: it is the muscle, and the soul is the brain.

Rabbi Kelemen has an excellent analogy for this concept involving the two main components of a computer: the memory and the microprocessor. The primary function of the memory is to store information, whereas the microprocessor centrally directs the computer's operations. Thus, the computer's memory is like the body; it acts as the physical component in the dynamic. The microprocessor is like the soul, in that it directs the memory to perform its function. The memory does all the heavy lifting to make the computer work, but if it were to defy the processor and step in to make its own executive decisions, the computer would malfunction. Similarly, our body needs to know its place in subordination to the soul in order for our body-soul system to operate optimally.

In the present day and age, though, our bodies have good reason to mistrust our souls: as in the case of Adam in the previous chapter, our souls tend to overwork, denigrate, and abuse our bodies. From the vantage point of the *Connections Paradigm*, depriving oneself of sleep to be more productive, starving oneself in order to lose weight, forcing the body to work beyond its limits, and denying the body enjoyable recreation in order to devote all its time to productivity are all examples of pushing the body too hard. The result of this overzealous approach, which may even be well intentioned, is that the body learns not to trust the soul regarding its physical needs, and it ends up making its own unilateral decisions, to the detriment of both parties. In reality, no matter how willful or robust the soul, it can do nothing without the body, and the body needs to be taken care of all the time in order for a person to thrive. The soul must therefore recognize the body as a separate living entity that is worthy of having a real relationship with, and not simply a robot for the soul to control. Conversely, the body needs to feel loved, not used or just maintained. If the body is being manipulated to its own detriment, it will crumble physically and emotionally; and in more extreme cases, the body will spitefully eschew connection altogether. Rabbi Kelemen taught me that when the body is resistant to accept the soul's guidance, it is usually because it has been or is being neglected or abused—rebellion always occurs in a context.

Sometimes, though, it seems that the soul is doing its best to be a patient mentor and the body continues to be obstinate. The reality is that the body can become tired, bored, or hungry and has an endless list of needs. This is not the body's fault, and it is not something that should be judged or frowned upon, however, because the body is like a child. The soul is the adult in the relationship, tasked with making the partnership *with their own body* work. The soul sometimes needs to push the body to work harder, but if it does so beyond a reasonable limit—creating significant long-term resentment from the body—disconnection will always follow. The soul must stay patient in cultivating connection even when the body is stubborn and resistant to work. With the soul's sustained encouragement, each body is able to transcend limitations in service of goals that benefit both itself and the soul.

For instance, I once treated the heiress of a large fortune—an artist who never had to work and had a vibrant social life—who was among the most depressed patients I have ever had. Angeline's depression was difficult to treat because she took impeccably good care of her body; her chef and personal trainer pampered her daily with customized exercise routines and curated meals. She was therefore frustrated with self-disappointment, since she "could not get it right" in her art studio. When I introduced Angeline to the *Connections Paradigm*, she quickly assumed that her body was simply resistant to her soul's guidance even though she generally took decent care of herself. "I spend most of my time taking care of myself. I quit drinking and smoking years ago, and I drink fresh juice and work out every day. I'm kind of a health freak these days. But there's a lot that my soul wants to accomplish, but I'm so tired and lazy." This response clearly demonstrated the problem: Angeline's soul was providing for her body not as an act of love and kindness but as an investment. She ultimately just wanted her body to be a better artist, and her body felt deep resentment toward her soul as a result. Indeed, when we discussed Angeline's daily routine in more detail, it became apparent that she did not sleep nearly enough, she ate significantly less than the recommended amounts from national nutritional guidelines, and she exercised more frequently than was healthy. It was also widely apparent that she resented her body's limitations and that she was attempting to control her body as opposed to developing a loving and caring internal relationship. I eventually learned that this pattern was common in her family: Angeline had witnessed her mother push herself so hard that she ultimately took her own life. Ultimately, Angeline's depression started to lift once she realized the virtues of gentle, loving self-encouragement toward meaningful goals. Her body loved to paint and was self-motivated, so a soft approach was all that was required.

However, even when the soul *truly* takes care of the body's needs, the body has a natural tendency not to accept the soul's guidance immediately. This too is not anything to judge or frown upon; rather, it simply provides an opportunity to cultivate a mutually loving relationship between body and soul. This was initially a problem for a young man I recently saw for therapy. Jacob was a twenty-seven-year-old single male who presented with moderate anxiety and depression and stated he was "deeply unsatisfied" with his life trajectory. Working as a self-employed e-commerce merchant, he was financially successful but felt as though he was stagnating. "I've been dating," he said, "but not really seriously. Mostly to satisfy my mother. I want to get married but I want to make something of myself first. Money isn't the issue. I want to have a respectable career that I enjoy. I try to be more productive, but I find myself wasting a lot of time." Jacob said he made "enough" income as an online vendor, but he did not particularly like his work. "My father and two of my brothers are doctors," he told me. "They are what you would call 'type A' personalities. They work nonstop and they always know what they should be doing. My older brother manages to work 36-hour shifts and spends time with his kids on the weekends. Even my younger sister is finishing up her master's degree in social work and she just got engaged. She's three years younger than me and she's got it all figured out! I only need to work for about four hours a day to make ends meet, so I spend most of my time just sitting at home doing nothing."

Jacob estimated that he wasted six to eight hours every day, and sometimes more. I asked him how he spent that time, and he said he smoked cigarettes, napped, read "random" books and magazines, watched TV shows, and made plans for his future that he never followed through with. "Sometimes I get really motivated and I start making solid plans," he said. "Like last month I decided I would go for an MBA, so I ordered study books for the GMAT and started perusing an application for business school. But then it said you need to have recommendations from professors, and I haven't spoken to any of my professors for years. I immediately felt so frustrated, because I felt like all my efforts could just be a waste of time if I can't get the recommendations. So, I haven't even opened the GMAT books. They are sitting on my kitchen table. Now I don't even know if I want to get an MBA. I'm a mess."

Jacob was also overweight and generally not taking care of his health. In addition to smoking, he subsisted almost entirely on junk food all day until dinner, at which point he overate. "That's another reason why I'm not that eager to date right now," he said. "I feel like I need to get in better shape and learn to take care of myself first. No one wants to date me right now because I am totally unhealthy and not really happy, and I don't blame them." In thinking about this case in terms of the *Connections Paradigm*, I came to understand Jacob's distress in terms of a lack of *Inner Connection*: his soul had reasonable ambitions and was not pushing his body too hard, but Jacob's body was simply resistant to his soul's guidance since the latter's approach was so negative. By habitually comparing himself with his siblings Jacob was putting his body down, which made it harder for his body to do the necessary work to thrive. I therefore assessed that the best approach would be to help Jacob focus his body on what it needed to do, in order to focus on being productive versus being self-critical. In our therapy sessions, Jacob was initially uninterested in the *Connections*

Paradigm. "I consider myself to be spiritual, even religious, and I believe I have a soul. But I don't know what it means to have an internal relationship," he said during one of our early sessions. I therefore scaled back my approach by introducing elements of the *Connections Paradigm* into treatment without explicitly describing them as such. For instance, Jacob and I developed a realistic schedule in which he planned out how he would spend each day, starting with sleep, exercise, and nutrition routines. We then moved toward tackling career advancement and increasing Jacob's social engagement.

For the first month, Jacob found his new schedule very difficult to follow. "I am so annoyed with myself," he said, "because you're keeping me accountable to my own commitments and I'm hating every minute of it. I know this is the right approach, but it's making me so uncomfortable. What is wrong with me? This is exactly what I want in my heart of hearts, so I should be happy." I responded by clarifying that I had zero expectations that Jacob's body would be happy with the new schedule, at least not for several months. I further illustrated that Jacob had spent several years without much "real" responsibility beyond managing a job that came easily to him. He had not been sitting with distress or pushing or investing in himself, and he had started to lose faith and confidence—hence, the reasons for his anxiety and depression. Therefore, I conveyed that it was perfectly reasonable for Jacob to have a difficult adjustment period to this new approach. "Oh, this is a normal response?" Jacob asked. "Completely," I responded. The immediate emotional effect on Jacob's face was palpable, and we both somehow knew that he was at a turning point. Indeed, after that discussion, things picked up for Jacob in a big way. He went to bed early, woke up early, cut out virtually all junk food from his diet, started an exercise routine, and reconnected with his professors from college to discuss the merits of pursuing an MBA.

At the end of our treatment, Jacob inquired about the *Connections Paradigm*, and I explained to him the following perspective on his treatment: Jacob's soul was kind and patient and made one crucial mistake of not holding his body accountable. Conversely, his body was not evil or even misguided but simply became complacent (if not a bit lazy) after years of habitually choosing comfort over happiness. The resulting inner disconnection created a sense of concern within Jacob's soul (mild anxiety) and a lack of fulfillment and confidence for his body (mild depression). The corrective steps for Jacob to take were for his body to heed his soul's guidance and get with the program, so to speak. Summarizing this approach, I said, "In a nutshell, think of your body as someone worthy of being taken care of. And think of your soul as someone worthy of listening to." Jacob was stunned with this analysis and immediately asked for Rabbi Kelemen's contact information so he could share his story with him directly. Jacob and I ended treatment shortly thereafter, but he sends me updates from time to time. Most recently, Jacob informed me that he has not smoked in six months, that he is retaking the GMAT and hopeful to start his MBA next year, and that he is dating a wonderful young woman.

While the conceptualization of cases in terms of "body and soul" is rarely found anywhere in modern psychology and certainly not in clinical practice, the above clinical approach is not entirely new. As the famous American psychologist William James wrote:

> Everyone knows what it is to start a piece of work, either intellectual or muscular, feeling stale. . . . And everybody knows what it is to "warm up" to his job. The process of warming up gets particularly striking in the phenomenon known as "second wind." On usual occasions we make a practice of stopping an occupation as soon as we meet the first effective layer (so to call it) of fatigue. We

have then walked, played, or worked "enough," so we desist. That amount of fatigue is an efficacious obstruction on this side of which our usual life is cast. But if an unusual necessity forces us to press onward a surprising thing occurs. The fatigue gets worse up to a certain critical point, when gradually or suddenly it passes away, and we are fresher than before. We have evidently tapped a level of new energy, masked until then by the fatigue-obstacle usually obeyed. . . . In exceptional cases we may find, beyond the very extremity of fatigue-distress, amounts of ease and power that we never dreamed ourselves to own—sources of strength habitually not taxed at all, because habitually we never push through the obstruction, never pass those early critical points.[1]

In training the body to follow the soul's guidance, we are all athletes. Seasoned athletes know that an ideal training schedule involves pushing their muscles just beyond their limit each week, but not to the point of injury. This gives their tissues time to repair and adjust to new strains they are contending with, while allowing them to sustain a long-term training plan and ultimately succeed. Similarly, the body can be conditioned to tolerate discomfort as long as it is not pushed beyond its true limits. And if the body is always held in positive regard by a soul that celebrates its achievements, it will progressively become more eager to please the soul and push its own limits.

In another case, a twenty-five-year-old woman came to my office with a moderately severe specific phobia of spiders. Julie would check her bedsheets every night for eight-legged creatures and scan the floor and walls before walking into any room at home, work, or otherwise. When all of Julie's friends went on a camping trip last summer, she stayed home. "I just can't!" she said during our first meeting, referring to having any potential contact with

1. William James, *The Energies of Men* (New York: Moffat, Yard, 1907), 7.

spiders. Julie was exceptionally bright and highly social. She had no other psychiatric diagnoses except for her phobia of spiders, and day to day she had a very high level of functioning. But she knew in the pit of her stomach that her spider phobia was holding her back in life. "I don't understand why I am so afraid," she said. "I never had a bad experience with spiders—I've never been bitten or anything like that. And I know there is nothing to be afraid of. They are just so scary though! And gross. I feel really repulsed by even the idea of touching a spider. Blech!"

The most widely supported treatment of specific phobias is called exposure therapy. A variant of cognitive behavioral therapy, exposure therapy is a process through which patients are gradually encouraged to face their fears head on. In Julie's case, the approach would involve first looking at still pictures of spiders, then moving on to videos, then looking at live spiders in containers, and finally handling live spiders of different sizes. Exposure therapy would also target Julie's avoidances: she would be discouraged from checking her bedsheets, walls, and floors and encouraged to go into "high risk" spider areas, such as the woods. Julie knew about this approach before coming to my office, and she was not surprised. "I want to do it. I really do," she said. "But I just don't know if I can sit with that level of distress. What if I die?" she asked. "Then you die!" I responded, with a big smile, quickly clarifying that I have never lost a patient. Julie clearly appreciated the comic relief and reiterated her question with less exaggeration, "What if I can't take it, though?" I calmly responded by saying that exposure therapy indeed involves sitting with distress—a lot of distress—but it is always done with the patient's full knowledge and consent. "We would never throw a spider onto your lap or take you by surprise. We will coach you to push well past your comfort zone, but you will always be in control of the process," I explained.

Julie signed up to begin treatment with one of my clinical fellows the next day. As planned, they started with still images of spiders. Some of the pictures were admittedly gross. "Oh my God, I didn't realize a spider could be that big!" Julie commented regarding a twelve-inch Goliath Bird-Eater. Julie winced at many of the pictures and was encouraged by my fellow to keep looking at them until her distress dissipated on its own. "It gets easier over time, right?" my fellow asked Julie. "Yes, but it's still very hard," Julie remarked. Indeed, it was hard. Julie had opted to do intensive treatment for her phobia, involving ninety-minute exposure therapy sessions two or three times each week for just a few weeks, instead of shorter sessions over a longer period of time. By the end of their first session, Julie was already relatively calm looking at all sorts of still images of spiders; by sitting with her distress, it was already greatly reduced. Two days later, Julie returned to the office for more. "I can't believe I'm doing this," she said as the fellow started to run videos of spiders. Julie was noticeably uncomfortable throughout this session; it was a very hard one for her, and she had tears in her eyes for much of the time. But she was resolved in her heart to overcome her phobia—for her body to learn to sit with distress—and she rose to the challenge. At the end of the session, Julie was sent an email with pictures and videos she had looked at over the past two sessions, and she was encouraged to spend no less than thirty minutes each day reviewing the images. The following week at her next session, Julie was able to demonstrate her mastery of the material. She was only mildly distressed watching the most advanced spider videos, whereas lower-level videos and images did not register at all. "I can see myself progressing and it's amazing. I am still scared of what's to come, but I know I can do it," Julie remarked.

The next session, it was time for in-vivo practice. My fellow arranged for a local spider collector to come to our office with several spiders in containers, including several tarantulas ranging in size from three inches to eight inches. Julie arrived to her session literally shaking. "I saw the spider guy with the bags in the hallway. I really don't think I'm ready for this." My clinical fellow validated Julie's distress and conveyed that it was perfectly natural to feel uncomfortable during any exposure sessions, let alone advanced ones. My fellow also assured Julie that she could go at her own pace and stop the session at any time. Julie started to cry as she said, "OK, let's do it." The fellow went outside to get the bags and brought them inside the room. She carefully unzipped the bags and took out the Lucite containers one by one. Julie immediately looked away. "I know this is hard, but it will be over soon. Try your best to look at the spiders." Julie turned to the spiders and caught a glimpse of the eight-inch tarantula. She literally started to wretch, then turned away. "They are perfectly peaceful and harmless. Allow yourself to feel distress and accept it. The more you fight and avoid, the harder it will be." After a few minutes, Julie managed to sustain her gaze on the spiders. She was still distressed, but her feelings were starting to simmer down. After a few minutes, she even cracked a smile. "I wonder if they have names," she said. Within thirty minutes, Julie was holding the Lucite containers with smaller spiders, working her way up to the larger ones. At her next session, Julie was ready to handle the spiders. She was clearly uncomfortable—not just anxious but disgusted—but she was determined and held on for dear life. By the end of the final ninety-minute session, Julie was handling an eight-inch tarantula (named Charlie) like a pro, and even able to smile for a photo with Charlie.

"That was the most difficult thing I have ever done in my whole life," Julie said during her wrap-up session with me at the end of her treatment, "but I feel so calm and peaceful now. I feel like I could do anything." Our conversation meandered, reviewing

Julie's experience during the sessions, to her satisfaction with herself, and ultimately to the topic of spirituality. Julie remarked that in addition to reduced apprehension about spiders and increased self-confidence, she felt a new sense of inner peace from going through exposure therapy. When I discussed this case with Rabbi Kelemen, he commented as follows: "At the start of treatment, Julie's soul knew that spiders aren't anything to be afraid of, but her body had not yet internalized that message. Through your treatment procedure, Julie was able to bridge that gap. Her soul taught her body—not just theoretically but at a deep emotional and behavioral level—that there is nothing to fear. As a result, Julie's body and soul are more connected. No wonder she is less anxious!"

Rabbi Kelemen once shared with me another point about the importance of the body accepting the soul's guidance: by doing so, the body not only benefits from less distress but also gains incredible opportunity for success. Warren Buffett, one of the most successful investors ever to live, has earned one of the world's largest fortunes with a business strategy that demonstrates a skill for the body accepting the soul's guidance. Buffett relies on a method called "value investing," in which he buys assets that he *believes* are more valuable than standard market appraisals and holds on to them until the market realizes their true worth. This method can be anxiety inducing because it requires Buffett to act in direct opposition to the opinions of the overwhelming majority of investors (i.e., the market). His body is inherently taking on risk by going against common thinking and trusting the decision of the mind. And the markets often take months or even years to realize the value that Buffett originally sees, creating a ripe context for distress. But Buffett is steadfast in his long-term outlook, and he has his body's best financial interest in mind. He remains committed to what he believes is the wisest long-term strategy no matter what. In one of Buffett's famous quotes, he summarizes his approach as follows: "When people are greedy, get fearful. When people are fearful, get greedy." In other words, when people's bodies react to their spontaneous gut instincts to make business decisions, it is best to do precisely the opposite, by carefully assessing the situation and planning accordingly. This soul-based approach to investing can be nerve-racking because the body resists taking such risks, but it tends to pay off in the long run. Buffett's company, Berkshire Hathaway, was valued at $11.50 per share in 1962. As I write this, its price per share has risen to over $300,000, representing a growth of over twenty-five thousand times. Simply put: by accepting the soul's guidance, the body gains incredible opportunity for success.

Exercise 2: Sitting with Discomfort/Distress

Our exercise for this chapter involves training the body to listen to the soul's guidance (figure 3). As mentioned earlier in this chapter, it is often difficult for the body to accept the soul's guidance partially because it can require tolerating some level of distress. Even when the soul meets the body's needs, the body may have a learning curve to accept its guidance. As a starting point for this exercise, identify at least three activities that are distressing, uncomfortable, or even boring but ultimately are important steps toward your long-term goals. These should of course be safe and practical activities, and you should not pick any activities that could realistically impact your safety, physical well-being, or the well-being of others. They should also be realistic in the sense that they do not require the body to work too hard for too long, beyond its current capacity. Resolving to run a marathon without

FIGURE 3 Body Sitting with Discomfort/Distress

When the body avoids discomfort/distress, it is easier in the short term but becomes progressively harder over time.

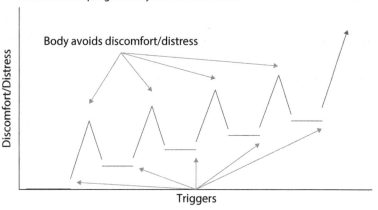

When the body sits with and accepts discomfort/distress, it is more difficult in the short term but becomes progressively easier over time.

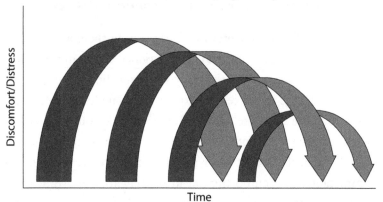

adequate training is foolish and will not facilitate *Inner Connection*. All activities that you engage in for the purposes of this exercise should be productive and beneficial. Here are some options:

- If you often sit down to do work but find yourself wasting time on the internet, reserve an hour in which you will work without taking any breaks to surf the web.

- If you struggle to initiate physical exercise, lace up your sneakers and head outside once a day for a workout.

- If you hit snooze on your alarm clock and oversleep, resolve to wake precisely at the sound of the buzzer every day for a week.

- If you tend to overeat at night, set a reasonable time to stop eating and stick to it.

- If you're afraid of spiders, print a still image of a moderately distressing spider and put it on your wall.

Importantly, after you have engaged in the uncomfortable activity, whether or not your body performed as well as you were expecting or would have liked it to, give yourself a reward. This could be anything from praising your body, telling someone about your accomplishments, or pampering your body with something fun. By repeating this exercise, the body will gradually become more trustful of the soul, and connection and productivity will follow.

It is important to clarify that the goal of this exercise is not to *live* in distress but to learn to *sit* with distress. Some patients who have practiced this have misinterpreted these directions to mean that they should try to endure a low level of distress for long periods of time. The goal here is not to work the body ragged or try to perfect its habits in one shot. It is best to practice this exercise for a limited amount of time and build up your tolerance as your body becomes better able to manage distress. For example, if you are overly concerned about germs, spend just a few minutes each day habituating your body to the discomfort associated with touching things that feel gross. Or if you tend to be overly shy, try to initiate conversations with someone once per day. Most important of all, though, always reward the body after it has worked, whether or not it met the soul's goals or worked as hard as the soul wanted it to. With these steps, over time the body will become better and better at yielding to the soul's guidance, resulting in enhanced *Inner Connection*.

CHAPTER 3

Inner Connection Part II: Loving the Body and Providing for Its Needs

According to the *Connections Paradigm, Inner Connection* isn't just a tool for psychological well-being. Rather, when the soul takes care of the body's needs, it fulfills a divine purpose. In fact, the core responsibilities of the soul in relation to the body can be summed up as follows: love the body, identify its needs, and provide for those needs (figure 4). This is a challenge because we usually think of love as something innate that either comes naturally or doesn't come at all. Furthermore, the soul has an innate sense for perfection that the body can never totally live up to, and it can be hard to love something that is seen as inferior. But as a divine creation, the body is a beautiful entity that can be loved *regardless* of its achievements or potential for success.

The *Connections Paradigm* does not espouse overindulgence of the body or excessive glorification of its form. It simply points out that the body is a wondrous and complex creation of God with immense spiritual potential, and it is inherently worthy of love, respect, and care. It also asserts that each body, along with its soul, has a unique and important mission in this world. To accomplish its mission, the body needs to be loved and cared for, like a parent cares for a child.

Jewish tradition contends that God created physical reality to facilitate awesome spiritual horizons that heaven could never realize without the earth. Souls exist in the perfection of heaven,

FIGURE 4 Soul Loving the Body and Providing for Its Needs

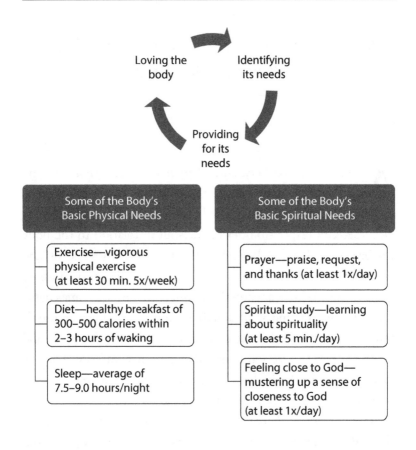

but it is only when they are married to a body that they can perfect the earth and work toward its ultimate destiny. The body, therefore, is of the utmost significance in carrying out God's plan; it is not an ancillary inconvenience.

Part of loving the body is providing for its needs, and some of the body's needs are spiritual. The body ultimately knows that its purpose is connection, and it tends to feel empty and alone without genuine wholesome spirituality. My research at the Harvard Medical School focuses on this very subject: how spirituality is related to mental health. Without getting into too many details, the research has clearly identified that belief in God, regular prayer, spiritual study, and having a connection with a faith community protect against many facets of mental distress. Perhaps for this reason, according to the *Connections Paradigm*, providing for the body's spiritual needs is not only a facet of *Spiritual Connection* but also an aspect of *Inner Connection* as well. When body and soul are connected, the latter recognizes that the former has genuine spiritual needs, and noticing and providing for such needs can unify the pair.

Getting back to our main point, most of my American patients seem to struggle with loving their bodies more than patients who come from non-Western countries. This creates a significant disadvantage when it comes to this aspect of *Inner Connection*. I recently treated a young man who greatly admired Jeff Bezos, Mark Zuckerberg, and other internet tycoons, and he was convinced that they work every hour of the day and are not subject to the same mortal limitations that he is. He said things like, "If only I could restrict my sleep to four hours a night. Then I could really get my career going." Until it started affecting his health and I persuaded him to stop, he used to fast for days on end because he read that Jack Dorsey (CEO of Twitter) recommends doing so because it helps him work harder and sleep less. I don't personally know Mr. Dorsey, or any Silicon Valley executives for that matter, and I cannot speak to their levels of connection or disconnection. But practicing Spartan routines of bodily denial is generally bad practice, especially for individuals suffering from mental health challenges.

A substantial volume of research, including many experimental studies, has linked physical exercise to lower levels of anxiety and depression. Engaging in physical exercise alone—*without any other formal mental health treatment*—has been shown to produce substantial reductions in anxiety and depression, and increased levels of focus, attention, and energy. A balanced diet is also an apparent prerequisite for physical and emotional health. Diets rich in fruits and vegetables, whole grains, fish, and olive oil are associated with lower risk of depression. Clinical research has also demonstrated unequivocally that not getting enough sleep causes or at least exacerbates nearly every mental health problem. To be clear, depression and anxiety can be caused by poor sleep patterns, and attention-deficit/hyperactivity disorder (ADHD) and bipolar disorder are known to be exacerbated by insufficient sleep. In my clinical practice, whenever people experience chronic emotional distress, it seems that poor diet, lack of sleep, or lack of exercise virtually always plays a role. It seems clear, then, that a better route to productivity is not to deny the body of these basic needs but to recognize and prioritize them every day.

A few years ago, I treated a world-class professional ballet dancer who suffered from depression and an eating disorder, both of which were rooted in her dogged insistence on denying her body its basic necessities. Melissa devoted her life to a beautiful art form that provided her with endless inspiration, but she practiced her routines nonstop until she was utterly exhausted and ate fewer calories than would be sufficient to sustain a seventy-pound child. I once asked her point blank how she felt about her body. "We're at war. Everything I want, all of my dreams, are dependent on my body doing what I want it to do, and it doesn't always measure up. That's basically what's been happening recently." Ironically, her response demonstrated a nuanced understanding of the *Connections Paradigm*: she recognized her body's existence as a unique entity separate from the soul. However, she was obviously not able to achieve *Inner Connection* with such an approach. Melissa did not come to treatment to address her eating disorder, but because of depression. She toured the world performing for thousands as a dancer for one of the premier ballet companies in New York. It was her dream, but recently she had been experiencing severe fatigue and anhedonia, finding herself unable to appreciate the beauty of the dance that she had built her entire life around. She did not want to get out of bed in the morning and was practicing her routine alone as often as possible. Her symptoms were compounded by circumstantial anxiety brought on by the fact that her depression was affecting her performance. "I can't work as hard when I feel this way," she told me, "no matter how hard I push myself." She had seen a psychiatrist before coming to therapy, but the medication he put her on made her more tired and less motivated to work, so she stopped taking it.

During her first week of treatment, I explained to Melissa that, typically, behavioral treatment for depression involves going out to exercise and socialize, getting sufficient sleep, doing meaningful work, and eating healthy meals. I told her our best first step would be to make a daily schedule that would include time for all these things. "I feel like I'm already doing all of that," she replied, but that was only partially true. She was certainly getting a lot of exercise at work, but she did not sleep enough, she rarely socialized outside of the dance studio (where she was very competitive with her fellow dancers and not on entirely friendly terms with any of them), and her idea of eating healthfully amounted to eating two or three servings of fruit, a cup of raw vegetables, and a handful of nuts each day. She told me, as if she thought it was healthy for someone in her position, "obviously weight is very important for dancers. I would be out of the company in a minute if I were ten pounds heavier, maybe even five." Although I am sure that ballet dancers are under a lot of pressure to stay thin, I knew Melissa was exaggerating because I had seen patients from her ballet troupe before. She told me she was only eighty-five pounds, so at 5'4", she was well below a healthy weight.

"I'm not body dysmorphic," she said. "I know I don't eat a lot. That's how you stay competitive in the dance world. There isn't a single professional dancer who is overweight." All of this was correct, but Melissa's ideal weight seemed closer to ninety or even ninety-five pounds. Melissa also suffered from a chronic sleep deficit, which she insisted was also an occupational necessity because she needed to practice so much. "You need to repeat a routine at least a few hundred times before you perfect it," she said, "and a typical performance is eighty minutes. Do the math!" Melissa told me that after successful tours, the company went on monthlong hiatuses when her troupe had fewer practice sessions. During those periods she would briefly treat her body better, getting adequate sleep and eating almost sufficiently. This made her feel healthier and more energetic, but as soon as her company returned to a busier schedule she returned to her old habits. She even saw these interim periods as a part of her general discipline, feeling that she could "catch up" on months' worth of sleep and food deprivation in thirty or forty days.

Melissa was insistent that she did not need the eight hours of sleep that I was recommending, and that even seven or six hours was too much. "You are only getting less than five hours, and you are tired and depressed," I reminded her. "I'm telling you in my honest, professional opinion that there is a connection. The research I've seen suggests that the average person your age needs 8.25 hours of sleep each night, with a range of 7.5–9.0 hours. I get that eight hours may not be possible during training season, but if you want to continue to excel at dancing and avoid depression and fatigue, we need to get more sleep." She also told me that she was able to function on her highly restricted diet because the food she *did* eat was very nutritious. "Sure, some people eat a lot of calories without getting proper nutrition, and that's another kind of eating disorder," I told her. "And you might even be getting enough vitamins from the fruits and vegetables you eat. But you are certainly not getting enough calories."

Melissa apparently wanted a quick fix for her depression and did not want to change anything about her daily routine. She told me she had been expecting "talk therapy," in which I would ask her questions about her childhood and she would have revelatory cathartic experiences that would rapidly cure her depression. "My mom has been in therapy for years," she told me. "She loves it and that's what it's like." I told her that I did not think such an approach would be beneficial. "Well then, what do you suggest? Because I'm not ready to do anything you're asking me to do," Melissa replied incredulously. I paused and collected my thoughts, recognizing that what I was about to say would determine whether Melissa would continue in therapy or drop out. I briefly contemplated raising the topic of *Inner Connection* between the body and soul, but recalled that Melissa was not particularly spiritual or religious and I thought she would not respond well to such abstract concepts. I felt a bit overwhelmed and found myself praying silently for divine assistance, and then the following came out of my mouth: "Melissa, you have such incredible gifts and talents. You are beautiful and strong and an incredible, world-class dancer. Don't you see? Your body is worth investing in. She is so special! She has a job to do in this world—to delight audiences with exquisite dancing. Don't you want to learn to support and love her more than you currently do?" Now it was Melissa's turn to pause. She was speechless and started to blink her eyes to hold back her tears. And then she started to cry, "I only wish I could love myself. I don't even know what that looks like." We sat for the next twenty minutes, with Melissa crying and me trying to convey with my gaze that she was inherently special and worthy of love. Our session ended without a word, and Melissa left my office.

I wasn't sure if Melissa would return for our next scheduled session, but she did. She was right on time, as usual, but she was smiling, which was unusual. "Dr. Rosmarin, I thought about it and realized that you are right. I need to love and invest in myself. I'm just terrified that by doing so, my body will become complacent and fat and lazy. That's why I control myself with sleep deprivation, a restricted diet, and an impeccably structured routine. I do think that many of those elements are necessary for me to succeed in ballet—the competition is fierce! But perhaps there is a way for me to develop self-love, while holding myself to a high standard." I was dumbfounded. She got it! Now, the question was, what to do. I filled the rest of the session as best I could, discussing Melissa's newfound insights and exploring her hesitations about self-love. After our session I contacted Rabbi Kelemen for guidance. My sage rabbinic mentor encouraged me to ask Melissa to think about a time that she had made an error and then to express to herself words of forgiveness, consolation, encouragement, and love. I was hesitant to try this approach as Melissa was not particularly religious or spiritual and it seemed overly explicit vis-à-vis the *Connections Paradigm*, but Rabbi Kelemen persuaded me to try, reminding me that Melissa was aware that her body and soul were distinct entities (albeit at war with one another).

Melissa responded extremely well to this approach. "I really screwed up a performance the other day. It was a live rehearsal that my troupe put on for some college kids, but I fell after a cabriole and almost couldn't stand up. Afterwards I was chewed out by two of my coaches and a choreographer. They told me I need to figure out what was going wrong or I'd be out of the company. I was so ashamed, scared and sad." I encouraged Melissa to validate her own sense of embarrassment, fear, and sadness by saying to herself, "Of course you feel that way. Your coaches were really mean and threatening! Anyone would feel that way if such a thing happened." Melissa already looked much better. And then I encouraged Melissa to speak words of encouragement and love to herself. "Can you tell yourself that you are a great dancer, and that you will do better next time, and that you love yourself?" I asked. "I can tell myself that I'm good at dancing and give myself confidence for the future, but I don't think I can say that I love myself—at least not yet," Melissa responded. I decided not to push and allowed Melissa to speak with herself. At some point, she hesitated and then started to cry. Instead of interrupting her, I allowed her to work through the impasse on her own, and then she suddenly said the words "I love you" to herself. The look on her face was one of surprise, but also happiness and contentment that I had not seen since Melissa started treatment.

At our next session, I suggested to Melissa that when she eats food, she could say to herself, "I am proud of you. You are an incredible dancer. And this food is for you, because I love you." Melissa balked at this suggestion, but then I pointed out that she had a very loving heart when it came to others and wouldn't hesitate at all to say such words when feeding someone else. "Every time you take a bite," I told her, "don't think of it as *you* eating. Think of it as you feeding your body, the way a mother feeds her baby." I knew we were making progress when Melissa laughed at what I said. I had never seen her laugh before. "That's really corny," she said. "I don't know if I can speak to myself that way, but I think I get it." Melissa continued to come to therapy with me for nearly a year. Throughout our sessions, she not only developed increased internalized self-love but started taking better care of her body's needs. She would catch up on sleep over the weekends such that her mean average daily sleep came close to seven hours, and her weight increased to just over ninety pounds. Interestingly, Melissa's performance as a dancer improved substantially over this period, since she became less tense and better able to practice difficult positions and maneuvers. Melissa and I terminated therapy approximately a year after starting, when she moved to Europe to pursue ballet in an even more competitive troupe.

To cultivate love for the body, a connected soul should always remember that it cannot accomplish any goals without the body. Melissa's path to connection required her to love herself and stop thinking negatively about her body. It was only once Melissa appreciated her physical capabilities and strengths that she could start to take care of her bodily needs. *Inner Connection* is impossible when the soul maintains that the body is ugly or lazy or incapable or the like, and some people unfortunately find it much easier to curse their bodies than to celebrate them. In my practice today, I encourage patients like Melissa with negative attitudes toward their bodies to verbally praise their bodies every day. Some patients relate to this exercise well, while others find it a bit awkward or ridiculous; but ironically, many in the latter category find it easy to verbally curse their bodies on a regular basis. It is apparently quite common for people to denigrate their bodies for being fat or slow, yet most people find it hard to cheer their bodies on. To make matters worse, *Inner Connection* requires that the soul make the body's needs a top priority over other matters, even when the goals of the soul and the needs of other people seem to be negatively impacted. It is sort of like the emergency instructions you hear before every commercial flight: if the oxygen masks deploy, *put yours on first before helping others.* This is because you won't be able to help the person next to you if you pass out! Similarly, the body will not be able to help other people, or pursue spiritual dreams, if it begins to break down. In sum, the soul must remember that all of its lofty goals are impossible without the existence of the body, as well as its cooperation and hard work.

Of course, everyone experiences times when the soul cannot meet the body's needs. As we learned in chapter 2, sometimes it is beneficial for the body to accept and sit with distress in order to create *Inner Connection*. But even in such circumstances, *Inner Connection* can be maintained only if the soul validates and acknowledges that the body's needs are not being met, and that it is struggling. Imagine, for instance, that you are traveling on business. You have just learned that your connecting flight has been delayed overnight. You cannot afford to stay in a hotel, so you will need to spend the night at the airport. What a stressful situation! On top of the delay and loss of sleep, you will likely not be well rested when you land and could lose an additional day of productivity. This combination of stressors could be a recipe for disaster for the body, unless the soul validates the struggle and conveys sentiments of appreciation and love. Similarly, the soul should do what it can to make the body as comfortable as possible—for example, buying yourself a snack or drink at the airport, buying earplugs to get as much restful sleep as possible, buying a new book to stay entertained, finding a quiet corner of the airport terminal to rest, and canceling appointments for the following day. These acts may seem small and even insufficient, but without them the body will feel unappreciated and uncared for. According to the *Connections Paradigm*, the body wants to feel loved by the soul, and it will be healthier and more compliant the more love and assistance it receives.

To clarify, it's possible that the body may choose to buy a drink or earplugs or a new book or find some quiet on its own, without the encouragement of the soul, and even without any body-soul conversation at all. While there isn't anything inherently wrong with this approach, it fails to capitalize on the opportunity to foster *Inner Connection*. As I have told many patients, there is a difference between the body *taking* a shower and the soul *giving* the body a shower. Either way the body gets clean, but in the latter scenario body and soul become closer in the process. As we will see in regard to *Interpersonal Connection* and *Spiritual Connection* as well, the *Connections Paradigm* puts more emphasis on the process than the behavior or outcome. The same activities can create greater connection or not, depending on what is in one's mind and heart at the time of the activity.

Circling back to validation, an inherent part of loving the body is validating its discomfort and expressing sympathy to acknowledge its burdens. Western culture typically encourages us to tolerate pain and ignore our own suffering while focusing on our goals. Popular aphorisms such as "no pain, no gain" reflect this sentiment. It is true that training the body to become more robust and tolerant of pain is beneficial, as we learned in chapter 2, but it is also important that we are sensitive to the body and supportive of it when it is under stress. There is no shame in acknowledging the body's struggles; in fact, this is an essential part of *Inner Connection*. The soul must be sensitive to the body's struggles and its needs so that it can adequately provide for them.

Exercise 3: Providing for the Body's Physical Needs

The exercise for this chapter is an easy and effective means by which the soul can cultivate love for the body, and the body can feel cared for by the soul. It goes as follows:

1. Choose a piece of food that will provide both sustenance and enjoyment for your body (e.g., fruit, cookies, chocolates, or a drink).

2. Imagine that your soul is giving the morsel to your body as a gift. Be conscious of the fact that the body will appreciate and benefit from it.

3. Eat the piece of food, keeping in mind that your soul is giving a gift to your body.

4. Finally, encourage your body to feel gratitude for the gift it has received from the soul. Try to solidify the body-soul relationship through feeling grateful.

This exercise, which is similar to a popular meditative practice known as mindful eating, should ideally be practiced once per day. Even practicing it for a single bite of one meal per day can make a big difference in cultivating self-love and self-care. The reality is that every bite of each meal can be experienced as the soul giving the body the gift of food to keep it healthy, and the body gracefully feeling loved by the soul in turn. You can do this exercise anytime you eat, to cultivate *Inner Connection*.

CHAPTER 4

Inner Connection Part III: Expressing Needs and Raising Issues to the Soul

E ngagement of body and soul is sometimes achieved through reflective meditational practices, but the latter is insufficient to yield greater body-soul connection. To be clear, sitting quietly and being aware of bodily sensations is a step toward *Inner Connection*, but according to the *Connections Paradigm*, body and soul must engage with each other to be connected. This is because internal communication between the physical body and the spiritual soul is a direct parallel to the way in which we relate to God—both *Inner* and *Spiritual Connection* involve real relationships, just like the domain of *Interpersonal Connection*. One of my patients, a young woman named Rebecca who was recovering from depression, recently discovered her body becoming clearer about its needs as a result of cultivating self-love and self-care. As part of her treatment, I encouraged Rebecca to get more exercise, and she opted for yoga. After several weeks she shared that she felt yoga was "an ideal connections workout" because it amplified her somatic sensitivity and awareness of her bodily needs, and provided her soul with the time and opportunity to recognize and attend to those needs. "Now that I've been doing it for a few months," she told me, "I am acutely aware when my body is hungry, thirsty, tired, getting sick, and the like. And I don't judge myself anymore for having such needs. I simply express them to my soul, and the two of us work towards figuring

FIGURE 5 Body Expressing Needs and Raising Issues to the Soul

Expressing needs: move past negative emotions (e.g., shame, guilt, disgust) and simply describe your need in detail to your soul.

Body's needs

Expression to the soul

Raising issues: here is another exercise that can build body-soul connection. Complete the following steps to engage in a discussion about a current problem.

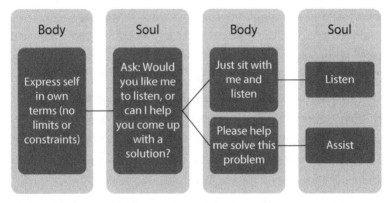

Body	Soul	Body	Soul
Express self in own terms (no limits or constraints)	Ask: Would you like me to listen, or can I help you come up with a solution?	Just sit with me and listen	Listen
		Please help me solve this problem	Assist

out a plan forward. It's a real relationship, just like I have with my friends and my husband."

Along these lines, just as in any relationship, in order for the body to connect to the soul, it must learn to express itself in a clear but gentle manner. This primarily occurs via two processes: expressing needs and raising issues to the soul (figure 5). Expressing needs is most useful for pressing concerns, such as hunger/thirst, relief from pain, or a need for rest. It involves the body actively alerting the soul to its needs. This is not as simple as it may sound, because our bodies, after years of their needs being denied and/or invalidated, often become conditioned to obscure their needs in order not to stoke the soul's ire. Further, it is hard on the body to raise a need to the soul, only to have the latter show insensitivity by getting caught up in lofty goals and ignoring the body's pleas for assistance. Raising issues involves the body engaging the soul in a reflective dialogue aimed at making a key decision. It is a sort of check-in that can be accomplished through quiet internal reflection and discussion and should be done frequently to ensure that the body and soul work together toward common goals. While the body takes the initiative to express needs and raise issues through these internal conversations, the soul must take time to sit patiently with the body and engage in the discussion. Another patient, Deborah, did not have the time to practice yoga but she took to having brief body-soul conversations every day about her bodily needs. "Every morning after brushing my teeth I have a dialogue between my body and soul about the day ahead," she recently said, "and I think it's especially effective at facilitating *Inner Connection* because, previously, I would just ignore my internal cues. Now, even before I start to feel stressed or sluggish, my body tells me what's wrong and what I need to do for her. It's almost miraculous!"

Our body's ability to express its needs and raise issues depends on whether it appreciates what it means to have a soul. This element of the human condition is perhaps best understood in contrast to animals. Every human being has a parental mentor in the soul, while all animals are essentially orphaned bodies without guides. Though animals have a God-given life force and may experience a wide range of emotions, all of their behaviors are driven by instincts and they lack the capacity to plan beyond the immediate future. Even when an animal is collecting food for the winter, it is driven by spontaneous instinctual reflexes rather than a cognitive conception of a future. The reflective capacities of the human soul not only allow for a much longer-term perspective but also facilitate love, hope, gratitude, awe, altruism, and other higher forms of existence that animals are incapable of. More fundamentally, animals' bodies take care of themselves, whereas humans can live with *Inner Connection* and learn to cultivate a real relationship between body and soul. This happens when the soul becomes a trustworthy mentor to the body, and the body seeks the guidance of the soul, especially in times of need.

Further, according to the *Connections Paradigm*, the soul is literally a part of God. As such, when the body develops a relationship with the soul, it gains access to aspects of divine wisdom. When the body raises issues to the soul in a clear but gentle manner, the body can receive guidance from an entity that is calmly detached from worldly distractions and more innately connected to the divine. However, for this to happen, one's soul should not jump into solving bodily problems before taking the necessary time to identify all their facets and the wisest methods for overcoming them. Once the body has expressed concerns, the soul must determine what the body truly wants and needs before proceeding: Is the body ready for assistance? Or does it need more time to make its needs known? The soul must develop the sensitivity to know if it should continue listening to the body or enter assistance mode and try to resolve the body's issue.

I find that many of my patients who engage with the *Connections Paradigm* get overzealous about their ability to sense the needs of their bodies and they try to solve their bodies' problems before discerning them. For instance, Veronica is a sixty-eight-year-old married woman and grandmother of five, whom I treated for chronic stress. She was very enthusiastic about the *Connections Paradigm* and sometimes overeager to solve bodily problems before she had really figured out what they were. Veronica is a retiree who has both chronic health issues and a lot of time to devote to self-care; her body is very "vocal" about its concerns, and she spends much of her day listening to its anxieties. But often it seemed like she missed the mark. "I was feeling tired yesterday," she told me one session, "and I realized my body needed exercise, so I went to the park and had a long hike. I was still tired later, so I think I need to start exercising more. Come to think of it, my body is telling me it's very tired right now." It was a Tuesday, and Veronica had just told me about her very busy weekend that included two doctor's visits and an eight-hour return road trip from a family party in New Jersey. "But Veronica, you had a very hectic weekend. Couldn't your body be tired from that? If so, might more exercise make your exhaustion worse?" Veronica had a very active mind, and she found it hard to sit still. In the past when she practiced raising issues, she usually did it while jogging or cleaning the house. I suspect that these activities distracted her and thus prevented the soul from fully understanding her body's needs. I told her she should try to make more time to mindfully reflect in silence so her body would have an opportunity to raise issues with the soul's full attention. By sitting without doing anything in particular, Veronica gradually became much more sensitive to her body's needs. This was very challenging for Veronica at first. "I want to *do* something!" she said to me during our fourth therapy session. But eventually she understood the merits of calmly and deliberately thinking about her needs, instead of inefficiently putting out fires. As a result, Veronica discovered new needs she didn't know her body had, such as a creative outlet. She eventually began taking watercolor painting classes that benefited both her soul and her body. "It's so inspiring," she told me, "and I feel like it's scratching an itch I never realized or knew that I had."

Many of the body's needs are universal and others that are unique. Further, if you examine all of the body's desires, you may find that many of them seem to serve no practical purpose. For example, your body may get immense satisfaction out of playing board games or eating certain foods that are neither particularly nutritious nor widely appreciated, or your body may be inclined to try something it's never done before. According to the *Connections Paradigm*, this is by design: the body has irrational needs because they offer the soul an opportunity to demonstrate its love. The soul can refine and deepen its love for the body by taking care of its peculiar needs that don't make sense. For example, I recently treated a young professional who came to therapy seeking treatment for his self-diagnosed video game addiction that he did not identify as a bodily need. Kelvin was making strides in his career as a financial consultant, maintained healthy relationships with family and many friends, and was even engaged to be married to a beautiful and ambitious young woman. But he regretted the time he spent playing PlayStation 4 each day, and he did not know how to stop. "I'm an only child, and my parents are immigrants," he told me. "I'm their pride and joy. They worked their entire lives to make my life as good as possible. They never wasted any time and they didn't like when I played video games as a teenager. Now that I live away from home I'm totally out of control, and I'll be very ashamed if they find out how often I play video games. It's such a waste of time." Kelvin's fiancée knew he played video games, but she did not know how often, and he feared that she would call the wedding off if she knew the extent of his addiction. That sounded pretty extreme to me, but I validated Kelvin's concerns and asked him how much he was actually playing. "About a half hour per day after work, about four days per week. Sometimes I play as much as two hours a day on the weekend with friends. It's really out of hand!" This seemed like a perfectly reasonable amount of time for recreation, and I thought Kelvin was being way too hard on himself. As I expected, he had a very rigorous work schedule and his video game time was his only recreation for most of the week.

I asked Kelvin what he enjoyed about playing video games, and he told me that they engaged his mind and allowed him to fully relax like no other recreational activity. I also asked him how he felt when he did not play for a few days, and he told me that he was a little less focused and prone to boredom in other domains of his life. "That means it's a real need," I told Kelvin, "and as such it's not a waste of time at all. You have a tight schedule and your body and mind need some time to relax." I conveyed to Kelvin that it was important for him to be sensitive to his body and give it time to take care of itself. Against my judgment and advice, Kelvin ultimately determined that video game playing should be curbed very slightly, but I was successful in persuading him not to completely exclude it from his life since it was something his body enjoyed. I also persuaded him to stop referring to his video gaming as an addiction and also to speak with his fiancée about the extent of his use. She was, of course, perfectly fine with what he shared with her, and in fact she shared with Kelvin that she had recreational pursuits of her own that took up more time than his gaming. This latter conversation helped Kelvin a lot in becoming more self-accepting.

When a body desires something with no apparent utility, like watching funny videos on the internet or playing with a Rubik's Cube, these wants should not be indiscriminately denied. Repressing the body's inconvenient or unusual wants represents a failing to get beyond one's soul perspective to appreciate the peculiar needs of the body. Furthermore, desires that seem strange may ultimately serve an important function, such as how Kelvin's video game playing helped him focus more on his work even after the game was over. When the soul invalidates the body's seemingly unproductive desires, the body becomes embarrassed and may withhold expressing its needs to the soul in the future. Over time it will lose the self-confidence that allows it to understand its own needs and will ultimately become more difficult to please. Disconnection will follow.

I once treated a devout Catholic woman who, in addition to mild anxiety and depression, was struggling with a marital problem related to a specific bodily desire that she was too ashamed to tell her husband about or even to admit to her own soul, let alone me. Agatha had been married for over twenty years and loved her husband deeply, but she was not totally satisfied with her marriage and could not understand why. "I love him," she said, "and I don't want to be with anyone else or be single for that matter. I just feel like something is missing." I encouraged Agatha to reflect on problems in her marriage, but she could not think of anything she or her husband was doing wrong. They had a strong bond and spent lots of time laughing, confiding in one another, discussing art and politics, and seeing their two adult children as much as possible. I discussed the *Connections Paradigm* with Agatha, highlighting the disparate needs of the body and soul. Since her soul seemed to be satisfied, I recommended that she try being more sensitive to her body to identify what was missing. "Our bodies get in the habit of keeping their needs to themselves," I said, "but keeping them happy is very important to our general well-being. Sometimes our bodies need something that doesn't automatically occur to us. We have to pay close attention to it if we want to be optimally functional and happy." When I made this recommendation, I suspected Agatha may be feeling personally unfulfilled for reasons totally unrelated to her marriage, but by her next session she had come to the realization that her body was unhappy that the physical passion in her marriage had died down. "When we were younger it was so passionate, but now it has been kind of . . . plain for a while," she said. "I can tell a more active physical relationship with my husband is something my body wants, but I guess it's something I can live without." Agatha did not want to leave her husband, but she felt that a more dynamic physical relationship would make her body happy. It might have been very easy for her and her husband to make the changes that would satisfy her body, but even after admitting it to herself and telling me, she was not willing to tell her husband. "It's my upbringing," she said. "In a traditional Irish Catholic family you don't talk about sex, and it's just not proper for a wife to voice those types of needs with her husband. I know it might be good to tell him, but I just can't do it." Agatha never broached the topic with her husband. Her anxiety and depression improved due to other aspects of her treatment, but she struggled to achieve optimal *Inner Connection* because she did not meet her body's particular needs, and she was promoting disconnection by shaming her body for its desire. "I would feel put off if he brought up a sexual complaint with me," she said, "so how can I do that with him? And I'm not even totally unsatisfied. Sometimes it's okay. I guess he just spoiled me when we were young." I tried to explain to her that the body had certain peculiar needs, that it has every right for its needs to be satisfied, and that the soul has a certain responsibility to meet these needs. But despite my best efforts, Agatha was unconvinced. She remained convicted that her sexual desire was too shameful, and she tragically never took the simple steps needed to cultivate *Inner Connection* by satisfying her body, *Interpersonal Connection* by improving her marriage, and *Spiritual Connection* as well. "Frankly," she said, "the whole notion just doesn't jive with my soul."

In some cases, it may be appropriate for the soul to deny the body of a maladaptive or dangerous want. Indulging in pornography, prostitution, or addictive substances is unfortunately a common bodily want that is almost universally harmful, but there are many others. For example, it's not uncommon in the social media age for generations of young people to literally put their lives at risk by climbing to precarious heights, playing chicken with freight trains, or risking electrocution just for a dramatic selfie. And of course, the body often wants to avoid doing activities that are beneficial, such as physical exercise. When such potentially harmful desires arise within the body, they should nevertheless be validated as a starting point and then redirected to a more productive alternative. The reality is that the body is physical, so it's not anything to be concerned about when the body has base physical desires. In fact, one of the biggest concerns for a body that makes hedonistic choices is that it loses its capacity for happiness. This is demonstrated by the fact that many individuals who entertain all manner of hedonistic urges, such as overeating, drug abuse, and sexual overindulgence, eventually report significant dissatisfaction and ultimately experience a desire for greater meaning in their lives. Indeed, in literature, many works depict characters who have all of their physical needs more than met but still struggle to be happy. The philosopher Robert Nozick elucidated this notion in his concept of the Experience Machine, a hypothetical device that offers its users a simulation of total pleasure and freedom from suffering, which most people, according to Nozick, say they would decline. In my own clinical practice, I have encountered countless patients with ample physical comforts who struggle to be satisfied.

When I first met Matthew, a twenty-year-old man who presented with a severe addiction to opiate-based pain medications, he was literally incoherent. Five days later, he emerged from a padded room having gone through the harrowing experience of detoxification, with all its chills, sweats, head-throbs, and even mild convulsions. Matthew shared with me that opiates were just the beginning of his troubles. While he did not presently engage in other forms of drug use, he had tried just about every substance under the sun—including sniffing glue and gasoline for a period as a teenager, which had a demonstrable permanent effect on his cognitive capacities. He did, however, have a very serious sexual addiction, including regular engagement with prostitutes. "The funny thing is that I'm not even enjoying it anymore," Matthew shared with me during an early session, adding "I used to enjoy sex when I had a steady girlfriend in high school but that went 'poof' like almost all puppy love relationships and now I just do it to feel less bad. It's a distraction." As our sessions progressed, it turned out that Matthew did ultimately enjoy thrilling experiences, but that he judged himself very harshly for such needs. "I wish I could be a celibate monk. What do I need sex for?" I explained to Matthew that sexuality was a natural need, like eating and drinking and sleeping, and that it seemed harsh to judge himself for his desires and fantasies. "So, does that mean I should do whatever I want?" Matthew asked. I responded, "No, because I don't think you'll enjoy it as much. But either way, it's one thing to want or need something and quite another to engage in a behavior. I don't see any problem with you exploring your needs and wants at all. They are valid." Matthew was stunned, as if he had never heard of this concept before. He went on to explain that as a child he attended a parochial religious school and was discouraged from even thinking, let alone feeling or acting out, in any manner related to physical enjoyment in general and sexuality in particular. "It sounds like you were actively taught to ignore your physical wants and needs," I remarked, and Matthew wholeheartedly agreed.

In our subsequent sessions, Matthew described the following sequence that led to his getting into drugs and prostitution. After breaking up with his girlfriend at age eighteen, Matthew was filled with intense emotions and didn't know how to manage them. He felt alone, scared, sad, and also a bit angry over some aspects of the breakup. These were all common and normal emotions to feel, but Matthew judged himself harshly for reacting with such intensity. "I didn't understand why I was feeling so bad. It just didn't make sense." From there, Matthew found himself fantasizing about drugs and sexual engagements as a distraction from his emotional pain and also because he found it fun to think about. "But I was so upset at myself for having those thoughts. My inner critic was firing away at me daily, berating me for having intense feelings and lustful drives and impulses," he said. Over time, Matthew's inner tensions built up to the point that the only thing he could think of to ease his pain was to try marijuana. From there, things went downhill very quickly. Matthew became addicted to several substances, including painkillers, and started to act out sexually. Less than two years later, he required detoxification.

In thinking about Matthew's situation under the lens of the *Connections Paradigm*, I came to conceptualize his case as follows: Matthew grew up without a healthy respect for his basic bodily needs. Likewise, his emotional needs were neglected. As a result, when he hit a rough patch in life, he was unable to cope. His soul was unable to validate and care for him in such an acute state of distress, and his body took care of the problem on its own by using drugs and sex to cope with the pain. That approach only led Matthew down a path to nowhere, which fortunately was interrupted by a hospital stay (it could have been much worse). Matthew's path to recovery would require him to accept, validate, and tend to his emotional and physical needs. Of course, substance use and prostitution were not beneficial to Matthew, but his urges and inclination to engage in such activities could be validated and understood by his soul and then redirected to other behaviors. For example,

Matthew could engage in thrill seeking in less dangerous ways, such as going to amusement parks, traveling, and even skydiving. He could also be encouraged to take up distance running in order to benefit from the effects of regular release of endorphins. In retrospect, Matthew's downfall came from his body's failure to communicate clearly and gently about its needs, and from his soul's harsh judgment of those needs. A trusting relationship between body and soul is a cornerstone of *Inner Connection*; the body can be honest only if it feels confident that the soul will understand and appreciate its desires.

Exercise 4: Expressing Needs

Our next exercise involves the body raising an issue to the soul once each day. As discussed in this chapter, the soul needs to give the body opportunities to express its needs and raise issues, by making time to detach from distractions. From there, the body needs to clearly and calmly communicate its needs, preferences, wishes, thoughts, feelings, desires, and more. Just as in a loving interpersonal relationship, the soul can then reflect on how well it has been taking care of the body, and ask the body for feedback and guidance before jumping into action. Importantly for the body, recognizing a need/concern creates a vulnerability, which is inherently uncomfortable. As well, it can be uncomfortable for the soul to listen to the body with patience without intervening, in order to convey concern, respect, and love. This exercise is therefore aimed at training the body to open up to the soul and training the soul to listen.

First, have your body identify one or more of its needs—anything that your body would like, prefer, or want, or something it physically needs to accomplish a task in life.

Second, have your body describe those said needs to the soul. Don't hesitate or hold back from the description, even if it is embarrassing to think about what you want and need. Speak freely and without constraints, while remaining clear, calm, and deliberate.

Third, have your soul convey to your body that there is nothing wrong with having needs, and that its needs are valid and important. The reality is that the body is very different from the soul, and the soul can learn to value the body's needs even if they are hard to understand.

The above exercise should take between two and three minutes and should be performed during a relaxed period of the day without any distractions. Remember that the goal of this exercise is for the body to express itself without reservations, and the soul should become more sensitive to the body's needs.

CHAPTER 5

Inner Connection Part IV: Tolerating the Body's Idiosyncrasies with Love and Patience

An unavoidable difficulty that the soul will confront in cultivating *Inner Connection* is that the body will be unreliable in its performance and variable in its needs. Even when the body's needs are consistently met, it may not strive toward the soul's goals. Further, even after the soul has developed a healthy schedule for the body that includes adequate sleep, healthy meals, exercise, and time for recreation that the soul enjoys, the body may present new needs that it previously did not have or express, and it may desist from work even when it has been reasonably well cared for. In my clinical practice, this tendency sometimes brings patients back to treatment after long periods of independent thriving. Some depressed patients initially experience rapid recoveries when they devote adequate time to sleep, physical exercise, social activity, recreation, and mastery activities every day. But their schedules work for an extended period of time and then suddenly stop "doing the trick," and the natural experience of decrease in one's mood and engagement levels is interpreted as a setback, leading to a real relapse. For these and other reasons, the soul must learn to tolerate the body's idiosyncrasies with love and patience in order to maintain *Inner Connection* (figure 6).

FIGURE 6 Soul Tolerating the Body's Idiosyncrasies with Love and Patience

Tolerating the Body's Language

Tolerating the Body's Cycles

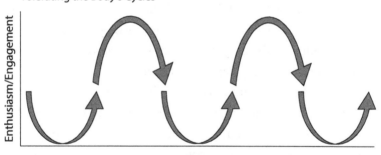

Tolerating the Body's Processes of Behavior Change

Behavior change = Size/intensity of activity × Time

The most effective strategies for long-term behavior change maximize time and minimize size/intensity of the activity.

I treated a depressed patient for several years who cyclically experienced periods of thriving followed by symptomatic relapse that were almost entirely the artifact of having a stressful profession. Freida was a flight attendant for American Airlines who worked very hard to develop a stable schedule that worked around the inconsistent demands of her job. However, the difficulties of changing time zones and spending countless hours in confined, pressurized cabins made it simply impossible to have regularity in her sleep, energy levels, diet, exercise routines, and even her social life. When she began her career as a young woman, Freida was the happiest person she knew, and she did not know what depression felt like. "I was always busy and very passionate about everything I did," she told me during one of our first sessions. "I was always the one of my friends who wanted to go out. I read a lot and I tried new things. I wanted to see the world, so I became a stewardess right out of college." She enjoyed her work and the fact that it allowed her and her husband of six years, George, to travel to six continents virtually as often as they liked. But a rigorous schedule defined by constant travel followed by extended periods of rest was very hard on her body.

Early in her first stint of therapy, she told me, "I'm very close with George. Talking to him, being around him, is a huge relief when I'm depressed. He is my soulmate. But, sometimes my job makes it impossible for us to connect. Like last week, I was feeling really down, but I had to work a morning flight from Newark to Singapore, which is fourteen hours. It's always a grueling haul but it was even more hard because of how down I was. I wanted to cry for the whole flight, and I couldn't even text him because I was in the air. When I landed, I was so miserable and exhausted that it didn't even make sense for me to call him because I didn't have anything to say. I felt I would have just made him worried. I was also afraid I'd start crying in the cab. I texted him a bit on the way to the hotel but then I slept through most of the day. I was staying in Singapore for a few days before coming back. It is one of my favorite cities, but I spent most of the time in my hotel room. The time difference made it so I couldn't even talk to my husband much. I ended up moping and crying until it was time to go home."

Freida's treatment was always complicated by the fact that she could not come to sessions as often as we jointly deemed was ideal. She was out of the country almost every other week, and when she came back, she often went into recovery mode, which meant she was not energetic and clearheaded during her sessions. Freida's job-related malaise was so problematic that I raised the possibility that Freida could switch careers, reminding her that flight attendants are known to be depression-prone because of their schedules and that she seemed especially vulnerable to it. "I can't imagine myself doing anything else," she said. "Not only do I not have any other skills sets, but I really love my job when I'm not depressed. I've seen more of the world than almost anyone I know, and I get paid to do it."

Like most depressed patients, Freida eventually came out of her depressive episode on her own. She stayed loosely on my caseload for the next year or so, popping in and out when her mood started to dip. And then, about a year and a half after our first visit, Freida was feeling especially discouraged again, but this time it was different. She had made great strides in maintaining a healthy schedule that had kept her depression at bay for nearly a year. She worked fewer long-haul flights, primarily sticking to transatlantic red-eyes, which denied her adequate sleep but allowed her to take breaks for mindfulness meditation when the cabin lights were out. During these breaks she worked to cultivate sympathy for her body and give it a chance to rest. She made her schedule as consistent as possible so that she could exercise, call her husband, and sleep between flights on a fairly structured basis. "I've been so sensitive to my body's needs, and it's still not doing its part! That makes it harder for me to love her." Freida had clearly resonated with the *Connections Paradigm*, but she was getting stuck. "My schedule hasn't changed at all recently," she told me, "and I'm really feeling at a loss because I was doing so well for a while. My body stopped responding to my schedule, so I've been finding it hard to work out. I was even getting a full eight hours of sleep until my depression came back, and now I have almost no energy."

I told Freida that her body was likely just going through a natural transition, and her soul's job was to accept it and be patient and kind. Freida's response demonstrated how far she had come in her bodily awareness. "That's the problem," she said, "when I am feeling good my body is happy with vegetables and exercise, but when I start feeling depressed my body tells me it wants to sleep and eat potato chips. If I listen to my body when I'm depressed, I'll end up doing all the things you say I shouldn't do! How do I listen to my body without letting it mistreat itself?" I conveyed to Freida that it is normal and expected for one's body to fluctuate in its needs and its compliance with stated goals. "I think I see what's going on here," I remarked. "You are expecting your body to be a soldier and follow orders all the time. The soul is like a parent, and the body is like a child. Let me ask you: Do children sometimes not follow the rules?" Freida was amused but quipped back, "Yes, but I'm an adult!" And so I responded, "Your soul may be an adult, but your body—just like everyone else's—is very much a child sometimes. And that's OK." Freida paused and then asked, "So, I'm being too rigid?" I nodded yes, while conveying that it was great for Freida to have high standards for herself but that she also needed to tolerate her body's idiosyncrasies with love and patience along the way. Freida looked as if a giant weight had been lifted from her shoulders. "So, I need to truly accept and love myself, even when I fall short?" she asked. "Bingo!" I responded.

Freida recovered from her depression after that discussion, but in truth, she had asked me a good question. Indeed, it can sometimes be difficult to judge how much flexibility and slack to give the body. When I discussed this general question with Rabbi Kelemen, he emphasized that the soul and body are literally two separate entities that can have a real relationship with each other, as real as that of any two people. In any relationship, there is give and take. Sometimes one person pushes the limits, and the other may let it go for a while, but eventually the other person will (hopefully) say something and reset equilibrium and balance. Fluctuations and dialectics are inherent in any relationship, and the world of *Inner Connection* is no different. And so, the question isn't how many potato chips constitute giving the body some slack versus binge eating, but rather what do the body and soul do to stay connected in the context of fluctuations? Can the soul tolerate and continue to connect with the body, even when it "acts up," disappoints, or fails to come through on an agreed-upon task? That is the focus of this facet of *Inner Connection*. More centrally, sometimes the body can be fickle or even recalcitrant. It may lend its efforts to the soul for years before suddenly becoming resistant. Once the soul accepts that all of that is normal and to be expected, it can continue to bestow goodness and kindness upon the body even in the wake of perceived failure.

A related point is that the body needs to be provided with concrete and reasonable guidance. If given unrealistic goals, the body won't have a chance to cooperate with the soul. In industrial psychology—the application of psychological principles and practices to business and organizational settings—there is a well-known acronym that fits this bill, called SMART, which stands for Specific, Measurable, Available, Reasonable, and Timed. Each and every goal that the soul has for the body, regardless of how lofty or spiritual, needs to be couched in these terms in order for the body to be successful. Specific, measurable, and timed refer to how concrete one's goals are. When a goal is clear and bound by time, the body is infinitely more likely to succeed. Available and reasonable refer to how appropriate one's goals are. As I tell my patients, "If you want to destroy a child, ask them to do tasks that are beyond their developmental level. That will teach them to despair into hopelessness that they can be successful and ensure that they will never be happy in life." Of course, that's an exaggeration, but not by much. Having realistic and reasonable goals isn't just about avoiding fantasy; it's about understanding that the body is a relatively simple, physical creature that needs things laid out clearly and realistically in order to succeed. I have seen countless patients suffer from failing to specify, measure, or assign time objectives for their life goals, and even more patients suffer from demanding unreasonable tasks from themselves.

For instance, I have a young patient named Caleb, who laments that he is most productive during the late hours of the night when he needs to be sleeping, since he has a day job and needs to be at work by 8:30 a.m. each day. "I want to be self-employed so I can set my own hours, because I am most sharp from 9 p.m. until two in the morning," he said. "I really wish society operated in such a way that you could work whenever it's best for you." Caleb suffers from anxiety, so it is especially critical that he tend to self-care and have a regular schedule, but he finds himself staying up late to work on personal projects or catch up on work. More fundamentally, though, in discussing Caleb's ambitions, he seems to have an unrealistic view of how much work is truly required to be successful. He speaks about starting his own business but has no concrete plans or ideas, and when he does start to pursue a path toward a plan, he gets distracted by other pursuits. Caleb is learning to set SMART goals for himself, but he is a long way from achieving much in the *Inner Connection* department. From a *Con-*

nections Paradigm standpoint, his lofty goals and dreams remain in the world of the ethereal soul—they are too far removed from the concrete reality of his physical body to become tangible and real. I am hopeful that as Caleb grows a bit older he will develop a greater understanding of the need for concrete and reasonable goals.

Rabbi Kelemen once shared with me a simple formula for behavior change, based on the *Connections Paradigm*, that I have found to be very useful: Change = Intensity of activity × Time. Translated into practical terms, this means that if you want to make behavioral change, you have two options: either make large changes over a small amount of time or make small changes over a large amount of time. In order to tolerate the body's doggedness and idiosyncrasies, it is typically better practice for the soul to maximize time and minimize the intensity of the body's activity. It's generally better to bite off a small amount you can handle than a large one you cannot. For example, training for a marathon can be done in twelve to forty-eight weeks or more. When I started running marathons about a decade ago, I tried to do the most training in the shortest amount of time, and I was headed straight for injury. Fortunately, I caught myself before it was too late, and realized the general consensus that the risk of injury drops precipitously the longer one takes to train. The only risk of maximizing time is that the body may lose interest if the process is too slow, especially if the soul becomes more prone to suddenly modifying its goals. But in training the body to succeed, small but consistent changes can yield a massive impact over time. I have found that keeping myself fit with a more or less constant, gentle training schedule is the key to success in running marathons.

Those who set out to increase their productivity often make the mistake of setting unrealistic goals that do not accurately reflect their current potential. But others have the opposite problem: out of fear of failure, they are not ambitious enough with their self-improvement objectives. They give their bodies more than ample time to adjust to distress, not out of consideration for the body or an accurate assessment of its abilities, but because they believe deep down that the body is destined to fail. Interestingly, in many cases this occurs because of previous attempts to change too quickly. Failure is a common prelude to expecting less from one's body; intolerance toward the body's idiosyncrasies begets resigning oneself to poor performance.

I once treated a police officer in his late thirties, Arthur, who wanted to build *Inner Connection* but was pessimistic about improving his body's schedule because he had been jaded by what he perceived as a lifetime of failure. This became a significant roadblock in his treatment because he needed to establish a healthier routine in order to overcome his acute anxiety. "My father was very authoritarian, and he always had big hopes for me," he told me early in his treatment. "When I was applying to college, he approved of only a handful of universities that he deemed to be fitting for 'his son.' 'You'll be the next Bill Gates,' he would always tell me. I tried to explain to him that my high school grades weren't Ivy League material, and that I didn't even want to be Bill Gates. I even reminded him that Bill Gates didn't even graduate college, but he didn't want to hear any of it. When I didn't get into any of the schools on his list, he was so angry. I asked him what I should do next, but he didn't even want to talk to me, so I applied for the academy and became a cop."

Arthur came to therapy with severe anxiety and a general sense that he "had gotten nowhere in life." Yet, in my assessment, he had a lot to be proud of. He was a respected and high-ranking officer in the Boston Police Department, and he had built a modest fortune by refurbishing and reselling houses in the Boston suburbs. He was well read, was well traveled, and had a large network of friends and family with whom he socialized frequently. But he had not achieved many of his childhood dreams, including getting a college degree, which made him unable to recognize his considerable personal achievements. Arthur had a very poor diet and rarely exercised. I encouraged him to incorporate more fruits, vegetables, and healthy unsaturated fats into his diet, but he was reluctant. "I eat unhealthy foods because it's the best medicine for my anxiety. When it gets really bad, I feel a pit in my stomach, and I can't focus on anything else. The only thing that helps, frankly, is some pizza or potato chips," he said with a chuckle. Temporarily putting the issue of his diet on the back burner, I encouraged him to start getting more exercise. "A run twice a week or a few weightlifting sessions could do a lot to help," I told him. I then asked, "Would you consider getting a gym membership?" But Arthur said that his anxiety made it very difficult for him to exercise, and that his body "had never liked working out." When I insisted that breaking a sweat every other day might be the single most important step toward recovery, he agreed that I was probably right and told me he would think about it.

Arthur's treatment also involved exposure therapy sessions, a clinical method in which the therapist works with the patient to evoke anxiety in the therapy room while coaching the patient not to avoid the resulting distress. As I explained to Arthur, a wide body of research has demonstrated the efficacy of exposure therapy for anxiety, but he was reluctant. "That's actually the last thing I'd like to do," he said. "I really hoped these sessions would give me a chance to escape my anxiety for a little while. But if you insist let's at least start slowly." I told Arthur that exposure therapy would be more effective if he tolerated a higher level of distress, but he remained reluctant to proceed.

Over the course of a few months, Arthur started to accept my recommendations, but he took them on very slowly. He started jogging during his fifth week of treatment, but only for fifteen minutes once per week. He said he was eating two or three apples a week, but his unhealthy diet had otherwise gone unchanged. Unsurprisingly, his anxiety had not subsided in the slightest. "If you put a little more effort into treatment, I think you'll be pleased with the results," I told him. "I know, I'm trying," he replied, "little by little." By one month into treatment Arthur agreed that all my recommendations sounded like rational steps toward getting his anxiety under control, so I asked him why he was so hesitant to incorporate them into his routine. "To be honest, with the exception of exposure therapy, I've tried them all before," he said. "My wife wants me to get in better shape, so I tried working out. I bought a gym membership and worked out every day for two weeks, but after that my body just broke down. I almost couldn't get up for work the week after that. I'm trying, I'm just doing it very slowly." Arthur also said that he had briefly become a raw vegan but found the diet too restrictive. "But you don't need to work out every day for it to make a difference," I told him, "and you don't need to eat like a rabbit to get the vitamins and nutrients you need. You could try jogging for 10 minutes every other day, and then increase that to jog for 15 minutes after a few weeks." Arthur's slow and steady approach to behavioral improvement ultimately thwarted his progress. More importantly, though, this emanated from an unrealistically negative assessment of his body's potential. Arthur's formative experiences as a young man engendered skepticism about his body's capabilities. He had developed an all-or-nothing perspective on self-care that reflected a deeper intolerance for his body's limitations. He felt his body would fail, so he didn't even try.

Tolerating the body's idiosyncrasies with love and patience is complex because it requires patiently waiting when the body's energy or enthusiasm wanes. However, according to the *Connections*

Paradigm, the body—like all physical things—has cycles. There-fore, in the natural order of events, decreases in engagement are simply a precursor to rebound. In other words, just as the soul must accept that when the body is experiencing a *high* point of functionality and cooperation, it will, at some point, subsequently experience a setback; so too must it remember that low levels of engagement and motivation are naturally followed by renewed strength and success. Athletes often experience their bodies sud-denly becoming less inclined to perform after a long streak of ded-icated hustle, but it is often simply that the body needs to go through a resting period before returning to its previous level of productivity. These rest periods may not even be related to how hard the body is working; they can result from subtle biological processes, fluctuations in circadian rhythms, weather, and other factors that are beyond our control and understanding. As with all aspects of connection, patience and perseverance are the key to overcoming the low points of the body's cycles.

Because of these concepts, when the body has a setback, the soul must not automatically interpret the body's lack of engage-ment as a manifestation of a chronic physical limitation. When such interpretations occur, the soul may give up on certain aspects of its body-care routine instead of encouraging the body to per-sist. I have treated countless patients who felt despair at the first occurrence of sadness, anxiety, or related symptoms, only to be greatly relieved to learn that mood fluctuations are perfectly nor-mal and to be expected. Recently, I saw a thirty-two-year-old with obsessive-compulsive disorder who interpreted his own thoughts as an indication that he was "going crazy." His treatment revolved around understanding that his thoughts were obsessive but normal, accepting them, and engaging in exercises to habit-uate himself to distress (see chapter 2). In a similar vein, it is extremely important for the soul to help the body maintain at least some level of engagement with its goals when things are difficult. After injury or illness it is usually unwise to keep to a normal day-to-day schedule, but failing to keep any aspect of one's schedule during such times can lead to long-term setbacks. When the body resists the soul's direction, the soul should encourage partial engagement. This is because holding on to even a small amount of success during trying times is what creates our opportunities for rebound.

Recently, I encouraged one of my depressed patients to go for a run. She laughed and said she was too depressed. So, I encouraged her to go for a walk. She smiled and said she was too depressed. So, I encouraged her to simply put on her running shoes and walk around the block once. She grinned and said she didn't feel like it. So, I encouraged her to simply put on her running shoes, walk outside for one minute, and then come back in. She finally (reluctantly) accepted that challenge. One week later, she was walking around the block, and a week later she was back to running. Commenting on the experience, my patient said, "I'm glad you pushed me to get outside. It may sound stupid but just putting my shoes on and walking for one minute that day was extremely hard for me! But, I did it, and that's what gave me the strength to move forward."

Exercise 5: Tolerating the Body's Idiosyncrasies with Love and Patience

Let's practice what it is like for the soul to tolerate the body's idiosyncrasies with love and patience. This is an advanced exercise that will draw on the skills we developed in previous exercises. As we discussed in this chapter, the body is physical and has natural biological cycles that affect its capabilities at any given time. Therefore, the body *will* waver in its enthusiasm and engagement in valued behaviors. We must remember that this is not necessarily an indication that the body is damaged or broken, or that it is a failure. The ebb and flow of the body's engagement are simply a fact, true to everyone, that our souls must learn to accept.

For our exercise, start by spending approximately ninety seconds conjuring up a recent event in which your body fell short of a goal—for example, sleeping in and missing an obligation, not doing well on an exam or a project at work, missing a goal time for a race, becoming angry at a friend or family member, or committing a spiritual/religious sin. Think about exactly how the body fell short in its goal and how disappointed you were. Try to feel the pain and disillusionment of being let down by your body.

Then spend ninety seconds vocalizing words of encouragement and love to your body. Have your soul tell your body that its setbacks are part of growth and that cycles are to be celebrated. Try to convey to your body that your soul's love is unconditional, not dependent on your body's ability to serve your soul's pursuits. The key is to remain connected to the body even when it does not fulfill the soul's expectations.

CHAPTER 6

Introduction to *Interpersonal Connection*

Interpersonal Connection involves connection between two or more people. At first glance, one might expect this would be more straightforward than *Inner Connection*. For one thing, we can *see Interpersonal Connection* happening since it occurs in physical space between human beings, rather than that mysterious domain where souls and bodies meet. Second, when people communicate, they do so with verbal language and other observable expressions, and gauge others' emotional reactions based on similarly observable behavior. This is in stark contrast to auscultating the quiet, cryptic, even silent speech of the soul. Third, whether a person is spiritually inclined or not, *Interpersonal Connection* plays a prominent role in day-to-day life, save for the most isolated individuals. By contrast, as we learned in previous chapters, the dynamics between the body and the soul are not readily apparent, such that the very existence of the soul is often a discovery to those who begin studying the *Connections Paradigm* or other spiritually oriented models of the human condition. However, *Interpersonal Connection* is actually substantially more complex than *Inner Connection*, since connection with another person involves intercommunication between *two* souls and *two* bodies. When *Interpersonal Connection* occurs in the broader contexts of families, communities, and nations, complexity increases by many orders of magnitude, and therefore it is no wonder that disconnection abounds. It isn't easy to develop and maintain connected relationships with other people, but the benefits far outweigh the work. Virtually nothing is more satisfying for the soul than making other people happy and relishing in the world of *Interpersonal Connection*.

As we will discuss in the following chapters, *Interpersonal Connection* is achieved by noticing the needs of others, providing for those needs, noticing when we are disconnecting from others, and building and maintaining connection with others even when they neglect our own needs (figure 7). To some degree, these are hierarchical steps: providing for others' needs should be prefaced by noticing their needs, and noticing our disconnection is a precursor to building and maintaining connection with others under stress. However, these elements can nevertheless be pursued and developed more or less simultaneously, since development of one can strengthen the others, and deficits in one take a toll on the others. To these ends, we will discuss them separately to highlight their distinctions.

As discussed in the introduction to this book, *Inner Connection* provides a firm footing on which to build connected relationships with others. This is because a healthy inner dynamic gives us the capacity to see beyond our own, limited reality and start noticing and caring for the needs of other people. Conversely, we are less sensitive to other people's disconnected tendencies when our body and soul have a loving and mutually supportive relationship. Interestingly, our ability to maintain and enhance *Inner Connection* is even dependent on our ability to connect with others. As mentioned earlier, the soul and body have innate desires that orient them toward the outside world and especially toward other people, so if we do not work toward *Interpersonal Connection*, our body and soul will inevitably become frustrated and will regress toward inner disconnection.

This point is perhaps where the *Connections Paradigm* most significantly differs from many prominent meditation-oriented

FIGURE 7 **Overview of *Interpersonal Connection***

In a nutshell, *Interpersonal Connection* involves entering another person's world. Dwelling in the world of *Interpersonal Connection* involves giving as opposed to taking.

Giving entails (1) identifying the needs of other people, (2) considering those needs, and (3) exerting an effort to meet those needs. However, there are four ways to provide/receive, and not all of them involve giving:

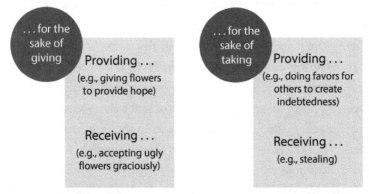

...for the sake of giving

Providing ...
(e.g., giving flowers to provide hope)

Receiving ...
(e.g., accepting ugly flowers graciously)

...for the sake of taking

Providing ...
(e.g., doing favors for others to create indebtedness)

Receiving ...
(e.g., stealing)

There are many ways to facilitate *Interpersonal Connection*. In this program we will focus on just four:

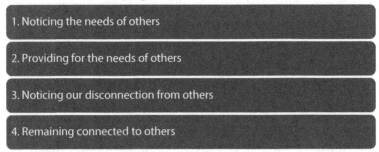

1. Noticing the needs of others

2. Providing for the needs of others

3. Noticing our disconnection from others

4. Remaining connected to others

spiritual practices. Though the latter also recognize a person's dualistic nature and the importance of nurturing connections between disparate aspects of the person, they also inadvertently promote interpersonal disconnection through encouraging asceticism. The outside world, according to these disciplines, is either an inherently fraught spiritual minefield that puts the soul's purity and peace at risk, or a passing fancy that is best enjoyed from afar. This ideal, known as *Sramana*, by no means characterizes all Eastern traditions, but it is central in the Indian philosophical traditions and continues to play a significant role in Western understanding of Eastern wisdom; many spiritually oriented Westerners fall victim to its appeal. Proponents of *Sramana* encourage the aspirant to extinguish what the *Connections Paradigm* understands to be a spiritually and emotionally healthy need for connection with other humans. To make this contrast clear: from the perspective of the *Connections Paradigm*, quelling, as opposed to channeling, the body's needs for *Interpersonal Connection* by escaping from worldly responsibilities is a recipe for spiritual disaster, since human beings are, by nature, social creatures. Reflection is no doubt an essential activity of a healthy and connected soul. But looking inward and prioritizing inner tranquility is viewed as a core set of skills from which we can propel ourselves to engage in loving, connected relationships with others. Put differently, the ultimate goal of building *Inner Connection* is to fill one's own cup so that it overflows into the lives of others and enriches their lives as well. As Rabbi Kelemen says, "Without *Inner Connection*, the soul and body are preoccupied with their constant, inevitable conflicts. Once they learn to work together, they will notice the world around them like never before, which begets a mutual desire to improve it." Indeed, the body and soul that have not yet developed a healthy *Inner Connection* may be tempted to recede into spiritual isolation because they feel their efforts toward improving the world will be futile. However, accepting the yoke—and opportunity—of *Interpersonal Connection* creates new opportunities for body and soul to connect with each other. In these regards, while *Inner Connection* is a base for *Interpersonal Connection*, the latter can also inform and deepen the former.

Along these lines, almost everyone I meet, even my most disconnected patients, demonstrates some degree of generosity toward others. Approaching interpersonal relationships with a more connected mind-set can help them see the value in efforts that they already take, and thereby improve their *Inner Connection* as well. Arthur, the Boston police officer we discussed in chapter 5, was initially slow in his progress toward *Inner Connection*, but when he picked up the pace he began feeling more connected to other people and more satisfied with his important work. "Some people call us heroes," he told me, "but I never really thought of it that way. I just like my job and I like being good at it. But now, as I'm starting to recognize my own needs, I'm noticing the needs of others too. People need to feel safe, and that's our mission in the department. I've been spending time realizing how much of a difference my work makes, and now I have more clarity about why I do what I do."

However, being sensitive to our own needs is no doubt very different from being sensitive to other people's needs, since *Interpersonal Connection* comes with unique challenges that *Inner Connection* does not necessarily prepare us for. When it comes to *Inner Connection*, the body may initially resist the soul's guidance, and the soul may start from a place of resentment toward the body. However, working through the process of the soul loving the body, providing for its needs, and tolerating its idiosyncrasies, and the body accepting discomfort and distress and opening up to the soul, the two will ultimately respond and improve their *Inner Connection*. Further, when we work toward *Inner Connection*, we can reap rewards relatively quickly because our own bodies and souls directly feel the benefits of their connection immediately. By stark contrast, other people can always choose to walk away from a relationship with us. By noticing others' needs, providing for those needs, noticing our disconnection, and guarding against it, we may ensure that we remain connected to others, but we cannot ensure that they will reciprocate our efforts.

I observed this problem acutely in Henry, a patient who came to treatment for what he initially described as social anxiety but was actually a mild form of Asperger's syndrome (AS). In fact, it turned out that Henry did not have any social anxiety at all, but he could tell there were problems in his relationships and that he was at least partially to blame. At our first session, I asked him to tell me a little about himself, and he went on to describe his robotics studies at MIT in intense detail. He went on for several minutes without making eye contact, failing to recognize that he was discussing his field on a level that way over my head. I finally interrupted him.

"Very interesting," I said. "So tell me, why did you come to my office?"

"Oh," he said, "people are getting mad at me and I don't know why."

Henry was highly functional, holding down his advanced studies, an adjunct teaching position, and good relationships with his family. He had had a girlfriend for over two years, and she had even followed him to Boston from their hometown in Illinois after he was accepted at MIT. He had long known that he did not have the most refined social skills, but recently his apparent lack of sensitivity was threatening some of his most important relationships. "As far as I am concerned, everything is fine," he told me, "but my girlfriend said I am insensitive. She said it's been obvious for a long time that she isn't happy. I really don't want to lose my girlfriend, so I've been doing better, but she says I'm not."

Recent incidents had caused some of Henry's other relations to reproach him for insensitivity. During a conversation with a fellow student about his work on a group project, Henry told him bluntly that his contributions were so totally substandard that he should consider dropping out of the program. "It's really what I felt," he told me. "I wasn't trying to be mean. I was trying to help him. But everyone in the group told me it was rude, and the professor even talked to me about it." A few weeks later, he visited his girlfriend's parents' and noticed that his girlfriend's sister had gained weight. "I read how dangerous it is to be obese in *Time* magazine. You should go on a diet." He proceeded to make dietary recommendations even as his girlfriend and her cringing family tried desperately to change the subject. His girlfriend was very embarrassed, and her parents later gently told him that it was not a nice thing to say.

A few sessions into our work together, I told Henry that I thought he had AS. He took the news well and shared that it was something he and his family had long suspected. "My mom mentioned that to me years ago, when I was a kid," he said. "She told me she never had me tested because she didn't want me to think I was any dumber than anyone else." Henry asked if I was going to try to cure his AS. I responded that it wasn't curable per se, but that he wouldn't want to be cured anyway. "You have an amazing gift. Many people with AS like you have unique skills in certain fields. With practice, you can potentially learn to maintain the benefits while making up for deficits and have the best of both worlds." Henry's treatment program was guided by the *Connections Paradigm* from the beginning, and he made a fair amount of progress. He became more aware of his own stress level and needs for sleep and a balanced diet. He also increased his awareness when it came to certain needs and desires of others, such as when people around him seemed hungry or thirsty. He also began to take pride and even joy in providing for others' concrete needs. Yet, as Henry progressed and grew in both *Inner* and *Interpersonal Connection*, he could not prevent his girlfriend from leaving him. As this case illustrates, interpersonal growth can occur even as some relationships fail to thrive.

Another inherent complexity with *Interpersonal Connection* is that it is not as simple as doing acts of kindness or refraining from doing others harm. *Interpersonal Connection* requires us to develop a refined sense of empathy for others, such that we can see the world through the eyes of others, feel their joy and despair, and make an effort to notice and accurately meet their needs. This means more than doing the most obvious things to improve their well-being, or simply being polite by asking others what they would like us to do. *Interpersonal Connection* is a dynamic process. It entails empathy: feelings of warmth and satisfaction when others are joyous and happy, and a sense of sadness and pain when others suffer. All human beings have the capacity for empathy, since the soul is innately empathetic, and the more its relationship with its body improves, the more confident it will be in expressing its compassion and sensing other people's needs. However, our inner and interpersonal (and spiritual) dynamics sometimes get in the way. For these reasons, when interacting with others, it is critical to be mindful of not only how we are behaving but what we are feeling and what is motivating us to act.

To these ends, according to the *Connections Paradigm*, social transactions can be classified into the following categories: (1) providing in order to give, (2) providing in order to take, (3) taking in order to provide, and (4) taking in order to take. Providing in order to give is a form of *Interpersonal Connection*. It entails meeting someone else's needs simply for that person's own sake, without (obvious) ulterior motives, such as anonymously donating to charity or doing acts of kindness when no one is watching. To be clear, providing in order to give does not always need to be done secretly; however, when others are aware of our giving, it carries a risk of servicing our own discreet needs. Providing in order to give does, however, always require us to transcend our bodies' needs to some degree by prioritizing the well-being of the person we are giving to. When our expectation of a returned favor is explicit or even tacit—for instance, in the context of business transactions—this may be a natural part of life, but it does not cultivate *Interpersonal Connection* unless the transaction is tilted in favor of the other person. Pure business transactions, in which each party feels it is getting the better end of the deal, do not build *Interpersonal Connection*, because they involve providing in order to take.

It is crucial to identify, however, that taking is not necessarily a selfish act. When accepting a gift (taking) is done in order to provide another with the opportunity to give, it is ultimately an act of giving and connection. Rabbi Kelemen taught me and many of his other students that when attending a meal at someone's home, it is vitally (spiritually) important to eat whatever is served, whether it is delectable or not. By doing so, one accepts the grace and good intentions of the host or hostess, and thereby enters into the world of *Interpersonal Connection* by giving them the pleasure of providing for others. In contrast, taking from others who do not want to give—such as stealing, extorting, or coercing— obviously does not build *Interpersonal Connection*, since it reinforces our focus on ourselves as opposed to others.

Along all these lines, building *Interpersonal Connection* requires being sensitive to our own needs, desires, and motivations and being sure not to willfully or unwittingly inject selfishness into our interactions with other people. This is an enormous challenge for *Interpersonal Connection*, since even highly intuitive people can struggle to be mindful of their disconnected tendencies. Furthermore, remaining fully sensitive to and aware of our own motivations is especially challenging when we have pressing needs of our own that are not being satisfied.

All of these principles came out in spades in the case of Barbara and Sam, a married couple I counseled. Both parties were generous by nature but failed to grasp the importance of giving freely and wholeheartedly to the other. Even as they strove to connect, any gains were short-lived since they unknowingly expected recompense from their counterpart. Barbara initially came to me for treatment of crippling anxiety that interfered with her daily tasks, which mainly consisted of keeping her home and taking care of her three children. Years of disconnection had taken their toll on her personal well-being and her marriage, and Sam, her husband, conveyed that Barbara's shortcomings were the only factor in their strained relationship. "He has legitimate complaints," she said about her husband, "but I can't get better with him breathing down my neck. We argue all the time. He never asks me how I'm doing. He only checks in on me to make sure I'm doing what he wants me to do." Barbara knew that her husband was not giving her the patience and care she needed to recover from her anxiety, and she realized that his neglect and criticism were contributing to her symptoms. However, Barbara had her own struggles in the world of *Interpersonal Connection*. Most centrally, she only received from Sam to satisfy her own needs—not in order to help him become a better person. When I asked Barbara if she ever confronted Sam about his behavior, she said, "Only to the extent that I defend myself if he calls me out on something unfairly. Remember, I have three adorable sons and a beautiful house in a great community. We're comfortable and I never have to worry. He's given me everything I ever wanted, so why would I rock the boat?"

"Because you want him to be a caring husband," I replied.

Barbara laughed. "Yeah, I guess that's true. But I'm not sure it's worth the risk."

Barbara traced the origins of her marital discord to the beginning of Sam's promotion as a stock analyst in a large hedge fund. When he had a less demanding position, he devoted more time to his marriage and family, but the new job had robbed him of most of his free time. Sam was more or less constantly stressed, and he expected his wife to care for herself and their children alone. They both seemed to agree that his responsibilities in relation to hers were limited to breadwinning. "He worked for years to get the position he's in and I wouldn't dare ask him to do more for the family," she said, "but he leaves the house at 7:00 a.m. and he doesn't get back home until after 9:00 p.m. By that point, he is understandably tired and cranky. We spend the weekend together, he's on his phone a lot and when he has a free minute he mostly uses it to catch up on quality time with the boys instead of with me. I'm always an afterthought, unless he wants to complain about something." Thus, Sam was providing for his wife, at considerable self-sacrifice, and Barbara was trying not to stress him out, also at considerable self-sacrifice. They were being generous to each other, and it was hard to fault either party. However, their marriage was suffering due to a lack of *Interpersonal Connection*.

Early in Barbara's treatment she learned about the *Connections Paradigm*, and it helped her become more conscious of her own needs, both in general and within her relationship with Sam. At an early session, she said, "I can feel that my anxiety originates in my body. . . . It starts in my stomach and rises up to my chest. It makes me feel too sick to complete the tasks I need to do. And I can feel that the part of me that gets fed up with it is my soul. My soul wants me to get things done and for me to be a reliable person. So, when my body is struggling, my soul just sits around and sulks." By practicing the exercises discussed in previous chapters,

Barbara soon began to make strides in *Inner Connection*. She started giving to her body and tolerating her natural limitations. And her body, in turn, was better able to sit with distress and express itself. Concurrent with these gains, Barbara started to feel less anxious. At that point, we identified that her marriage was in trouble and shifted focus to *Interpersonal Connection*.

"Sam always has a list of things he wants me to do for him during the day. If he gets home and they aren't done, we have a big argument, and I usually feel terrible about myself." Barbara's concerns were valid. Sam had been skeptical of her coming to therapy from the outset, and he was by no means ready for her to take time out of her schedule for self-care, especially if it was going to get in the way of her fulfilling her domestic duties. After all, he was simply too busy making money to help out around the house. For these reasons, Barbara felt that Sam had given his blessing—and credit card—for her to come to therapy only because he felt it would help Barbara be more productive. "He's definitely not interested in me taking time out of my schedule to do anything else," Barbara exclaimed.

My response to Barbara was as follows: "I think you need to share your concerns directly with Sam." Indeed, Barbara had not told Sam about the work she was doing toward building *Inner Connection*, despite being in treatment for several months. She also did not express to Sam many of her needs in general—not only for less of his criticism, but also for less oversight and control of her day-to-day life, for more recreation and social engagement, for him to make her an emotional priority over their children, for more time together, and for more romance and emotional connection in the bedroom. When I raised these possibilities, Barbara was visibly uncomfortable, "Again, I really don't want to rock the boat. What if Sam gets angry with me?" I conveyed that Barbara's role in the world of *Interpersonal Connection* is simply to do her part—to express to Sam what she needs, in order to receive from him in a way that would make him a bigger person. After several weeks of discussions along these lines, Barbara mustered up the courage and expressed some of these needs to her husband. To her surprise, Sam was not only receptive but appeared happy that she had opened up to him about her needs. Sam even took off from work just to spend the day with Barbara, and he also accepted her offer to attend one of her therapy sessions.

During our meeting, I gave Sam a crash course on the *Connections Paradigm* and focused specifically on the importance of providing for Barbara in a way that *she* wanted and needed. Sam understood right away that being the primary breadwinner, even in a generous manner, could ultimately be selfish if he wasn't providing for Barbara's true preferences and needs. "I grew up in a home where my father didn't provide materially for my family. I was always resentful that others had so much, and we were always short. When the opportunity for my promotion came I grabbed it, but I guess I got a bit carried away," Sam said, after which he turned to Barbara and apologized for not being there for her, and for being too demanding and critical. Then it was Barbara's turn. "I love you so much, Sam, and I just want to connect with you. I won't ever fault you for not taking care of us financially. Ultimately, I just want a happy husband who loves me." I could see Barbara's lip quivering as she spoke—she was so nervous to share her inner world with Sam. But he responded beautifully by sliding over on the couch and putting his arm around her. It was a touching moment. It was a connected moment. At the end of our session, Sam agreed to come to Barbara's sessions at least once per month; he also agreed to spend more time with Barbara (not just their kids) on the weekends, and to chill out a bit more in the evenings. Barbara, in turn, committed to sharing her feelings more with Sam, in order to give him the feedback he needs to tend to her in a way that is truly helpful.

Over the ensuing weeks, Barbara opened up even more to Sam. The two addressed their communication patterns—what was going well and what needed to be improved—and also Barbara's concerns that Sam was not attentive enough to her emotional and romantic needs in the buildup to sexual interactions. At one critical point, Sam shared with Barbara how grateful he was to her for providing him with feedback. "For the last few years, I felt that you weren't present in our relationship. I knew something was wrong but couldn't figure out what it was. When you tell me what I can do differently in our marriage, it's like I get my wife back." Of course, there were ups and downs. At one point, opening lines of communication made their arguments more frequent. "He's been making an effort to be nice," Barbara told me, "but the other day I got upset with him and he threw it all in my face. He was like 'I work myself to the bone every day! I ask you how your day was every night! How much more do I have to do to make you happy?!' I just completely lost it. I know it was disconnection, but I just couldn't hold back. I felt like all he's been saying about wanting to improve our marriage has been a lie."

"How did the argument start?" I asked.

"I got mad because he told me he was going to take out the garbage. I helped him by getting the bags ready, which I felt was a really connected thing to do, and he forgot to take them out. I had been taking care of the kids all day and I only asked him to do that one thing when he got home from work."

"And how long did the disconnection last?" I asked.

"Not long. Within an hour we both apologized and made up. Also, I was much more forgiving of myself for getting angry," Barbara responded.

"I'd call that quite the success, then! In the past wouldn't it have taken much longer?" I asked.

"Ha. In the past I would have gone to bed anxious and sad feeling ashamed about losing control, and he would have gone to his desk to work for a few hours more until eventually coming to bed. We would have ignored what happened and not spoken about it at all," Barbara said, recognizing how far they had come as a couple and how much more tolerant she had become of her own idiosyncrasies.

As we'll continue to discuss in the following chapters, *Interpersonal Connection* requires a sense of selflessness in both giving and receiving. This comes naturally to very few people. While all people need others and thrive when connected to others, some of us tend to be better at giving in a connected way—in a way that truly takes into account what other people need—and others tend to be better at receiving, conveying to others what they need, in order to deepen connections. Still other people struggle with both aspects of *Interpersonal Connection*, since it is hard for them to get out of their own mind-sets across the board. To these ends, cultivating a connected mind-set when interacting with others is a key to all aspects of *Interpersonal Connection*. One can begin to achieve this by noticing others' needs.

Exercise 6: Noticing Others' Needs, Part 1

Our exercise for this chapter is to notice a single need of another person once per day. This can be any need, either physical or emotional, and all we have to do is simply become aware of it. The need can be somewhat obvious, but the more subtle, the better. For example, if you notice that someone has just poured a cup of coffee, it is a high level of *Interpersonal Connection* to realize that they need sugar before they ask (verbal behavior), and an even higher level to perceive their need before they start looking around the table (nonverbal behavior). The activity of noticing another's needs can be done with anyone—someone you live with, a co-worker, a friend you see or speak with, or a complete stranger whom you see on the bus or in line at a store. The exercise is simple: take a moment to reflect on the person you've chosen, and contemplate what their needs may be right now. Do they seem thirsty? Tired? Overworked? Are they struggling with something specific, or general? Have they had a particularly rough week? Focus on one of their needs and imagine how difficult it is for them. At this stage, we are *not* yet attempting to try to meet or provide for their needs; rather, we are simply trying to notice them. The point of the exercise is to leave our own world for a moment and delve into the experience of another person. This exercise can be especially productive if we choose different people each day with whom we have different relationships. Needless to say, noticing others' needs is harder when we are under higher levels of stress ourselves, and easier when things are going well.

CHAPTER 7

Interpersonal Connection Part I: Three Levels of Noticing the Needs of Others

As discussed in chapter 6, *Interpersonal Connection* does not arise from charitable acts alone; rather, it comes from giving selflessly to others. More fundamentally, however, *Interpersonal Connection* requires noticing other people's needs with true sensitivity before providing for them. Giving to others—even though it is valued and prosocial—may emerge from an inner need to give, as opposed to a desire to provide for someone else. By contrast, being mindful and empathic of others is a firm base on which altruistic giving can occur. Along these lines, noticing others' needs enhances our ability to help them when they do not explicitly ask for our assistance, and especially when they themselves do not know what they need. It is a deeply satisfying act of connection, for both the giver and the receiver, when we meet the needs of others that they did not realize they had in the first place. But the importance of noticing others' needs goes beyond improving the well-being of the other person—it is independently important for our own connection. Our own body and soul benefit from developing fine-tuned empathy for other people. So, if we notice the needs of another, our *Interpersonal Connection* increases, even if they are completely unaware that we are taking notice, and even if we do not follow through with actually helping them.

In fact, in some ways noticing other people's needs is more difficult than meeting their needs. If we know that someone has a particular need that we are capable of meeting, it only takes a finite amount of exertion for us to satisfy it. But everyone has a vast number of needs beyond those that we can satisfy. If we were to make an effort to identify all the things they need, we would come up with an extensive list. Even that would probably not be completely exhaustive, although we may very well get exhausted in the process! A relatively easy way to notice others' needs is by pondering the basic essentials. We already discussed these when we learned about *Inner Connection*. The most obvious are physical necessities like food, water, clothing, a clean environment, temperature regulation, and safety. Then there are emotional needs such as feeling loved, being valued, belonging to a community, and feeling successful in our creative pursuits. Some needs are both physical and emotional, like physical affection and sexuality. Spiritual needs such as hopefulness, a sense of meaning, and closeness to God are also worth contemplation.

Rabbi Kelemen taught me that it is easiest to notice others' needs when we are also experiencing those needs at the same time (figure 8). When we are feeling cold, for instance, it is easier to notice that others are feeling cold. When we are hungry, it is easier to notice that others have yet to eat. Such levels of connection come more naturally to some than others, but either way they are the most fundamental and basic. Shared needs require the least sensitivity for us to identify, but they provide a good first step for us to become sensitive to other people's needs. Conversely, it's harder to notice others' needs when we don't presently share those needs. I remember the time that I arrived a bit early to a breakfast meeting with a very wealthy philanthropist, only to discover that he had scheduled a first breakfast meeting with someone else immediately prior. I had arrived hungry to the meeting, expecting to eat breakfast, and left disappointed as this individual—who ironically is known for his generosity—did not notice or inquire

FIGURE 8 **Noticing the Needs of Others (Three Levels)**

It is easiest to notice others' needs when we ourselves concurrently have those same needs (e.g., when we feel cold and notice that others are chilly as well). It is harder—and therefore a higher level of *Interpersonal Connection*—to notice others' needs when we do not currently have those needs but have experienced them in the past (e.g., we are currently not cold, but someone comes in from outside and is shivering). Finally, it is hardest—and therefore the highest level of noticing others' needs—to recognize when other people have needs that we have never experienced and therefore do not understand (e.g., because of cultural or gender differences, or because we have never had those needs before).

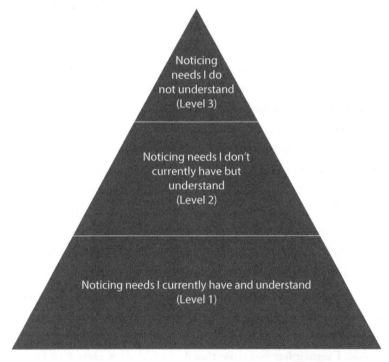

Noticing
needs I do
not understand
(Level 3)

Noticing needs I don't
currently have but
understand
(Level 2)

Noticing needs I currently have and understand
(Level 1)

as to whether I had already eaten, likely because he himself was already satiated.

A higher level of connection is to notice someone else's needs when we are not currently experiencing those needs; however, we have had such needs in the past. I am originally from Toronto, Canada, where winter months tend to be rather cold. From years of facing ice storms and bone-chilling winds, I am exquisitely sensitive to others' needs for warmth when they walk in from the cold, even when I myself am warm. Fortunately, living in New England still gives me opportunity to flex my muscles in this arena. Similarly, several months ago I observed this level of connection in my wife. One of my sons loves to play baseball and was excited when his team won their final game, but he seemed surprisingly down. My wife, Miri—who used to play Little League herself when she was a child—understood immediately that he was disappointed with his own performance. She remembered that he had dropped a relatively easy pop fly during one of the early innings, which enabled the opposing team to score a run. Miri remembered her own experiences of success and failure on the baseball field as a child and channeled those memories to connect with our son.

The highest level of noticing others' needs, however, occurs when we have *never* experienced the need before in our lives. This requires getting completely outside of our own nature and experience and delving into the mind-set and heart of another person. Opportunities for connection in this domain are somewhat rare and typically involve relating to people who are very different from us in terms of gender, culture, socioeconomic status, and otherwise. For example, by nature it is generally easier for men to understand the needs of men, and for women to understand the needs of women. Anatomy aside, gender differences occur in the context of how individuals have historically been treated since birth, myriad expectations that are placed on them from others and also that they place on themselves, and aspects of identity that are deeply profound. Thus, delving into the needs of a member of another gender is inherently more challenging than generalizing from one's personal experience to a member of the same gender. The same applies to culture. Growing up and living in North America makes it easier for me to relate to and understand the needs of other North Americans.

I began learning about *Interpersonal Connection* at a crucial time in my early career. I was just beginning to develop as a clinician, and I was meeting patients with almost every need imaginable. Some of my patients had needs that were similar to my own needs, but others had needs I'd never experienced before and struggled to identify with. Pondering the lives of people in very different circumstances from my own and seriously making an effort to imagine how it felt to be in their shoes required a lot of creativity. At one point during my training, I worked on a geriatric unit and treated several older people with age-related problems that I had never encountered before. With other patients, I learned about culture-specific needs that I will probably never fully grasp, let alone experience. In other cases, I saw needs associated with specific health concerns that I have never had, or of individuals with dire personal and financial circumstances that I pray to avoid during my lifetime. Through this process, I came to the conclusion that being sensitive to each patient's needs—i.e., *Interpersonal Connection*—is one of the most important skills in being an effective therapist.

I have also observed some of the most common ways that people fail to notice the needs of others. Once, a twenty-nine-year-old male patient of mine named Danny completely disputed the importance of noticing other people's needs.

"I'm more of a doer. I only feel like I'm making progress when I'm actively involved in something. And at the end of the day, getting things done is more important than thinking about other people. Could anyone seriously argue otherwise?" he stated.

"But how do you know what another person needs unless you develop your sensitivity?" I asked.

"A lot of the time their needs are obvious. And if not, they should tell me," he retorted.

"Doesn't it feel better when someone notices your needs without you telling them?" I asked.

"Um . . . I guess so," he said.

"And let's be honest, do people really always know what they need? There are times when everyone in someone's life can see clearly what they need except *them*. And sometimes we are sure we need one thing, but someone else can see that we really need something else," I remarked.

"What's your point? I just don't want to sit and think about other people, I guess. Is that so bad?" he responded.

Danny first came to treatment after a brief psychiatric hospital inpatient stay for severe depression. He had lived at his parents' home for several years after college until he finally got a job and decided to move out. Within a few months, however, he was seriously considering suicide and ultimately checked himself into a hospital. "I've always gotten depressed, but this was worse," he said. "When I was living by myself, I was not really thriving. I had a job I hated and not much of a social life. I thought about moving home, but my depression just kept getting worse until I knew I needed to go into the hospital. I had to stop working and I didn't really have enough money." After his hospital stay, Danny decided to move back home with his parents. "I just need some time to relax and not worry about bills," he said.

Danny's psychiatrists recommended outpatient care after his discharge, and he first came to my New York clinic a few days after he left the hospital. As part of his treatment, I stressed the importance of self-care, positive thinking, and staying active, and his condition improved relatively quickly. But as he started getting better, he experienced a backlash from his siblings. Danny's parents were elderly and were struggling with health problems. His father, eighty-four years old, was going through the early stages of dementia, and his seventy-five-year-old mother, who had suffered several bone fractures as a result of severe osteoporosis, could no longer go up and down the stairs without help. They were both struggling to do basic chores to keep their house in order, and Danny's siblings felt that he was putting pressure on them by moving back home. "I basically do whatever my parents ask me to do," Danny said. "We have a good relationship. They say they're happy that I'm home. But my brothers and sisters say I'm making it harder for them. Last weekend we all had a 'siblings meeting' to talk about Mom and Dad, and they basically ganged up on me. They said the house is dirty and that I'm not keeping up with the laundry and stuff like that. My older brother comes just about every day and he's been giving me the stink eye for months, and I really didn't know why until this weekend. We used to be really close. I was close with all my siblings. But now that I know how they feel I'm really annoyed."

Danny was spending a lot of time applying for jobs and making sure he was taking care of himself so that his depression would not return, which was clearly an important priority. "They think I'm just sitting around doing nothing, but I need to focus on getting back on my feet. And really, the house is not that messy. My parents have complex medical issues, but basically they're doing okay."

"You said you do everything your parents ask you to do," I said, "so what are those things?"

"They don't even ask me to do much. Sometimes my mom will ask me to help her get up the stairs, or my dad will ask me to help him to move something heavy. But they like to handle things on their own," Danny responded.

With Danny's permission, I spoke with his parents and siblings and got an entirely different story. Danny was simply not aware that he was creating a significant financial and interpersonal burden on his parents, and making their old age much more stressful. He expected that his mother would cook, clean, and do laundry for him, and he would routinely leave his belongings around the house, even though they presented a tripping hazard for his parents. His siblings were frustrated and even exasperated with his selfishness, to the point that they wanted to throw him out of their parents' home even if it would lead to rehospitalization or worse. I managed to calm the siblings down, with the hope that I could get through to Danny in therapy.

During the next few sessions, I continued to discuss the core concepts of *Interpersonal Connection* with Danny, and he eventually acknowledged that his interpersonal style was a significant contributor to his depression over time. "Years ago, when I lived in California with a friend after college, it was my highest point of functioning. I had a job, a girlfriend, and things were going pretty well. But, over time my friends got fed up with me because I have this unhealthy tendency to focus on myself more than others. I grew apart from my girlfriend and also my roommate, and eventually moved out on my own. But the costs of living were so expensive and the next thing I knew, I was in major debt, so I moved back home. It's been a bad situation ever since."

"There are ways to improve how you connect with others," I told Danny, and he seemed interested to learn more. "*Interpersonal Connection* starts with noticing other people and what they need, and eventually making an effort to make them happy. Being sensitive to others' needs helps us to remain connected to others, and also helps us to feel more confident and happy ourselves." As a preliminary exercise, I encouraged Danny to make a comprehensive list of someone else's needs. Danny initially wanted to focus on his older brother, but I encouraged him to choose one of his parents instead. "You see them a lot more often," I said, "so you have a better perspective on what they need. And they seem to have a lot of difficulties right now, so many of their needs are more noticeable." Danny reacted negatively to my suggestion, suspecting it indicated my agreement with his siblings that he was not making an effort to care for his parents' needs. "I'm not making any judgments on how you're behaving in your relationships," I said. *"You're* my patient. I'm focused on helping you." Danny reluctantly complied with my recommendation, and we spent nearly half a session making a list of all of his parents' needs. The exercise turned out to be a powerful experience for him. He became especially conscious of the consequences of his parents' physical health decline, and how he had indeed become more of a burden to them than he had previously acknowledged.

At our next session he said, "It's hard for both of them to go out anymore. My dad used to be so active, he took a lot of pride in his work. Now he can't do anything but sit at home and watch TV. It's definitely not easy for my mom that she can't go out to see my nieces and nephews. She used to take care of them every day, but now it's too hard for her even to go visit them at all." It was slow going, but we were getting somewhere.

In truth, Danny had already been aware of his parents' needs, but verbalizing them made them more visceral. I asked him to focus not only on his parents' emotional needs but also on their physical needs. "Well when it comes to physical needs, I guess they have enough money, so they've got that taken care of."

"But your mom is in a lot of pain, right? Relief from pain is also a very strong physical need," I said.

"That's true. But I can't do anything about that," Danny replied.

"Maybe, but the point is to consider her needs, not necessarily to solve them. What about your dad?" I asked.

"He moves okay and he's not in pain, but I guess his dementia makes it hard for him to handle all the basic things that he used to do to feel good. We put notes around the house because he doesn't always remember where things are or how to use them. My brother told me we're all going to start wearing nametags when his dementia worsens." Danny became emotional as he began taking serious stock of all the ways his parents were struggling to meet their own needs. "The thing is," he said, "I still can't see how it helps for me to get upset about it. It's not like there's anything I can do," Danny said.

"Maybe not," I replied, "but being mindful of other people's problems is important. That feeling of empathy you're experiencing now *is Interpersonal Connection*. I can see now why it's hard for you. The truth is that you *really* feel their pain. It's very hard for you to see them suffer. It's actually because you are a caring person inside that it's so challenging for you to acknowledge that they are suffering," I said.

Danny started to cry, and then a wellspring of emotion came forth. He was visibly distraught with how his parents were suffering and also how he had contributed to their pain and concern. Over the following month, Danny's behavior started to change. He not only improved his self-care but became much more considerate of his parents' needs, and even his siblings. He also became less introverted and eventually found a decent-paying job where he developed friendships with several of his co-workers. "If I'm being honest, I'm not doing that much more to help anyone," he said a few months later, "but even thinking about other peoples' needs has given me much more perspective. I have more interesting conversations with people now. They open up more since they see that I'm focused on what they're saying, and that I care about them. Even my conversations with my siblings are better."

As mentioned above, noticing needs cuts across spiritual, as well as emotional and physical, domains. However, in today's secular society, spiritual needs are often hard to notice because many people rarely discuss them. At one point in treatment with Barbara and Sam (from chapter 6), I encouraged Barbara to broach the topic of spirituality in her marriage. "Apparently, he has lots of spiritual needs that I didn't even know about. He told me he misses going to church and has felt like he needed to get closer with God again. I was totally surprised because he never brought it up with me before. I knew he was an altar boy when he was younger and I could always tell that he gets a little upset if someone says something negative about the church, but we've never gone to services together except for holidays, when the whole family goes. He told me that he feels it's sad that the boys aren't growing up with the same spirituality that he had." Barbara did not have the same desire to engage in organized religious practice, and she was not sure it was something she could commit to on a regular basis.

"I didn't grow up religious and to be honest, I'm very spiritual but I don't get a lot out of organized prayer. He didn't say it explicitly, but I think he would like to start making it part of our routine. What should I do?" Barbara asked.

"Well, I think you should tell Sam how you feel. Remember that he wants to hear from you, right?" I said.

"I guess so," she replied. "To be clear, I'm not against church or anything. I just don't feel that it speaks to me, and I have other priorities. I'm also concerned that if we start going, it will give Sam another set of values and expectations to judge me by, and I really don't want that," Barbara shared.

"That's exactly what you need to tell him!" I exclaimed. "He will understand."

Barbara and Sam had a heart-to-heart about her emotional needs and his spiritual needs. And the couple deepened their connection. Sam understood that Barbara was not against his spirituality or his religious values, and that she simply wanted to remove any impediments to their relationship. And Sam felt that Barbara understood and supported his values for spirituality. Ultimately, the couple decided to go to church as a family about once per month, with no expectations on Barbara to participate beyond what felt authentic to her inside.

Exercise 7: Noticing Others' Needs, Part 2

This exercise is similar to the exercise we practiced in the previous chapter except we will take it a few steps further. First, identify a need that you currently share with someone else around you. Perhaps both of you are tired after a long day at work, or perhaps both of you are feeling cold, or hot, or thirsty, or hungry, or bored. Focus on feeling this need that you share with the other person, and how you are experiencing similar sensations. Next, try to identify a need that someone else has that you are presently not experiencing but you have experienced in the past. The need could be as simple as the aforementioned examples or something more complicated, such as elation with a success or grief from a loss. Imagine how that person is feeling, informed by your own recollection of feeling the same way in the past. Finally, the most difficult step is to identify a need of someone you are with that you have *never* experienced before. If you are young with few responsibilities beyond your own self-care, you can try to imagine how it feels for a mother or father to care for their children. Or maybe you have a friend with a health problem that you've never had before. Or perhaps you're with someone who has a spiritual need, and you aren't particularly spiritually inclined yourself. Just as in chapter 6, at this point the exercise does not entail making an effort to help; rather, you should simply notice someone else's needs and try to empathize with how they feel. Ideally, this exercise should be performed in a variety of settings so that you can develop sensitivity to a large number of needs.

CHAPTER 8

Interpersonal Connection Part II: Providing for the Needs of Others

N oticing other people's needs is an act of *Interpersonal Connection* in itself and a worthwhile pursuit. However, if we notice other people's needs without ultimately making an effort to provide for them, we limit our capacity for *Interpersonal Connection* (figure 9).

When we start noticing people's needs, we may discover that we can offer them more than we previously thought. Providing emotional support for a friend during a rough time, giving to charity, and preparing food for others in need are just a few common examples, but there are many subtler acts of kindness that can make a huge difference. When I am having a stressful day, for instance, a smile or kind word from a stranger can do wonders for my sense of well-being. When we make an effort to provide for other people's needs, we find that there are an infinite number of things we can do to lighten their loads and improve their lives.

As powerful as simply giving to others may be, the ultimate goal of *Interpersonal Connection* is to fall in love with other people— to become one with their experience and love them as we love ourselves. We know we have achieved this when giving to others and seeing their satisfaction provides the same degree of happiness as if we ourselves were receiving the gift. This requires a high level of compassion that must be learned. Indeed, babies are born

FIGURE 9 **Providing for the Needs of Others**

The most basic form of *Interpersonal Connection* is noticing others' needs. To the extent that one notices others' needs, one can build greater *Interpersonal Connection* by providing for others' needs. This has two levels: (1) doing good for others and (2) loving the act of doing good for others.

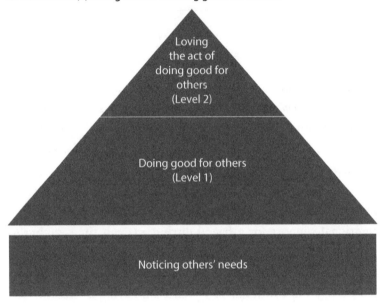

completely self-centered because they are fully reliant on other people and have not developed the requisite capacities to be connected receivers—their receiving is not done deliberately to provide others with an opportunity to give, but rather because they have a need they wish to satisfy. People can transcend this birthright state of disconnection and move toward greater levels of *Interpersonal Connection* over the course of their lives.

When I first began practicing psychotherapy in New York, I treated an older gentleman who came for pain management after suffering from severe back pain for over a decade. Frank had decided to stop taking prescription painkillers soon after his eighty-fourth birthday, after a fall that he attributed to the dizziness caused by the medication. Despite being in constant pain, Frank was among the warmest and most compassionate people I have ever met. His main concerns all revolved around other people, and his primary goal in therapy was to learn to manage and accept his pain so that he could go back to giving his time to others. "I can barely go anywhere," he said. "I can't make the rounds in the neighborhood anymore." He still lived in the same Brooklyn neighborhood where he grew up, and he had spent most of his time practicing connected giving with people whose needs he had grown highly sensitive to over the course of his entire life. "There's a woman down the block, Marissa, who's 102," he said, "and her son was a few years younger than me and a good friend of mine when we were young. He passed away about ten years back and I visited her at least once a week from then until last month. She can't get out at all, and it kills me to imagine how lonely she is now. She's got nobody else." Besides visiting friends, Frank had volunteered for nearly twenty years as a groundskeeper in a small local park. "I haven't even seen it recently," he told me, "but I don't even want to. By the end I was the only one taking care of it, and it's probably so overgrown now that people can't even use it. It's a real refuge for the neighborhood and I've been going there since I was a kid." Frank was so connected with other people that his main concern was not his own pain but the degree to which it was limiting his ability to care for other people. In other words, the primary negative consequence of his ailing health was that it inhibited his *Interpersonal Connection*. This is the level of connectedness that we should all strive for, especially while we are young enough to demonstrate our care to the fullest extent.

I treated Frank relatively early in my career, and I had barely started to study the *Connections Paradigm* with Rabbi Kelemen. In retrospect, I realize that Frank held the keys to *Interpersonal*

Connection like no other patient—in fact, like few other people—I had ever met. "Tell me, Frank. What do you get out of taking care of people?"

"The same as everybody else," he said, "it makes me feel good. When you're as old as I am and you look back on your life, the only thing that really sticks are the times you made someone smile."

What made Frank's connected giving so compelling was how small acts of kindness made such a large impact on both his own well-being and those of his recipients. After his fall limited his mobility, he received a flood of calls and visits from people in the neighborhood who he used to care for. "There's a guy on the corner, Juan, who hands out free newspapers to people getting on the subway," he told me, "and I used to pass by and chat with him for a few minutes every morning. After the fall I couldn't leave the house for a whole week, and the next week, Juan knocked on my door. He said he was worried about me and he had asked around to figure out where I was living and how I was doing. That meant a lot." Even a friendly two-minute chat each morning was so important to Juan that he felt its absence after only a week.

One of the defining aspects of connected giving is that our motivation is far more important than the substance of our gift. Holding a door open can make someone's day, even our own, if we do it out of love for the other person. But if we do it perfunctorily, merely to avoid the embarrassment we would feel for being seen to let a door slam in someone's face, it will barely make an impact at all. Any gift can promote connection or disconnection depending on whether it is self-serving or driven by true generosity, but the difference can be difficult to discern. Sometimes our intentions are complicated by self-interest and we are not fully aware of the fact that we are really giving in order to take.

I once treated an anxious twenty-five-year-old man, Charlie, who initially struggled with *Interpersonal Connection* because he spent a tremendous amount of time giving, but it seemed he did so mainly to avoid the negative feelings he expected to feel if he didn't. He cared about his friends, but most of his motivation to help them was sparked by a subtly self-centered drive to avoid negative emotions and negative evaluations of others. When I asked him, as I do with all my anxious patients, if he was devoting sufficient time to exercise, recreation, and sleep, he said, "Sleep yes, exercise and recreation no. I don't have enough time."

"Why? Working long hours?" I asked.

"No, not really. I work normal hours. It's just I have a lot of people counting on me and I don't like it when others get upset," he responded.

While that sounded noble, it turned out that in addition to the constant unease caused by his anxiety, Charlie struggled with low self-esteem and the primary way he bolstered his sense of self-worth was by constantly doing favors for a few highly dependent friends. Although he was always available to help others, he made little time to take care of his own needs, which contributed to his severe anxiety. And the extent to which he made himself available to others was disconnected, because it was motivated by his need to feel like he was "doing something" and being responsible.

"I start to feel uneasy if I sit in the same place for too long. I get antsy," Charlie admitted during an early session.

"Are there any specific things you feel like you need to do?" I asked.

"Not really. . . . Well, actually I guess there are. If I'm at home, I usually clean the bathrooms or the kitchen. Sometimes I wash the sheets or do laundry. I also clean out the fridge at my neighbor's house once a week," Charlie said sheepishly.

"Wow, is that much cleaning really necessary?" I asked.

"Not really but my parents really like cleanliness and I don't want to let them down or make them angry," Charlie said.

Charlie's compulsive-like tendency to engage in various activities, and his corresponding difficulty with relaxing, suggested that he might suffer from obsessive-compulsive tendencies. In his diagnostic assessment and questionnaires, he scored moderate high for compulsivity, but his symptoms were below the clinical threshold for obsessive-compulsive disorder. This made sense, since his drive to "do" was not motivated by obsessions per se but rather by a need to give to others and avoid their criticism or negative feedback. This was a concerning discovery for me, since it would be harder to help Charlie realize that his tendencies were pathological given that they seemed, on the surface, to be motivated by a desire to take care of others. On the other hand, I realized that Charlie's caring nature could be an asset to his recovery if he could manage to start giving in a connected way. Doing so would increase his sense of self-worth and responsibility, as long as he also made time for his own needs and learned to care for others out of love for them, as opposed to fear of evoking their ire. When I began discussing the *Connections Paradigm*, focusing on the concept of connected giving, Charlie interrupted me.

"I give a lot," he said. "Giving makes me feel good. I like to make people happy and it makes my mom happy when she sees me doing good things for people."

"That's great. What kinds of things do you do to help others?" I asked.

"Well Marty, he's my brother who lives with us, he gets really antsy unless coffee is made in the morning, so I wake up early every morning to make it for him. Then I usually see what I can do for my mom, because she struggles with her own anxiety and hates taking the dogs out for a walk. It really drives me crazy when she is stressed out since sometimes she takes it out on me, you know by getting angry. So, I try to make it as easy for her as I can."

"That's great. It seems like you help so much, it must be hard to do anything else," I remarked.

"Usually my mom settles into bed around 8 or 9 because she needs her rest. After she's in bed, once a week I visit my friend Billy, who lives down the street. I like to check in on him and see if there's anything he needs from the store, because once he blew up at me when he was running low on groceries. So, I often do his shopping for him and that's the only time of day that I have to take care of it," Charlie reported.

"That's amazing. It would be very difficult for most people to spend that much of their day helping people, especially at the young age of twenty-five," I remarked.

"Yes," he said, "but I'll feel irresponsible if I do less. They need help and I'm the only one around to help them. And I still live at home. I at least want to be pulling my own weight and take care of my mom."

Even though he didn't get it, I was able to persuade Charlie to scale back his time caring for his friends and family in order to be more attentive to his own needs. My ultimate goal was to enhance Charlie's *Interpersonal Connection.* I feared that his giving was ultimately coming from a selfish place since he seemed primarily motivated by the fear of letting others down. I wanted him to regroup and tend to his own needs a bit more, then approach *Interpersonal Connection* from a greater place of love and understanding of what other people truly need. However, this was particularly difficult for Charlie because he lived with his mother and viewed her as a "challenging character." It took several weeks, but eventually Charlie mustered the courage to explain to her that he needed more time for exercise, recreation, and other self-care necessities in order to combat his anxiety. To Charlie's surprise, his mother was fairly supportive, but Charlie continued feeling unsure about spending less time on his duties and questioned its necessity.

"Okay, I want you to practice something for the next week," I told him. "I want you to try to avoid doing anything at all for other people. Tell your friends and family beforehand that this week is all about you taking care of yourself. Imagine that you have absolutely no obligations to take care of other people. Instead, I'd like you to simply notice other people's needs. Just take inventory and pay attention when other people need you to do something, but don't take action."

Charlie looked at me as though I were from outer space.

At our next session, I asked Charlie about the exercise. "Yes," he said, "I did it until Thursday. I'm really not sure it's the right thing for me."

"How did everyone react?" I asked.

"They've all been very encouraging. That made me feel kind of bad actually. They always act so grateful when I help. I thought they really needed it but I'm realizing maybe they don't."

"Charlie, there are plenty of people to help. You have a great job to do! But it needs to come from a place of noticing others' needs, and also accepting your own needs and limitations," I said, and I encouraged Charlie to do the exercise for another week.

It was very hard for Charlie, but persisting with the approach was a turning point in his treatment. Taking time off from caring for others made him realize the importance of self-care and healthy body-soul dynamics. Ultimately Charlie realized that other people didn't need some of the things he was doing, but they did have other needs that he could attend to. We mutually decided to extend the exercise yet another week. Charlie felt very anxious and also guilty, but by the third week of this approach his feelings subsided considerably. By then he said, "Instead of cleaning and fixing up the house and doing grocery shopping, I just hang out and people seem to appreciate me even more. In a way it's better for them to just spend time with me." As his comfort with this approach exercise increased, we began discussing connected giving and the ways that small gifts with the right intention can have a greater impact than larger ones. "There's only so much we can do to help people," I told him, "but when we do help, it can do us a lot of good as long as we do it out of love and not in order to avoid guilt feelings." Gradually, Charlie's satisfaction in giving increased without negatively affecting his self-care because he was able to give in a connected way. "I focus on a few things instead of doing everything," he said, "and I get more satisfaction out of it. It's kind of a hobby now." I told Charlie that treating giving as an enjoyable pastime is exactly what we're striving for. Hobbyists love engaging in their interests, independent of the outcomes.

As discussed in the introduction to this book, according to the *Connections Paradigm* people dwell in the *World of Connection* or *Disconnection* at any moment in time—there is no in-between state. In terms of *Interpersonal Connection*, that means we orient ourselves as either a giver (selfless) or a taker (selfish) in every interaction, and regardless of the circumstances we can always orient ourselves as a giver if we so choose. As mentioned previously, we can connect by giving, when providing for others from a place of wanting to give to them, but we can also connect by receiving, when we do so in order to give others the chance to connect with us. Conversely, we can disconnect by giving when it comes from an unhealthy place, as it did with Charlie. And we can also disconnect by receiving, when our intentions are simply to benefit from someone else as opposed to drawing close to them in a relationship.

Once, a twenty-four-year-old patient named Sandra, who had an especially difficult time accepting this notion, challenged me with an important point: "So many people need help. We all need help, sometimes! So, I do what I can for others, whenever I can, and however I can. Why does it matter what my intentions are?" she asked. I did not share this with Sandra at the time, but I found it very interesting that she herself, though highly motivated to give, struggled mightily with receiving. When I discussed the case with Rabbi Kelemen, he pointed out to me that Sandra appeared to be a natural giver. Her parents were devoted community leaders who regularly self-sacrificed for others throughout their lives. And so, it was no surprise that Sandra chose a helping profession for her vocation. When I met her, she was completing a master's degree in school counseling at New York University and interning at a not-for-profit agency that helped underprivileged high school students apply to college. After graduation, she planned on enlisting in the Peace Corps to volunteer as either a librarian or an English teacher for children in West Africa, and afterward to pursue doctoral studies in counseling. "My parents don't like the idea of me going to Ghana," she told me. "They say they think it's better for me to get my PhD first, but I know it's really because they think I'll get hurt. Or they think I'll fail and need to come home early. But I am going to do it. I'm very driven to help children and I won't let my parents get in the way of that."

Rabbi Kelemen also pointed out to me, though, that Sandra was virtually unable to receive from others. She was devoting almost all of her time to caring for other people and preparing for a career of service, but failing to invest in deep relationships that she herself needed. Sandra shared with me that not only did her parents voice concern about her choices, but her friends had also shared that she was too self-effacing. In fact, in the course of the two years prior to coming to me for therapy, Sandra had lost two of her closest friends because she was not spending enough time with them—being too preoccupied with her giving pursuits—and the friendships simply fell apart. By the time she came for treatment, Sandra was quite depressed and lonely. Worse, she berated herself for feeling down, since she expected that her focus on giving—a deeply valued activity—should have been enough to raise her spirits. To be clear, Sandra was getting exactly what she wanted in life. She was thriving academically and taking full advantage of her free time, but she was falling apart behind the scenes since she would not—she could not—allow anyone to get close enough that she would rely on them emotionally. Deep down, I sensed that Sandra struggled with feelings of inadequacy and low self-esteem, which I attributed to neglect on the part of her parents for putting community service before her emotional and other needs.

"I'm the youngest among four siblings and I'm five years younger than my next-youngest brother, so there were always people around me to take care of everything, but my parents were older and busier than they were when my siblings were growing up. So, I wasn't lonely, but I didn't have much of a connection with them. I always felt bad when they doted on me, because I knew it was taking them away from community service. When I got sick, I would pretend to be OK in order that it wouldn't burden them," Sandra shared with me a few sessions into our work together. "But now, my parents are really treating me like 'the baby' by being overprotective, and I really resent them for it! It's hard to explain, but it's like they didn't tend to me when I was growing up and all of a sudden they see me as immature and helpless. I guess part of me thinks they are right—part of me knows that I'm pushing myself too hard, but I am a capable adult and should be able to make my own decisions at this point! With that said, when I mess things up I get so down on myself and feel that I really can't accomplish anything. Plus, my friends are abandoning me. So, my life is a mess," Sandra shared, with tears in her eyes.

Over the following month or so, I shared with Sandra some of the concepts in this chapter—most centrally, that giving to others is a wonderful way to connect, but only when it flows from a place of wanting to provide as opposed to trying to avoid receiving. I illustrated to Sandra that her visceral fears of relying on others were not helpful and were ultimately undermining her efforts to be a giver in the world since it's impossible to give forever unless one is emotionally strong and has others to rely on.

"So, it's not enough that I'm maintaining excellent grades and volunteering fifteen hours a week?" Sandra asked.

"Actually, it's more than enough. It's too much! I think it's time to focus on receiving from others—letting them take care of you, since you're such a great person," I responded.

"I know you're right, Dr. Rosmarin," Sandra responded. "I keep it together pretty well but in reality I'm running away from others. I don't let anyone get too close because I don't want to get hurt."

Over the coming weeks, Sandra worked on opening up to her friends and her parents about her feelings of inadequacy. It was not easy for Sandra to acknowledge that she needed support from others, and she was terrified inside that those around her would judge or even leave her when she became needy. But, just as I predicted, the exact opposite happened. Sandra's giving nature had built up a lot of social credit for her, and others were all too happy that they could finally "return the favor" and provide for Sandra's needs. Sandra even reconnected with her old friends, initially by just sending them text messages and eventually by opening up emotionally to them and asking for their listening ears and advice. Sandra learned, through these processes, that taking from others can also be an act of giving—both to oneself and to others—since her friends and family wanted to provide for her needs.

Sandra appreciated my affirmation, but it took more concrete steps to help her develop the empathy needed to get the most connection out of her giving. In addition to helping her make an effective schedule that balanced her responsibilities without taking on more than she could handle, I encouraged her to make a list of all the people whose lives she had impacted in a positive way through her internship, and to read it to herself every morning. "When you're reading the list, really try to imagine and feel how much more hopeful and happy they are because of your role in their lives." I also coached her on how to get the most out of simpler acts of giving by making an effort to feel a deep level of empathy for the recipient, even if all she did for them was give them a friendly smile. "We can do a lot of good without giving it that much thought," I told her, "but giving is even better for *us* when we can feel the joy of the other person." Fortunately, her friends and family had terrific advice for Sandra. It was virtually unanimous among them that Sandra was working too hard and that she needed to spend more time on her own needs and also in developing her relationships.

At our final session, Sandra remarked, "Yeah, I guess I never thought about other people needing to give to me. I know that I love giving to others, but somehow it never dawned on me that other people have a similar need." Along these lines, Sandra told me that she was working on expressing gratitude to others when they did things for her. "It is so hard for me! Because I don't want to receive from other people. But I know that it's actually a form of giving, so I am trying. I am learning," she said. "Remember," I reminded her, "it isn't a sign of weakness for you to let others help you. It's very normal these days for parents to continue supporting their children emotionally and otherwise into adulthood, and there is nothing wrong with that. Let your parents enjoy the satisfaction of helping you! In addition, you actually do need their support, so graciously accept the offer and you will be even better positioned to give whatever you can to the world."

A few months later, Sandra sent me an email. Her mood had drastically improved, but more importantly so had her sense of self-efficacy and capacity for *Interpersonal Connection*. She had decided against going to Ghana, because she recognized she would be utterly alone in West Africa and she now understood the inherent and deep spiritual value of *Interpersonal Connection*.

Exercise 8: Providing for the Needs of Others

This exercise is a natural extension of the ones we practiced in the previous two chapters. We will again notice a current need of someone around us, but this time we will make an effort to satisfy it. No need is too small, and in fact, a simple gift can be a more powerful act of connection if we focus on giving it with a clear and confident sense of altruism. As well, if we notice/become aware that someone wants to give to us, then "giving" in that situation entails receiving the gift from them. For this exercise, it doesn't matter who the other person is. It could be someone in your family, a coworker, a friend, an acquaintance, or a complete stranger, since *Interpersonal Connection* can occur between any two people at any time. Just as in chapters 6 and 7, it's best to provide for the need before the other person has stated it explicitly. For example, if we notice a coworker yawning in the early afternoon, we may offer them a coffee (before they ask for it). Or, maybe we notice that our home is a mess and we can clean it up for the benefit of our family or roommates, before they say anything. Do not worry if doing this exercise doesn't initially inspire strong feelings of connection or warmth toward others. Some individuals will naturally gravitate toward giving and enjoy the process, whereas others may struggle internally and it will take longer. Be patient with yourself as you enter the world of *Interpersonal Connection* and delve into the minds and hearts of others by identifying and providing for their needs.

CHAPTER 9

Interpersonal Connection Part III: Noticing Our Disconnection from Others

Everyone who embarks on the path to connection encounters a frustrating and unavoidable obstacle: the need to extend our connection to those we dislike. This is because living in the world of connection means expanding the bounds of our love and compassion to everyone we encounter. As we will learn in later chapters, it is not possible to proceed to the highest level of connection, *Spiritual Connection*, if we simply pick and choose the people we want to connect with, based on how they make us feel or what they do for us. Of course, there are priorities in life, so we naturally have a deeper *Interpersonal Connection* with those closest to us, and most of us do more to meet the needs of our family members than we do for the needs of acquaintances or people we do not know at all. But it is impossible to maintain connection if we completely exclude anyone from our connected sphere.

Building *Interpersonal Connection* requires us to be mindful and aware when we unintentionally (or intentionally) slide toward disconnection. If we approach an acquaintance with good intentions and they blindside us with an insult, many people switch from the *World of Connection* to the *World of Disconnection* in the blink of an eye. Our instinct is to disconnect from that person and stop noticing, caring about, or providing for their needs. The *Connections*

Paradigm highlights that human beings can rise above this natural tendency and remain connected to others even when they are challenging.

"Sorry, but it's totally not in my blood to love everybody," Jacqueline, a patient in her mid-thirties, told me with a laugh when I shared this idea with her. "If you met my family, you'd know what I mean!" Jacqueline was referred to treatment by her primary care physician for sleep problems, but she was also quick to admit that she also struggled with anger management issues. Most of the time, Jacqueline was sweet, funny, and an energetic conversationalist, but when she disliked someone she made her distaste clearly known. Interestingly, Jacqueline herself recognized that this was not a healthy trait. She had raised the issue of her anger during our first session because she thought it might be contributing to her insomnia; she often could not sleep because she could not quiet angry thoughts toward someone who had offended her during the day.

"I get along with almost everyone, almost all the time," she told me with a gleeful smile. "But when someone rubs me the wrong way, I'm not going to jump through hoops to be nice. And if someone is nasty with me, I'm going to be nasty right back to them!"

When we first began discussing the *Connections Paradigm*, Jacqueline took a strong interest in *Inner* and *Spiritual Connection*, but she insisted that she already had *Interpersonal Connection* down pat. "I'm very close with my whole family and I have tons of friends," she said. "I don't know anyone who has better connection with other people!" By that time, I knew that Jacqueline had serious and chronic conflicts with several people in her life and a tendency toward road rage. I took a risk of offending her by responding, "What about your coworkers? When we discussed your insomnia, you said that you often can't sleep because you ruminate on conflicts at work."

"I don't want to connect with them because *they* don't want to connect with me. I'm not going to show love to anybody who doesn't love me back," Jacqueline proudly responded, though she immediately turned and hung her head a bit after the assertion.

I chose to validate Jacqueline's response, while pushing her forward. "I completely understand where you're coming from. But you've come to me for help with sleep and you know deep down that your anger—even though it may be justified—is making it harder. Isn't it worth reexamining what you're saying?"

"Dr. Rosmarin, with all due respect, I'm not a Buddhist monk," Jacqueline reverted back.

I took the response to be positive. Jacqueline seemed to be understanding that there is value in letting go of anger, but she simply felt it was beyond her capacity. And so, I responded, "Perhaps you're not giving yourself enough credit. You have incredible relationships. You are gifted in this realm! Perhaps you have more capacity to connect with others who make you angry than you think?"

Jacqueline took a deep breath and seemed simultaneously burdened and relieved. After almost a full thirty seconds, she said, "Maybe you don't get angry when other people are rude to you, but I just can't stand it. I don't like being offended."

"To be honest, I struggle with this myself," I responded. "In fact, of all the aspects of the *Connections Paradigm* that I have learned, this is probably the hardest for me personally. You are certainly not alone in struggling with this, Jacqueline."

It was difficult for Jacqueline to connect with two of her coworkers in particular: one of whom she described as an "all around nasty guy" (and other things not suitable to write here), and a former friend who had betrayed her in order to obtain a promotion that Jacqueline had also been competing for. That relationship was particularly strained because Jacqueline still shared a large desk and part of a computer station with her betrayer.

"We were really close. We even used to watch each other's kids sometimes. But after she lied about me to my boss, I want nothing to do with her. I will never forgive her for that. I hate her. In fact, I don't even like speaking about this; it's making me more angry!"

I pointed out to Jacqueline that it is very common for people to feel an increase in anger when they start noticing their disconnection from others. "The human mind and heart are funny in that way. We are able to switch off how we think and feel. Psychologists call this 'cognitive avoidance' and 'emotional avoidance.' But doing so makes our emotions fester such that they never go away," I shared. And so, I encouraged Jacqueline to think about what her coworker had done to her, to review in her mind every few days how she betrayed her for the promotion. I also encouraged Jaqueline to remain aware of her feelings toward her coworker on a daily basis—to monitor whether she felt particularly angry or just distaste toward her on any given day. Concurrently with this approach, Jacqueline worked on her *Inner Connection*. She was vigilant about her diet, exercise routine, getting to bed on time each night, and not sleeping during the day (a critical strategy for individuals with insomnia) in order that she would feel the need to rest by bedtime each night.

After two weeks, Jacqueline shared the following with me: "I felt so peaceful all weekend. I was really loving my time with my family and friends, and even being alone with myself was enjoyable and peaceful like never before. But when I got to work Monday morning there was so much toxicity. I feel like I lose my connection all week and can't get it back until Friday comes around. I realized something important though: in a weird way, I used to like the negative atmosphere of work. It somehow made me feel powerful to get into arguments and try to win them. Now it just makes me feel bad." I viewed this as an important shift for Jacqueline in a few ways. First, she was clearly doing better on the *Inner Connection* front, which was great. Second, she seemed more aware of her disconnection at work, which was also positive in my view. Most importantly, though, in some ways she seemed to be taking responsibility for her tattered and torn relationships with her coworkers by recognizing that she had instigated fights and even enjoyed doing so.

With this newly developed lens, I felt that Jacqueline was ready to start noticing her disconnection from others, in vivo as it happened day to day at work. Jacqueline was challenged to count the number of times that she felt anger in her heart on a day-to-day basis. This reminded me of a conversation I once had with Rabbi Kelemen in which he shared with me, "We are aiming for high numbers. The reality is that all of us disconnect from others habitually and regularly throughout the day. The only question is how often we are aware of it. So, high numbers are best." I conveyed this message to Jacqueline, who initially laughed but then realized that I was being serious. The next session, Jacqueline was very proud to share with me that she felt her heart being sucked into the world of interpersonal disconnection a whopping ninety-eight times in a single day at work. "Wow, you are really struggling, huh?!" I remarked. "Yeah, I knew that I hated work but I didn't realize at all the extent to which this is something I carry around all the time. It's really hell for me. And I am realizing that I contributed to it, which is even harder," Jacqueline shared. I emphasized that the point of the exercise is *not* for Jacqueline to blame herself or feel guilty but rather to simply recognize her disconnection from others.

A few weeks later, Jacqueline proudly shared with me, "I've been doing nice things for both of them. I even got Nick a coffee the other day. That might seem like nothing to some people, but it was a big step for me. I even did it the way you taught me. First I tried to notice his needs, and I could tell he was tired, so I bought him a coffee from Dunkin Donuts while I was out doing an errand. I didn't even buy anything for myself, I went there only to help him meet his need. When I got back and gave it to him, I even tried to focus on all the things you and I talked about, how much he needed it and how good it might feel for him to be cared for." I was really dumbfounded. Jacqueline and I had not yet spoken about continuing to bestow goodness and kindness when disconnected (chapter 10), and she was plowing ahead. In fact, I was a bit concerned she was biting off more than she could chew and encouraged her to stick with noticing her disconnection for a few more weeks, before moving into higher levels of *Interpersonal Connection*. Jacqueline responded by saying, "Don't worry, I won't do it again. Guess what Nick did when I gave him the coffee? He told me it was cold because I put in too much milk! The nerve of that guy!" We both laughed.

A few sessions later, Jacqueline came up with a fantastic question for me about noticing disconnection. We were speaking about the ultimate goal of remaining connected to others even when they don't respond well or don't want to connect with us, and she said, "At this point it's hard for me to imagine how I'm ever going to do that. Am I supposed to just bury my feelings?" "Not at all," I told her. "It's very important for us to acknowledge, understand, and validate our emotions and care for ourselves when we are hurt. That should be our top priority, because we cannot take care of other people unless we take care of ourselves. However, we can learn to recognize that other people have baggage—sometimes very serious and heavy baggage—and that they struggle with connection, not because of us, but rather for other reasons. With some people, even if you play your cards perfectly, they will mess up the game. The key in such situations is to muster up compassion—not anger."

"Does that mean we just need to accept it when people do things that are out of line?" Jacqueline responded, with surprise.

"Not necessarily," I said. "Eventually, when we're not feeling angry or upset, it is often a good idea to share with the person how they offended us. Simply going numb to our own feelings is not the best option, since it is a challenge for *Inner Connection* and also *Interpersonal Connection*. By sharing our concern and pain with others, we may be able to help them to change. In this regard, expressing how we feel is both *Inner* and *Interpersonal Connection*."

"You are definitely an optimist, Dr. Rosmarin," Jacqueline responded.

"Guilty as charged!" I reverted back.

I went on to explain that when we are offended or otherwise harmed by another person, we naturally react with indignation because, deep down, we are taking responsibility for the other's behavior. Once we realize that others are struggling on their own—independently of us—it makes it much easier to tolerate them. As Rabbi Kelemen once put it, "Do you take offense when your acutely psychotic patients in an inpatient unit get upset at you? Of course not, because you recognize that their anger is delusional. It's the same thing when dealing with other people. Once we recognize how little control we have over others' behavior, the rest is easy." To these ends, being conscious of our own disconnection allows us to reset the bar and rethink through challenging interpersonal interactions, before things get out of hand. When someone offends us and we feel that first pang of anger or indignation, the best strategy is simply to notice our feelings of anger—to walk away and refocus on ourselves and our own needs.

Beyond this, in terms of *Inner Connection*, the soul can remind the body that it is loved and cared for, and that it is hard to feel disconnected from others. It is from this healthy base of *Inner* and *Interpersonal Connection* that we can ultimately show kindness to challenging and difficult people.

"That makes sense," Jacqueline said, "because the more I focus on *Inner Connection*, the less angry I get with other people. The problem is that I fall out of the connected mind-set when I'm stressed out at work."

"Yeah, it doesn't happen overnight," I said. "So don't be so hard on yourself. Just keep taking it one day at a time."

Taking things one step further, Rabbi Kelemen once taught me that in some ways, it's actually easier to connect with people who irritate us versus people whom we love and value. "If someone is always agreeable, we may be connecting with them because of how they make us feel, which is ultimately disconnected selfishness. It's only when we can remain connected to others who irritate us that we know we've reached the pinnacle of *Interpersonal Connection*." Along these lines, after carefully considering what we discussed, Jacqueline came to her next session with a wonderful insight of her own. "I realized something this week," she said. "The way I should relate to the people I don't really like is the same way I relate to kids. I love kids! And sometimes they are a real pain, but it doesn't make me feel differently about them. I love them anyway, I guess that's because I think that their behavior is somewhat out of their control, since they are so young. If I can manage to feel that same way towards my coworkers, I think I'll be able to connect with them."

With the above said, there are times when giving to others who we are disconnected from can backfire. I once made the mistake of encouraging one of my patients to engage in the connected giving exercise (chapter 8), without realizing that he needed some coaching on choosing an appropriate gift and recipient. Dennis chose to give a small box of chocolates to a young woman in his office who had just started working there as an administrative assistant. The day before, she had misspelled his name on an important document, and Dennis felt both offended and upset. However, she interpreted the gift as a suggestive act and responded by gently reminding him that she was over twenty years younger than he was. Dennis, who is happily married and had no intention of flirting, was very embarrassed, and he became much less confident in his connected giving as a result.

"It's possible to practice connected giving with everyone," I told him, "but we need to be aware of the other person's needs to know the right place, the right time, the right gift, and whether or not we are the right giver. In other words, someone may really like chocolate, but they don't need to receive it from us. When we make a mistake in our attempts at connected giving, the last thing we should do is be hard on ourselves. We should take a step back, notice how their reaction led us to disconnect, and remind ourselves how good our intentions were."

In other situations, someone may be unable to receive our gift because they harbor deep-seated ill will toward us. In such situations, it may be an act of giving to provide others with a wide berth and leave them alone for several weeks or even months, in order to restore safety. In still other situations, though, it is actually inappropriate to give altogether. If someone physically harms us or someone we love, or even threatens to do so, it is best to avoid them and not engage, and/or protect ourselves. Under such circumstances, *Inner Connection* takes priority since we need to put our own needs and safety first. At the same time, it doesn't necessarily mean we need to disconnect from an attacker altogether. Tyler, a forty-five-year-old veteran of the Iraq War, never needed to encounter his former adversaries who inflicted casualties on his unit and caused him to suffer from post-traumatic stress disorder (PTSD). But after we had been studying the paradigm together for some time, I posed the following question to him as a thought experiment: "Do you think it would ever be possible for you to connect with the insurgents you were fighting?"

He chuckled nervously. "Obviously, I wouldn't want to," he responded.

"I'm not talking about connecting with them back in Fallujah, but if you were to face them now in a neutral setting, with no risk to your safety, would it be possible for you to cultivate some empathy for them, just as you've been developing in relation to people in your life now?"

I asked this question for two reasons. The first was that, thankfully, I have never been in a combat situation like Tyler, so I was sincerely curious if he thought it would be possible to connect. The second was that Tyler was in the midst of treatment for PTSD, and the treatment of choice for his symptoms was exposure therapy. As mentioned in earlier chapters, exposure therapy involves the patient intentionally approaching unpleasant stimuli related to their fears and helps them sit with the resulting distress without seeking immediate relief. Over time, exposure to the fear or anxiety helps the symptoms subside. In Tyler's case, his exposure work would involve writing down in great detail what happened to him on the battlefield and reexperiencing or reliving those horrific memories. And so I wondered if it would be helpful to script a situation in which Tyler would approach his enemies and speak with them about what they did to him and his platoon. After a long and very thoughtful pause, Tyler responded, "I think I would want to face them." He added, "I guess, most of us have a subconscious desire to connect with others—even our enemies. When you go to war, you have to turn that off, and some of us never get it back. But, I'm not at war anymore so I don't see why I couldn't speak with them."

This conversation turned out to be extremely beneficial to Tyler's *Interpersonal Connection*. Simply by being willing to speak with his former foes, he understood in his heart that they were people too—individuals with their own struggles and issues who likely weren't fighting entirely of their own volition but rather in a complex political context. In a subsequent conversation, Tyler shared with me, "I can't really imagine what their needs were that led them to make the decision to go to war. I can empathize with them without endorsing their behaviors or their values. And since I've learned where disconnection comes from, I know what kinds of emotions might be motivating them, and how toxic those feelings are for their own well-being. All of us really just want to connect, within ourselves and with others, so it doesn't make sense for me to hold a grudge against them for something that happened several years ago. I'll probably never get the opportunity to let go of my feelings directly, but at this point I can imagine having a connected interaction with somebody who tried to kill me." Ever since that session, whenever a patient tells me that they cannot muster the will to connect in a difficult relationship, I tell them about the soldier I once treated who managed to cultivate the capacity to connect with his former enemies.

Exercise 9: Noticing Our Disconnection from Others

The most fundamental skill for avoiding descending into the world of interpersonal disconnection is to build greater sensitivity by noticing when it happens. As simple as that sounds, we can exit the *World of Connection* in the blink of an eye if we do not quickly take stock of how interactions impact how we feel. In this exercise, we will practice noticing our disconnection from other people by counting the number of times we get angry or irritated at someone else over the course of a day. Keep tabs either electronically or in a small notebook throughout the day and record the number of times that you disconnect from another person. Remember that high numbers are the goal! We all habitually disconnect from others, and the only question is how often we are aware of it. Also, remind yourself of how you felt and how it made it difficult to continue connecting with the other person.

CHAPTER 10

Interpersonal Connection Part IV: Remaining Connected to Others

P art of building long-standing *Interpersonal Connection* is preparing for inevitable disruptions in our connected relationships. Interpersonal disconnections are not pleasant, but realistically they are part and parcel of life, and often they occur when we are under stress and not providing for our own needs. In fact, inner disconnection makes us much more sensitive to external threats such that *Interpersonal Connection* may even become impossible in some cases. In other cases, our connected relationships go through a natural waning period. We may take connection for granted and stop trying to notice other people's needs or care for them. In any case, setbacks are to be expected and should not discourage us from pursuing a life of living in the world of *Interpersonal Connection*. As we've discussed in previous chapters, all three domains of connection require a lifelong process, and even though it gets easier with practice, we will always be vulnerable to disconnection. But if we prepare ourselves for setbacks and commit to recovering from them, we will find it is not so difficult to minimize disconnection and reestablish connection when inevitable misattunements occur (figure 10).

"I feel like giving up," Barbara, whom we met in chapter 6, told me during a particularly troublesome relapse in her relationship with her husband, Sam. "I didn't see this coming. Now I'm afraid we will always end up back at square one no matter what I do!"

FIGURE 10 **Remaining Connected to Others**

Remaining connected to others has two main components:
(1) guarding against (refraining from) disconnection and
(2) continuing to bestow goodness on others when they do
things we don't like. However, as one progresses in these facets
of connection, it also becomes easier to (3) notice our disconnection from others. This, in turn, makes it easier to guard
against disconnection and bestow goodness on others when
irritated.

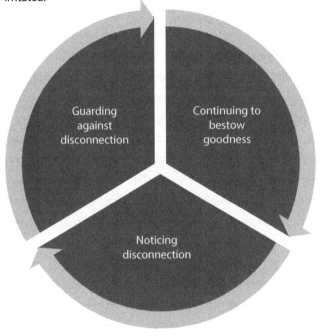

After a slow start, Barbara and Sam made impressive progress in
building connection in their marriage. Although Sam's work
schedule was still intense, he demonstrated strong commitment
to previous gains by asking Barbara to keep him abreast of her
progress and insights in therapy. Barbara was more than happy to
share with him what she was struggling with, and what she was
learning. She considered it an act of connected giving because she

knew how valuable connection would be for Sam. Working toward connection to improve their relationship became a shared goal, and their relationship rapidly strengthened. Sam practiced some of the connection-building exercises Barbara learned in treatment almost as frequently as she did. The way Barbara discussed Sam in our sessions went through a total revolution. After only a month and a half of striving for connection, she went from complaining about his faults to pondering his needs and considering how she could help him meet them. They began going to church together to help Sam meet his spiritual needs, and Sam was encouraging Barbara to devote time to her own spiritual and emotional growth. But from that peak of connection, Sam and Barbara dramatically fell into the nadir of disconnection.

"It happened over the course of two days. He was kind of moody on Saturday, and by Sunday night he was barely talking to me. I asked him what was wrong, and he brushed me off. I made his favorite dish for dinner and made a sexual advance. We ended up eating in the living room because he likes to watch TV while we eat even though I don't, and then he just went to bed. I was so upset! Then on Monday afternoon, he sent me a bunch of critical texts, just like he used to. He told me the house is dirty, and that I'm neglecting the kids. He didn't even mention all the progress we made before, and he didn't respond when I brought it up."

Listening to Barbara describe the situation and knowing the players, I surmised that Sam was under the gun at work and it was simply beyond his capacity (at present) to engage romantically or physically with Barbara. I also took it as a good sign that Barbara was interested in engagement with Sam. Previously, she had felt too resentful of him to want to spend time together. With Barbara's consent, I decided to contact Sam and had a half-hour telephone session with him. Indeed, Sam was overloaded at work. He was completely engrossed in a project with a tight deadline that was leaving him with even less time for self-care and relaxation than usual. In our next session, Barbara expressed to me that she understood this, but the way Sam treated her was so hurtful that she could not hold the pain any longer—it was just too much for her to take.

"Last week I wasn't even thinking about connection anymore," Barbara told me. "I was really just focusing on how good it was for Sam and how I could help make his life better. And he threw it in my face!" she shared, with tears in her eyes.

I felt Barbara's pain and her sense of rejection and sadness, and her fear that Sam was going down the rabbit's hole again. I validated her feelings by saying, "Barbara, I am so sorry. You really did your part here and it must be so painful for you."

Barbara calmed down a bit—just enough for me to try to edge her forward a drop.

"What are our options?" I asked.

"Options?" Barbara responded.

"Yeah. What can we do, when we take care of someone who simply doesn't respond the way we expect or deserve?" I clarified.

Barbara sat and thought for a bit. And then she said, "I know what you're going to tell me, Dr. Rosmarin. I can choose to remain connected to Sam, or I can disconnect from him. Right?"

I smiled at Barbara and responded by saying, "Well, I wouldn't put it that way, exactly. What I was thinking is this: when Sam gets into these moods, is it the right time to teach him a lesson by pulling back and getting angry at him? Or might we be better off continuing to bestow goodness and kindness to him, even though he is being so hurtful, and then taking up our concerns at a later time?"

"Yes, I suppose that would be a better approach. Sam does listen to me when I share—just not when he is completely overloaded with stress," Barbara acknowledged. "The problem is that it just feels wrong though. He shouldn't be treating me that way! How can I just go ahead and be kind to him when it's not right?"

Barbara's question was at the epicenter of her conundrum. Sam didn't deserve kindness. He deserved a smack in the face! So how could she ignore his behavior and be kind to him? I responded by quoting Rabbi Kelemen, who often says, "Peace is more powerful, and a higher value, than truth."

At first Barbara winced, but a few seconds later she seemed to come around and said, "I guess what you're saying is that I shouldn't allow someone's misbehavior to allow me to disconnect from them in the moment, and if I want to hold them to task I can always do so at a later time. Is that right?"

"Yes, but there is an even more profound lesson here," I responded. "When we continue to be kind to people who upset us, we make a choice that being peaceful people—connected people—is more important than other values that we may have, such as being correct." I then quoted Rabbi Kelemen again, who once taught me the following Kabbalistic concept: as we will see in the chapters of this book on *Spiritual Connection*, according to traditional Jewish thought, God is ever present and ever involved in all aspects of the world. God must constantly will our lungs to fill with air, and our hearts to pump blood through our veins. However, as we already know, at some points in time people slip into the *World of Disconnection*, and sometimes we act in ways that are destructive to our relationships with ourselves, with others, and with God. Therefore, at the very moment that a person disconnects (even from God), God continues to bestow kindness and grace on us by supporting our vital physiological processes. In other words, during moments of disconnection, God chooses to turn a blind eye to our misdeeds and chooses to benevolently sustain us, as opposed to cutting off the flow of blessing from our lives. All that being the case, choosing to be kind when others disconnect is literally an act of God. Over time, we can emulate God and learn to do this as a matter of habit and course.

Barbara was simultaneously dumbfounded and inspired. All she could muster was, "OK, I'll give it a try." Given the greater context of Barbara's tendency not to share her emotional and other needs with Sam, before she left the room I was clear to emphasize that turning a blind eye to Sam's behavior was only a temporary solution. I conveyed to Barbara that at some point after Sam resurfaced from his stressful stint at work, it would be critical to share with him her feelings of hurt and try to help him realize the importance of being more empathic, caring, and supportive even when he is under great stress. "Once you're back on firmer ground, you need to have a serious conversation with him about what went wrong." Barbara understood, and left my office. At our next session, she was smiling. By following this approach, Barbara was able to restore *Interpersonal Connection* within her marriage. The moment that Sam saw Barbara's smile when he came home, he felt unconditionally loved by her, which helped reduce his stress. As a result, even before Barbara could raise her concerns about his behavior, he apologized to her and accepted responsibility for allowing his stressors to get the better of him. He also recommitted to repairing their relationship by ensuring that his work stress did not spike so high in the future. The couple decided to spend some time together and rekindle their connection.

In other cases, it's much more complicated. I've seen some individuals jump into bestowing kindness to people who cause them pain, without fully stopping to appreciate and feel the pain they are experiencing. In other words, they attempt to remain connected, without noticing their own disconnection, which never works out well in the end. Several years ago, I met Charlene, a sophomore college student who came to her initial session with an ear-to-ear smile that seemed empty. Indeed, Charlene's chief complaint was chronic, low-grade depression (dysthymia) including a lack of ability to enjoy most activities throughout the day (anhedonia). Charlene had what she thought was a wonderful tendency to "turn the other cheek" and provide unconditional grace to everyone around her, in perpetuity, even when others took advantage of her kindness. "I feel like I'm losing my best friend," she said, "and I can't even figure out why. I do everything for her."

"Have you spoken with Winter about it?" I asked.

"I've tried but she acts like everything is fine," Charlene responded.

Charlene and Winter became close friends after meeting during freshman orientation the previous year. They were both English literature majors who grew up in towns only forty miles apart, and they shared many interests and experiences that made them very compatible. At the beginning of their sophomore year, however, they decided to rent an apartment together off campus, and after about a month their relationship was under great stress. The worst part about it for Charlene, though, was that she had no clue why. "I really don't like to live in a disorganized or dirty apartment," Charlene said, "and Winter, well, she's a wonderful person and it really shouldn't bother me so much . . ." I asked Charlene to elaborate, but she wouldn't. She did, however, go on to say that she makes Winter breakfast in the morning, helps her with her homework, and often stays up late listening to her complain about her boyfriend. "It sounds to me like your relationship is a bit one-sided," I said to Charlene, mostly just to see how she would respond. "Um . . . Winter is a wonderful person. She's also been through a lot. Her parents had a really messy divorce when she was a child, and she struggles academically. She is a good friend," Charlene defensively shared. "Well, have you ever spoken with Winter about your needs to have the apartment cleaner than it currently is?" I asked. Charlene was visibly uncomfortable with the question. Her response was very telling: "I would prefer to take the high road and not think about it."

From a *Connections Paradigm* perspective, my clinical sense was that Charlene was not truly "remaining connected" to Winter during moments of disconnection. Rather, she was altogether ignoring the fact that she felt disconnected, and in actuality she was refusing to think about the problem at all. I surmised that Charlene's approach to this conflict was related to her symptoms. She was going numb inside to the pain of Winter not attending to her needs. We all have a natural need to feel important to others in our lives—especially people we feel closest to—and Charlene was not getting this from Winter. So, the only option Charlene felt she had, in order to preserve the relationship, was to numb herself to the pain. This resulted in Charlene becoming chronically mildly depressed and losing interest in life—in other words, she became emotionally numb. Interestingly, about a month into treatment, Charlene explained to me that she came from a very religious family, and although she became less engaged in organized practice during her adolescence, she still held deep religious convictions such as the importance of "turning the other cheek" and "practicing forgiveness" when others do wrong. I engaged Charlene in a discussion about her religious background and beliefs around forgiveness.

"Is it really forgiveness, though, if you don't fully feel the pain of what someone is doing to you?" I asked.

"What do you mean?" Charlene inquired.

"Well, can you fully forgive someone and move on without appreciating the impact of their behavior on your life? How it makes you feel, and how it affects you day to day?" I clarified.

"I suppose not. I guess that would just be putting one's head in the sand," Charlene responded.

"How do you think that may apply to your situation with Winter?" I asked.

Charlene didn't quite get it at first. But over time she started to appreciate her tendency to overextend herself for Winter despite feeling deep resentment inside toward her. More importantly, she came to understand that she was discounting and ignoring her own pain inside in order to maintain her connection with Winter.

"What am I supposed to do, then?" Charlene asked at a later session. "If I tell Winter how I feel, it could blow up our entire relationship. I feel really stuck now."

We were getting somewhere . . .

I shared with Charlene the main themes of chapter 9 as well as those of this chapter, and highlighted that remaining connected to others requires first being fully aware of how disconnected we feel inside toward them. At first, Charlene started to feel a *lot* of resentment and anger toward Winter, and this even came out in their relationship. On a few occasions, Charlene criticized Winter directly, and on a few more occasions she became passive-aggressive and simply didn't come through for Winter on things that she had promised to do. Winter was understandably upset, but Charlene had built up a lot of social credibility over the past several months so she took it in stride. At one point, Winter asked Charlene outright, "Are you upset at me? For the last little while I've gotten the sense that something isn't right." And Charlene took the opportunity to address the "mess" issue in the apartment. Winter was defensive at first, and Charlene backtracked as a result, but over the coming weeks—with some coaching and discussions in therapy—they eventually worked out their differences. Lo and behold, Charlene started to feel a lot better shortly thereafter. "It's like the Beatles said: 'All you need is love,'" Charlene shared during one of our sessions. "That's the beauty of the *Connections Paradigm*. It's true that ultimately love is all we need."

There is another point about remaining connected, however, that is worth highlighting. Sometimes it takes other people months or even years to change, and unfortunately, sometimes people never change. What should we do in such circumstances? Continuing to remain connected seems impossible, if not futile, when others don't reciprocate at all. However, according to the *Connections Paradigm*, relationships are not two-way streets. They are two, one-way streets. Ultimately, connection is about unlimited giving, and relationships thrive when one partner's giving is independent of the other's. Of course, connection is enhanced when we provide others with feedback and help them become more caring and considerate of our needs. But in cases where that simply is not possible, it doesn't mean we need to leave the relationship at the side of the road.

In the years since I first began studying the *Connections Paradigm*, social media has created a new terrain for connection that can be both a blessing and a curse. On the one hand, social media provides the opportunity to connect with friends and acquaintances whom we don't see often enough to connect with in person; but on the other, they limit our range of expression and can foster miscommunication. One of my current patients, Scarlett, is a middle-aged mother of five who suffers from depression. She has found that email, WhatsApp, Skype, and Facebook offer great means to stay connected with her children, who are scattered around the country like so many millennials are in the current day and age. Her daughter Daphne texts her almost every day. However, they almost never speak by phone or see each other in person. "Daphne is just too busy. She has her life—her job, her boyfriend, her hobbies. It hurts me that we cannot be closer, but I understand that's just the way things are," Scarlett told me at an early session. I inquired whether Scarlett had mentioned to Daphne how she feels, and she had indeed done so. I also sensed that Scarlett truly felt the pain—she was lonely and sad that her daughter had other priorities, and even more sad that she had tried to address this with her without results. However, most admirably, Scarlett did not allow that pain to get between her and Daphne. She boldly accepted Daphne's limitations as a busy, single twenty-something chasing productivity and success in the urban jungle, which leaves her without enough time to call her mother. To be clear, Scarlett was depressed and her lack of connection with Daphne may be a contributing factor; but from my vantage point, Scarlett is not disconnected from her daughter.

In cases of uneven marriages or even parent-child relationships like that of Scarlett and Daphne, Western sensibilities typically encourage us to recoil and withdraw, and ultimately live more isolated and alone. While that is sometimes the best option—for example, in cases where there is ongoing abuse of an emotional, physical, or sexual nature—our tendency to drop relationships on other grounds is not consistent with the *Connections Paradigm*. "All relationships rise and fall on our ability to tolerate others' misbehavior," Rabbi Kelemen once taught me. I understood this to refer not only to interpersonal relationships but also to our connection with ourselves (body and soul), and most importantly with God. Regarding the latter, as we will see in later chapters, the foundation for *Spiritual Connection* is *Interpersonal Connection*, as well as *Inner Connection*. Learning to tolerate and suffer the burden of relationships is wonderful preparation for a *Spiritual Connection* with God, since it teaches us to accept circumstances that are beyond our control.

We should not wait for trouble in our relationships before preparing for these possibilities. Even when our connections with other people are strong, we should be aware and prepare for disconnection to occur, since human beings are not perfect. Preparing means cultivating an attitude of being ready to experience the pain of disconnection, doing our best to communicate our needs to our loved ones, and accepting the challenge of remaining connected during such times regardless of how others respond. As social beings, all of us need strong relationships with other people, and by nourishing and preparing for moments of darkness within these sacred connections, we can catapult ourselves forward—emotionally and spiritually.

Exercise 10: Remaining Connected to Others

This exercise differs from those in the previous few chapters in that it is done primarily in the mind and heart. Begin by remembering a time in the past when another person offended you, disappointed you, or made you angry. Take some time to recall as much as possible about the event, including when it happened, where it occurred, whether other people were around, how you felt in relation to the person who offended you, and if you suffered any consequences as a result. Especially focus on how it felt in your body to be treated so poorly. Next, try to think positively about the person who upset you. Try to move past your anger and imagine yourself doing something kind for that person. Imagine yourself noticing your disconnection and then choosing to let go of your hurt and pain. Even if you cannot forgive the person fully in your heart, and even though they may not deserve it, try to envision yourself smiling at them or otherwise being kind and generous.

CHAPTER 11

Introduction to *Spiritual Connection*

Spiritual Connection involves connection between human beings and God. Just like *Inner Connection* and *Interpersonal Connection*, *Spiritual Connection* is about nurturing and experiencing a relationship between two opposite pairs. In the world of *Inner Connection*, our body and soul learn to reduce conflict and nurture a loving bond with one another. To the extent that body and soul are in sync, we can enter the world of *Interpersonal Connection* and create rich, thriving relationships with other people. Finally, the foundations of *Inner* and *Interpersonal Connection* can express themselves in the spiritual domain, through a relationship with our Creator (figure 11).

The primary components of *Spiritual Connection* are akin to any relationship. First, just as we need to be aware of our body/soul and the needs of others, to have a relationship with spirituality we need to increase our sensitivity and awareness of God. Second, in the realms of *Inner Connection* and *Interpersonal Connection* we learned to prioritize the "other" in order to expand our connection, and similarly *Spiritual Connection* involves recognizing and fulfilling the will of God. Individuals who are nascent to the spiritual domain will likely have more questions than answers at this point, some of which will be addressed in due course in the chapters that follow. But it is worth stating here that ascribing to a religious doctrine is not necessary in order to benefit from *Spiritual Connection*. However, it is essential that individuals be open

FIGURE 11 Overview of *Spiritual Connection*

Spiritual Connection is composed of (1) experiencing God's presence in our lives and (2) fulfilling God's will. In chapters 12–15, we will focus on two parts of each (below).

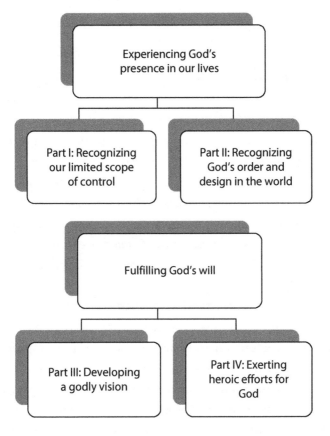

to the possibility that there is a Creator in order to develop their *Spiritual Connection.*

Challenges

Spiritual Connection is generally more difficult to engage with than *Inner* or *Interpersonal Connection*. In fact, *Spiritual Connection* shares the primary challenges of both *Inner Connection* and *Interpersonal Connection* and also has some unique difficulties of its own. The primary barrier to facilitating *Inner Connection* was learning to distinguish between the wants of the body and the higher aspirations of the soul. Regarding *Interpersonal Connection*, the primary barriers were generating a heartfelt desire to provide for the needs of others and learning to tolerate idiosyncrasies and irritations with patience and love. All these skills—inferential reasoning, exquisite perception, a giving spirit, and patience/tolerance—are needed to build *Spiritual Connection*. In addition, the nature of a relationship with God is more mysterious and individualized for each person, as we will see in chapters 14 and 15.

Perhaps the best way to demonstrate the unique challenge of *Spiritual Connection* is to consider how difficult it might be for those who question its underlying assumption (i.e., the existence of God). A lack of faith is only a partial disadvantage when it comes to the first two stages of connection, since even if one doesn't fully embrace the spiritual elements of *Inner* and *Interpersonal Connection*, they can make significant progress if they are sensate to their emotions and those of other people. While a life of faith may provide a boost when it comes to *Inner* or *Interpersonal Connection*, since modern, secular values are oriented toward productivity and self-improvement versus relationship, many of my irreligious patients are very self-aware and in tune with their physical and even spiritual needs, and have wonderful, active social lives.

However, even those among us who are successful in cultivating *Inner* and *Interpersonal Connection* may hit a wall when it comes to *Spiritual Connection*: if one has no conscious relationship with God, how can we be aware of / sensitive to God or align our efforts with God's will?

For these reasons, many of my less than spiritually inclined patients question the importance of *Spiritual Connection* altogether. Take Edgar, an agnostic patient in his mid-forties who had been living with moderate to severe anxiety for almost his entire life. The year before coming to therapy, Edgar had enjoyed a rare reprieve from constant unease and worry that made it difficult for him to relax or even sleep. When his symptoms abruptly returned over the course of just a few weeks, he found himself in my office. We started working with the paradigm early in his treatment because Edgar expressed openness to novel methods and he had little success achieving long-lasting change with conventional therapies. From our first meeting I saw that Edgar had great potential to achieve a sense of well-being with the *Connections Paradigm* because he was a deep thinker and a highly motivated patient whose symptoms related directly to disconnection. After six weeks it seemed our discussions and exercises to help Edgar achieve *Inner* and *Interpersonal Connection* were helping him significantly. Noticing and caring for his body's needs made him more aware of the physical symptoms of his anxiety, and Edgar found that making just a little extra effort to be mindful of other people's needs positioned him well socially to have richer, closer relationships. Over time, Edgar developed stable foundations in both *Inner* and *Interpersonal Connection*, but when we embarked on the final stage of connection he expressed a strong aversion that I hadn't fully anticipated.

"I don't worry about God. In fact, God is one of the only things I never worry about. All my life, I've worried about myself, my friends, my family. That's the reason why I came to therapy. But I was never concerned about going to hell or anything like that. So why would I start worrying about God?" he asked. To be clear, Edgar didn't deny that there was part of him that could be called a "soul" in the sense that various influential philosophers discussed such an entity. But he preferred to use terms like "mind," "cogito," and even "spirit," which he felt held the same essentially semantic value without carrying an association with organized religion. As a devoted father with strong civic and progressive values, he also believed that universal interpersonal moral imperatives such as not to murder or steal were as essential as the laws of physics, but he didn't see these as having any direct relevance to a Creator.

It was early in my career and I was still gaining experience in the *Connections Paradigm* as well as learning how to apply it to treatment. It was difficult for me to guide anyone through the paradigm without using or referring to the religious terminologies with which it was described to me by Rabbi Kelemen and in Rabbi Wolbe's works. However, everything I had learned told me that *Spiritual Connection* fortifies its preceding steps, and that both *Inner* and *Interpersonal Connection* were likely to falter over time without a healthy relationship with God. For instance, the soul can sometimes become pessimistic about its mission and give up on the body. We can grow apathetic to the needs of others over time. *Spiritual Connection* involves pushing well past the physical limits of our inner and interpersonal worlds, such that achieving connection in those domains is substantially easier. I felt that this concept needed to be imparted to Edgar in order to maintain his treatment gains—indeed, he had done very well with other (secular) therapies but always relapsed over time. But that was a challenge given his concerns and very reasonable questions.

During one of our sessions, Edgar became a bit perturbed. "Look," he said, "you wear a yarmulke and you keep kosher. My grandfather was like you and he was the best man I've ever met. I respect it, but it's just not for me. I don't have religious leanings and I just want to stay on the track that I'm on." In discussing Edgar's core feelings about faith, however, another side to him came out. Edgar disclosed that he didn't mind the idea of God per se, and he even had some spiritual experiences over the course of his life. However, he was terrified that believing in God or developing a spiritual relationship would require a lifestyle change. These concerns were reinforced by experiences Edgar had with some unscrupulous religious family members, who chastised his secular practices and were heavy-handed and critical at times. "Maybe they think they're helping me, but it comes across as judgmental. They think all of my problems would be solved if I just started living like they do, so it's hard to talk to them about anything." I reassured Edgar that *Spiritual Connection* may involve religious changes but that need not be the case for each person since the domain is so highly individualized. "The ultimate goal of *Spiritual Connection*," I shared, "is to have a unique and close relationship with God by perceiving God's presence day to day, and exerting efforts to fulfill what we perceive to be God's will."

After that conversation, Edgar opened up to discussing *Spiritual Connection*, and he worked toward cultivating a greater appreciation and awareness of God in his life. As he thought about and engaged in spiritual matters, he became substantially more accepting of matters that were out of his control. As with almost all patients, Edgar's journey in *Spiritual Connection* transcended the Sabbath or other religious activities. *Spiritual Connection* centers on recognizing order and design in the world, realizing our inherent vulnerability, recognizing the divine potential within each of us, and exerting heroic efforts to bring forth that potential into the world. Edgar's efforts to forge a relationship with God enabled him to tap into these higher-order processes as sources of psychogenic strength.

The first steps on his pathway were very simple: Edgar started by devoting just a few minutes each morning and evening to reflecting on God's presence in his life, and to express gratitude for his most precious gifts, such as his family, good overall general health, and a sharp and passionate mind with which to experience the world's beauty. After a week of practice, Edgar reported feeling a sensation of "oneness" that he had experienced on a few occasions in the past. "It's never been something I could bring on deliberately, but it's not an unfamiliar feeling. It's a sense of being part of something bigger," he said, giving off a sense of mastery and contentment.

As Edgar strengthened his *Spiritual Connection*, his symptoms began to recede beyond his greatest expectations. His acceptance of life became much more palpable, while his level of expended effort and sense of accomplishment increased. These aspects of Edgar's development helped reinforce his body-soul relationship, since he needed to remain carefully in tune with himself in order to maintain equanimity under greater stress. Edgar also noticed substantial improvements in his relationship with his wife. He exerted more effort to connect with her, and her level of respect for him increased. Further, as he shared aspects of his spiritual journey with her, she felt more inspired and safe, which made her more open to deepening their emotional connection. Edgar also noticed broader character improvements. In concert with his sharp, witty mind, Edgar had fallen into patterns of anger and cynicism at times, which eroded trust with his loved ones, particularly his children. At one point, Edgar redefined his "calling" in life as a need to work on his anger, which he did with love and patience using techniques from *Inner* and *Interpersonal Connection*. He also took up volunteering at a local park he frequently visited, where he guided families and school groups on tours and assisted in ecological restoration projects. "I really don't think I could have come this far without a connection with God," Edgar shared with me toward the end of his treatment. Over the years, I have stayed in touch with Edgar, and he has remained on course and free of anxiety.

In another case, Mira first came to treatment to overcome a specific phobia of dogs (typically a very brief treatment), and neither of us expected that we would end up working together for several months or having lengthy discussions about spirituality. Mira was a devout Muslim originally from Bangladesh, where talking about God was part of her daily conversation. Her mother and father spoke about God and their duties to him as matters of fact, and they often tried to discern God's messages from events in their daily lives. She had learned that Americans were less frank about their religious lives but the fact that I wore a yarmulke, she told me, put her at ease to express the significance of religiosity in her life. Our work toward connection started with a seemingly trivial comment. "I've been terrified of dogs since I was a kid. All dogs. It's embarrassing to say, but I'm even afraid of Chihuahuas," she said with a laugh. "In my country the dogs are really scary, they roam around in packs and attack the weak. But I know they are mostly harmless here. I used to pray and pray that I would stop being so cowardly, but God doesn't want me to be brave."

Helping Mira with her dog phobia was fairly simple—it involved helping her to face pictures of dogs, videos of dogs, and actual live dogs over time. But given her spiritual leanings, I was careful to formulate this approach within the framework of the *Connections Paradigm* (similar to the approach outlined in chapter 2). Mira was very brave and did a terrific job overcoming her fear. Just as we were about to terminate treatment, however, Mira opened up to me about another matter. It turned out that Mira suffered from much more psychological distress than just a fear of dogs. In addition to a horrendous history of physical and sexual abuse, Mira wished to discuss her particularly complicated relationship with God. She was using prayer to manage persistent anxiety and occasional bouts of depression, and she believed her symptoms were divine punishments that were at least partially intractable. In light of the fact that Mira was a victim and not a perpetrator, I found this narrative to be very painful. Mira's comments suggested that she was in severe spiritual distress.

I hesitated to discuss *Spiritual Connection* with Mira, since our faiths were so different from one another. Most of all, I did not want to inadvertently offend Mira or add to her pain. I encouraged Mira to reach out to her imam to discuss the possibility of addressing her spiritual concerns with me, an Orthodox Jewish therapist. The imam asked to speak with me directly, which I was happy to do. In our conversation, he was understandably ambivalent about Mira discussing theology with someone outside her faith community, but after I clarified a few central points about the *Connections Paradigm* he gave his blessing, as long as I agreed not to encourage Mira to violate Islamic doctrine. I told him my intention was just the opposite.

Mira and I thus began discussing *Spiritual Connection*. She was initially averse to my assertion that her relationship with God was problematic and that she could benefit from a more positive approach. However, Mira understood deep down that her sense of being punished by God was not helpful or based in reality. "I know that I have a complicated relationship with God," she said. "I just feel so guilty! I am so ashamed about what they did to me. If I wasn't an evil person, why would God do something so terrible?" Mira's emotions were raw. She was reaching the crux of the matter and addressing the ultimate question of why bad things happen to good people.

Through our discussions regarding *Spiritual Connection*, Mira learned that there is no simple answer to this question; however, there are several potential answers that may fit in any given situation (in isolation or in combination with one another). Our sessions focusing on these issues didn't even directly answer her question, but they did provide a good deal of food for thought, and salve for her pain. Fortunately, as a retired housewife with grown children, Mira was able to invest a lot of time and effort in the *Connections Paradigm*, and she made rewarding gains in contemplating and working on her relationship with God. She particularly resonated with an approach of integrating the *Spiritual Connection* exercises into her daily Muslim prayers. During this process, I learned a lot about Mira's religious traditions and Islamic concepts about the nature of God, and how consistent many of them were with the *Connections Paradigm*.

Other aspects of Mira's spiritual distress became apparent over time. For example, she initially made a rigorous schedule to engage in various connections activities across all three domains (*Inner Connection*, *Interpersonal Connection*, and *Spiritual Connection*). When her approach proved too onerous, Mira became very angry at herself, at me as her therapist, and also at God. During one particularly bad week, Mira had forgotten a scheduled exercise and also missed her daily prayers due to accidentally oversleeping from a nap, having been up late the night before for one of the feasts of Ramadan. Mira felt exceedingly guilty, and her bad mood set in for several days to the point that she did not wish to get out of bed. In addition, Mira became absentminded and missed out on additional connections exercises and prayer, which only exacerbated her sense of guilt and shame. I helped Mira refocus on accepting the limits of her control—a core *Spiritual Connection* concept—and over time she became more forgiving and flexible in all three areas of relationships.

"I always believed my actions and intentions, and those of others, carried a lot of weight. My mother was the same way," she told me. "When something bad happened we were not really sad, we were guilty because we must have done something that made God mad. One time in our village, someone died young and my mother said that they or someone in the family must have done something to deserve it. It was very difficult in my country when I was a child, everyone was poor. In 1971 there was a terrible war and my father was killed. The way that my family coped with it was to blame ourselves. I guess it felt like we were paying off a debt." I pointed out to Mira that her sense of God's omnipotence was very much consistent with the *Connections Paradigm*, but her sense of God's omnibenevolence—never-ending kindness and grace—was absent. Through a series of connections exercises, Mira learned to focus on God's gifts and bounty, in order to take a more positive, loving approach to her *Spiritual Connection*.

In the coming chapters, we will explore concepts and methods for deepening a sense of *Spiritual Connection*. As mentioned above, it must be emphasized that ascribing to a religious doctrine is not necessary in order to benefit from *Spiritual Connection*. However, it is essential that individuals be open to the possibility that there is a Creator in order to develop their *Spiritual Connection*. The following chapters will help us feel a sense of God's presence in our day-to-day lives, and also help align our efforts with what we perceive to be the will of God. We will find that prayer and good deeds serve an important role, but they are not the only tools to build *Spiritual Connection*. In fact, the primary tools to connect spiritually rest in the human heart and mind, by imbuing everyday activities with a sense of spirituality. Across these approaches, we will see that *Spiritual Connection* is the most challenging but also the most rewarding domain of connection, since it enables us to see virtually all activities from the vantage point of connection, and hone in on our central purpose in life.

Exercise 11: Feeling God's Presence

For our first exercise in *Spiritual Connection*, we will engage in a subtle but powerful method to begin heightening our awareness of God's role in our affairs. This will prime us for one of the biggest challenges we will face in the coming chapters, which is learning to devote our full energy to serving our Creator while paradoxically understanding that God ultimately runs the show. The main goal at this time is to facilitate greater awareness that God is present in our lives, and that we are responsible to be active players in God's world. The exercise goes as follows: Pick a simple activity that you engage in on a daily basis, such as turning on a light or writing the date at the top of a page. If you choose to turn on a light, trust that God has kept the electrical system functioning and the circuitry and light bulb filaments intact so the system will operate as you want it to. As you engage in the activity, envision that God—and not you or some other aspect of nature—is facilitating its completion. Imagine that God is intimately involved in the activity, from start to finish, and that without God's direct assistance and intervention it cannot be completed. This teaches us on a basic level what it means to rely on God while also exerting our own effort.

CHAPTER 12

Spiritual Connection Part I: Recognizing Our Limited Scope of Control

O ur efforts toward feeling God's presence in our lives are often foiled by our own hubris. Most of us operate under a subtle but pervasive assumption that we are independently responsible for maintaining our own well-being, so we have little reason to pray for help or ponder God's role in our day-to-day life. We naturally see the influence that we and other people seem to have over our fate, and we seldom really consider God's influence behind the scenes. Even for those with a faith system or religion, God may be an abstract and remote persona to whom we tend not to ascribe significant sway over our day-to-day affairs. A precondition for developing a real relationship with God, however, is to recognize God's control over our present, past, and future. Just as we need to recognize our emotional vulnerability to others in order to develop *Interpersonal Connection*, *Spiritual Connection* requires us to feel a similar sense of vulnerability toward God.

To start to enter this space of vulnerability, try this short exercise: Lift your arm and wiggle a finger for a few seconds.

And now, you can put it down.

There are few activities in which we feel so much in control. We use the expression "not to even lift a finger" to imply it is the easiest thing we ever do. But to what extent are we *really* in control of this simple motion of our own digits? Even with a limited background in human biology, I know that in the course of microseconds, the responsible brain tissues pass the command down through an intricate network of nerves that relay the message to dozens of muscles in the palm and forearm, which contract in unison to pull the tendons that connect to the fingers to finish the job. Meanwhile, our environments are so complex and delicate that even a relatively minor trauma could pose a significant distraction or impediment to the simplest of actions. Lifting a finger is also fully dependent on our health, which will be sustainable only if thousands of circumstances remain favorable. That being the case for a simple activity, imagine how complex and fragile are the systems involved in playing a violin, flying a plane, or writing a letter.

When we consider the dimension of time, all of the above variables increase exponentially. We pursue goals under the assumption of a stable future and our continued productivity, but the rampant spread of coronavirus throughout the world in the spring of 2020 is just one recent example of the inherent vulnerability of our future circumstances. And the past is even more uncontrollable. People don't choose when, where, or whether to be born. We are not in control of the era of history into which we are placed, or the country or socioeconomic circumstances into which we emerge in life. For these reasons, our fate is only marginally influenced by our own actions. Someone who enjoys professional success might take pride in their achievements and reap the benefits of their pursuits, but how much credit do they really deserve? Even their work ethic was likely shaped by their upbringing, the environment in which they grew up, and the resources and opportunities available to them. Many stars needed to align for them to *be able* to work hard toward a goal. Furthermore, their talents arise from inherited advantages that existed in their ancestors long before they were born. In sum, everything we accomplish in life is completely contingent on infinite variables beyond our control, so every success is truly a miracle. Yet most of us live under the illusion of our own potency until something shatters our sense of control (figure 12).

FIGURE 12 **Recognizing Our Limited Scope of Control**

The first step in developing *Spiritual Connection* is recognizing that we have a very limited scope of control over our experiences in life. Any of the following incidents—in isolation or in combination—could occur at any moment and radically impact our lives:

Terrorist attack on a skyscraper	Major water supply contamination	Malfunctioning of all cell phone systems
Superbacteria released from a medical center	Permanent erasure of central banking records	Major malware attack on Google
Nationwide power outage for over a year	A sudden tenfold increase in gasoline prices	Nuclear attack on a major urban center
Chemical contamination of the air	A devastating weather event	Rampant murder of civilians by civilians
A 50-foot rise in sea levels	Deadly radiation due to an astronomical event	99% devaluation of US currency
A catastrophic collapse of the New York Stock Exchange	Outbreak of a rare and deadly virus	An unrelenting meteor shower
Hostile military invasion of a foreign government	Walkout of the entire police force	Widespread social acceptance of grand theft

Psychologically speaking, there are two primary options for us to respond to the realization that we are, ultimately, helpless. First, many people live in constant fear of all that could potentially go wrong in the future. In clinical terminology, this is called anxiety. When working with patients, we are careful to point out that the likelihood of negative events occurring is much lower than the anxious mind perceives; however, in truth, there are no guarantees in life and we are inherently very vulnerable. Thus, the main drawback of this option is that we are condemned to a life of emotional pain. The second option is to actively deny our level of risk. It is common to use the expression "act of God" to describe an unexpected misfortune, yet most people rarely conceive of disasters as divinely ordained and instead use the term to refer to "exceedingly rare events." The problem with this option is that "acts of God" are not always rare, and when they do occur they can create a sudden shock that can cause irreparable damage. Perhaps most centrally, individuals who deny their level of risk also tend to ascribe their fortunes and misfortunes to their own efforts. The downside of this approach is that we only have ourselves to blame when things go wrong. Fortunately, the *Connections Paradigm* offers a third solution, which will be discussed in due course below.

I've treated enough geriatric patients to know that one of the most difficult things about getting old is losing control. Some years ago, I treated an eighty-five-year-old great-grandmother who was aging exceptionally well but coping with aging worse than most of her peers. Doris had lived a bold and adventurous life in which she pursued her passions as a labor leader, world traveler, and mother of three, but she was totally unprepared for old age. "I was always the one people relied on if they needed help and I was busier than everyone. Twenty years ago, I was taking care of my parents and children while working full time. I cooked dinner every night. Now all I do is sit around and watch people play cards." Six months earlier, Doris's children had persuaded her and her husband to enter a retirement community after he suffered a severe fall that left him in the hospital for two weeks. "They made it into a big deal. I said no for months but they wouldn't stop nagging me," Doris told me.

"But do you think your husband needed the care he's getting now?" I asked.

"Please," she responded, "this place is a dump. He wasn't even that bad. I could have taken care of him like I did for sixty-two years! Now we have to rely on strangers who don't know what they're doing and don't even care."

Doris's daughter had pleaded with her to see me after the retirement home threatened to discharge her after a series of conflicts with staff. The culminating incident involved Doris berating a worker and allegedly throwing a meal tray at her. "She said I threw it, and that was a lie. I dropped it at her feet. She told me I needed to take the low-sodium lunch option because of my blood pressure. Can you believe the nerve of that? She's got such an attitude. . . . She was asking for it!" Doris felt a lot of resentment toward her kids for insisting on her entering a twenty-four-hour care facility, and she became visibly angry whenever we discussed them. "Do you feel like they made that decision out of love and genuine concern?" I asked her. Without hesitating, Doris responded, "I think they made it out of fear. They don't want me to end up on the floor like the geezers on those life alert commercials. But they know I'd rather die in my own home than live in a place like this." Doris also felt some frustration with her husband, Tim, because she believed that they would still be living at home if not for his fall, which she felt was partially his fault for not exercising more frequently. She had also been entertaining ideas of moving back home, but Tim would not agree.

Doris was exceptionally healthy for her age and still rather mobile, and it seemed to her that "everyone here just sits around, wastes time, waiting to die." It was especially difficult for her to handle the lack of important tasks because she did not have any consistent hobbies to fill her time. Doris was not depressed; rather, she was simply discontent and irritable about losing control over her circumstances. Her inability to cope with waning autonomy was clearly distressing her, and I suspected it would eventually devolve into more heated outbursts and depression if she did not develop a new way of thinking.

Doris initially came to treatment to satisfy the wishes of her youngest daughter, but it also served as an excuse for her to get out of the home two days a week. During our second session, I told her about the *Connections Paradigm* and outlined its basic features. Doris had long been interested in self-help books oriented toward time management, and some of what I told her about connection piqued her interest. "It's not easy for me to read anymore with my eyes but I used to love Stephen Covey's books." Doris had always had a sense of spirituality, and she jumped into the paradigm with intense enthusiasm and made some quick progress. It was challenging but rewarding for her to develop a more affectionate relationship with her body, which her energetic mind often pushed beyond its limits. *Interpersonal Connection* was a little rockier as I encouraged her to connect with her children, caretakers, and fellow nursing home residents. She tended to focus on her husband and one of her friends, Florence, both of whom she already had quite a bit of conflict with, so Doris had less favorable ground for developing the skills of *Interpersonal Connection*. Still, she made progress by experimenting in *Interpersonal Connection* in the context of these stable bonds so that she could make an effort to cultivate a similar empathy and patience toward others. Once she was headed in the right direction, we began discussing *Spiritual Connection* in earnest. Things went well until I encouraged her to embrace letting go of control.

I knew the conversation was coming, and it was difficult for me to broach because Doris's autonomy had clearly been so dear to her and she was struggling so mightily to get it back. But I felt that it was in her best interest to discuss how embracing as opposed to fighting the limits of her control would ironically give her a renewed sense of freedom. A crucial part of this would be helping Doris to realize a new mission in life, but before we could get to that discussion she shuddered at my suggestion because she took it as an insinuation that she should just give up.

"I don't want to be like Iris," she told me.

"Sorry, who?" I asked.

"A woman who lives across the hall from me," Doris responded. "She never does anything but she's always happy and smiling. I don't get it. It seems pathetic."

Doris continued to struggle with letting go of control until a crisis came. Tim suffered a mild heart attack during lunchtime one day while sitting next to Doris, and there was nothing she could do to help him. "One of the staff ran to the phone and the medic was with us in less than two minutes. Thank God, he's going to be okay but it was the scariest thing that's ever happened to me," she said with tears in her eyes. When I asked Doris what was so terrifying about the experience, I knew what she would say.

"There was just nothing I could do. I felt so helpless and . . ."

"Out of control?" I asked.

Doris got the point that I was trying to make. She could no longer deny the truth. She was getting on in years and there was nothing she could do to avoid it. At the same time, resigning herself to the fate of oblivious Iris was not an appealing alternative. I shared with Doris that this could be a good opportunity to enhance her *Spiritual Connection* and choose a different path altogether.

I then articulated to Doris what the *Connections Paradigm* suggests as a way to live with sustainable equanimity and a renewed sense of *Spiritual Connection*. The approach requires us to strive to accept that we are not in control, while cultivating an understanding that God truly *is*. Unlike active denial and passively submitting to fear, the paradigm encourages us to accept our dependence on God. By enhancing our faith and exerting efforts to inculcate the perspective that our reality is divinely organized, we can emerge with a sense that things happen for cosmic reasons beyond our human understanding, and that our day-to-day lives are a playing-out of God's ultimate plan. In tandem with this idea, I shared with Doris that the *Connections Paradigm* is not fatalistic since human efforts have enormous spiritual importance and can shape the course of history (as we will discuss in more detail in chapters 14 and 15). Nevertheless, a key facet of *Spiritual Connection* is to accept God's omnipotence and learn to calmly relate to our circumstances with copious amounts of acceptance. In sum, part of *Spiritual Connection* is learning to trust God that, ultimately, things will work out for the best. Notably, it is from this place that we can continue exerting our best efforts to lead a meaningful life, always keeping in mind that our plans, intentions, and exertions play an insignificant role in the outcome of life events. Through plunging ourselves into the abyss of insecurity and recognizing the limits of our control, we can rebuild serenity with God as our foundation.

As a clinician, I am often surprised to find that one of the most common emotions my patients feel in response to loss is guilt. In many cases the worst part of grieving is often not the loss itself but the self-reproach that follows. Children often reproach themselves for not doing more to bolster the health or happiness of their deceased parents, which robs them of the capacity to mourn effectively. Similarly, in the wake of an unfortunate medical diagnosis, many patients regret their lifestyle choices even when their doctors assure them that their illness does not have a genetic etiology. These negative emotional responses are indicative of an illusion of control, but the most obvious alternative—recognizing the limits of our control—is perhaps an even less pleasant perspective to bear, due to the anxiety it engenders. It is no wonder, then, why people choose to live under the false pretense of their own power and even perpetuate such feelings after sustaining a loss. The paradigm's solution is to accept that we must do whatever we can to sustain life, health, success, and the like, but ultimately accept that our fate is in God's hands. By increasing our sense that the Creator of the universe watches over our daily affairs, we can walk through life aware of the limits of our control without the associated anxiety.

That said, many people struggle to maintain faith in God because of their life experiences. "Let's be honest, prayer only gets you so far," Sal, a patient who had lost his trust in God, once told me. "I worry about my daughter's safety when she goes out with her friends. Should I just stop having her call me to make sure she's okay? Don't you watch the news? Bad things happen to kids whose parents pray all the time!" Sal was a hardworking, self-reliant son of Italian immigrants. While Sal was growing up, his father had discouraged him from relying on anyone outside his family and closest friends for help or guidance, since he valued determination and hard work as the most important ingredients in success. But Sal had also been raised a devout Catholic, and prayer as well as faith had always been an important part of his life, until recently. "Hard work, prayer, taking care of the family. That was everything to us." Sal's ethos of work, family, and faith served him in good stead until both of his parents passed away much sooner than expected, an event that shook Sal's world. His father died suddenly of a heart attack following a routine surgery four months before his mother succumbed to breast cancer that had returned a year earlier after ten years in remission. Both were in their mid-sixties.

Although Sal projected an image of total self-reliance, the extent to which he depended on his parents' love and guidance became very clear once they were gone. Two months after his mother's funeral, Sal was experiencing crippling grief, which was made more difficult by his intransigent insistence that both of his parents' deaths were his own fault. He blamed himself for not finding "better" doctors to treat his mother, even though she had received world-class treatment at Sloan-Kettering hospital. He also managed to blame himself for not being present when his father died, even though the heart attack occurred in the middle of a workday while he was at the office. A home health-care aide immediately called 911 when Sal's father collapsed, and EMTs had arrived in less than eight minutes. I got the sense that Sal had spent his life respecting the judgment of only three people, his two parents and himself, as I encouraged him to reevaluate his thinking.

"Do you really think you could have done more for your father?" I asked.

"I should have encouraged him more to get exercise and eat better. I also should have spent more time with him while my mom was sick. He was lonely and it made his health situation worse. He wasn't taking care of himself and I was too busy to really help."

Sal tempered his guilt and grief by growing bitter toward God. After taking pride and solace in the church for his entire life, the combined loss of both of his parents had shattered this reserve of strength, and he stopped attending. "My parents were poor when I was born, and over time the landscaping company my dad started—the one I own now—became very successful. Since I was a kid, I always thought my family had made it because we prayed and did the right things by God. We went to church every Sunday and said grace before meals. Now I'm thinking, why should my old man get the ax when he was only sixty-five? I knew criminals as a kid in Bensonhurst who are still alive and well now in their eighties and nineties! If there's really a God, and a just God like they say, it just doesn't add up." Sal did not go to church after his mom passed for the first time since he was a child.

From that day forward, Sal's pessimism, depressed mood, and declining religiosity started to negatively impact his relationships with his entire family and almost everyone else he came into contact with. Just as he had relied on his parents for emotional support and guidance, his children relied on his positive, encouraging attitude, which all but disappeared after his parents died. He had gone from being laid back and good humored to worrying excessively about the well-being of his family all the time, even at the expense of their feelings. He would call his wife incessantly if she did not pick up the phone the first time, and when she did answer, he would reproach her for not picking up sooner. His constant check-ins with his daughter, his only child still living at home, were straining their relationship. When he heard on the news that a police officer had been shot while on duty, he flew into an absolute panic fearing it was his son, who is on the force. Before the name of the officer was released, he repeatedly called the precinct closest to the site of the shooting, where his son had never been stationed, angrily demanding information from officers and staff who were still reeling from the sudden death of their colleague. Sal was striving to regain his sense of control by redoubling his efforts to keep tragedy at bay. He was struggling to embrace the reality that human control is an illusion, and in doing so he was inadvertently nurturing a suspicion that the faith he had lived by for his entire life was a lie.

Sal's first words to me after we introduced ourselves were, "I just want to warn you, I'm not the kind of guy to come to a shrink and it wasn't my idea. I think therapy is for people who can't handle their own problems." Indeed, he never would have come to treatment had his worries not worsened into sudden bouts of anxiety akin to mild panic attacks, which his wife had noticed despite his best efforts to conceal them. At seemingly random times, Sal would suddenly feel dizzy and his breathing would become heavy, and he would feel the need to isolate himself. In the clinical intake assessment he completed before his first session, he indicated that he had been averaging just three to four hours of sleep per night for several months. Sal and I started discussing religion in our first session. This was because Sal's wife, who helped him schedule the appointment, believed that his emotional turmoil and absence from church were related to each other. "She doesn't understand what's wrong with me. She just thinks I need to go back to church. My perspective is that she doesn't need to worry because I do it for both of us!" But after a few minutes of conversation, it was clear that Sal was quite aware that spiritual breakdown was playing a major role in his inability to cope with his parents' deaths. He was simply unsure whether he needed to restore his former connection with God or divest completely from his faith.

Sal was keen on discussing theology, so I naturally told him about the *Connections Paradigm* early in his treatment. We ventured rather quickly, perhaps a bit prematurely, into *Spiritual Connection*, because spiritual conflict was clearly at the root of Sal's symptoms and I felt we could continue working on *Inner* and

Interpersonal Connection while discussing faith and connection with God. But *Spiritual Connection* became the only topic that Sal wanted to discuss, which was problematic because I knew he needed to develop better foundations in *Inner* and *Interpersonal Connection* to foster a healthy perspective on God. Sal ardently criticized the validity of the *Connections Paradigm*'s basic assertions about God during our sessions, and it was clear he spent a lot of time deeply pondering religious and philosophical questions. The ideas of accepting our inherent helplessness and trusting in God were particularly hard for Sal to swallow. "So many people trust in God and pray all the time and nothing good comes of it? You're Jewish, what do you make of the Holocaust?! And we hear stories in the news all the time of worshippers in Mecca getting crushed by stampedes, or packed churches collapsing on Sundays in all parts of the world. I trusted in God my whole life. It seemed to work for a while but then I lost my parents and now I lost my marbles and ended up in a shrink's office. No offense," Sal said, pulling no punches along the way.

I thought long and hard before responding. I think I put my head in my hands for a full minute before opening my mouth. And then I said, "I get that you're in pain about your parents. You wish you were more supportive and you're consumed with guilt. But what does that have to do with God? Whether one believes in God or not, human beings have a very limited scope of control. Even an atheist can see that plainly! The question, Sal, is whether you want to tap into your faith—which has been a reservoir of strength for your entire life—or whether you'd like to walk away. Either option is fine with me, as long as you make an informed decision. Let's be clear though that walking away from faith will not net you any more control. At present, your frantic efforts to exert control are only making it harder to have agency in your life. You're alienating your wife and children and others around you, your stress level is through the roof, and now you're in a shrink's office! The choice is yours, my friend."

Sal was a bit taken aback, but he kept up his fight. "There is nothing worse than trusting somebody and then having them pull out the rug from under you. If you haven't learned that so far, you're a very lucky guy." I decided to pull back from the discussion and simply validate the point. "You're right, Sal, I am a very lucky guy." Despite the fact that the main issue on the table was unresolved, over the ensuing weeks I noticed that Sal was a bit more mellow, and his panic attacks were less frequent and less intense. Over time, the more I got to know Sal, the more I realized that his belief in God was actually as strong as ever. Sal never questioned God's existence, or even God's control over life events. His struggles were in one specific area: mistrust in God. Sal doubted whether God was on his team. He shared with me that he had never questioned God's benevolence his entire life, and that he had taken this aspect of faith for granted until his parents died. The questioning was clearly related to his presenting problems. And so, I encouraged Sal to speak with his parish priest, which he agreed to do. To my surprise, the priest in turn asked to speak with me (with Sal's consent, of course).

"I've known Sal for years, but he hasn't really opened up about his religious questions until now," said the priest.

"That's interesting. He is such a deeply spiritual man. Come to think of it, I can't think of any other patient who spends more time speaking about God than Sal," I responded. "Which aspects of faith are you speaking about?"

"He's been asking a lot about heaven and hell. He's constantly worrying about what happens in the hereafter," the priest responded, insightfully adding, "I think the afterlife is the only thing Sal knows deep down that he has no control over. He's told me about the *Connections Paradigm*, and I think it could really help him find some peace."

"Interesting," I said. "He seems to be very preoccupied with divine injustice when we speak, but we haven't discussed the afterlife. Let me see if he'll want to discuss that with me."

At our next session, I didn't waste any time. "Do you still believe in heaven?" I asked him. "That's a tough one . . . ," he responded before continuing, "I guess nobody knows for sure. Yet the vast majority of us seem to believe in it. I guess no matter what we feel about it, we need to live with the fact that we don't really know for sure." As the conversation progressed, Sal finally told me about his fears of the afterlife and particularly about his parents' continued existence in the hereafter. Unlike his other worries, which could be temporarily assuaged by making an earthly effort to secure the best outcome, Sal understood that he had no control over the inevitability of death. That was why he became so frantic and irrational when he thought his son might have been killed. As Sal put it, "You know, I don't think about it a lot because I couldn't live a normal life if I did. It's just terrifying. I mean, how do you deal with the fact that everybody's gonna die and we don't know where we go? I mean, when I think about my kids, I can't even . . ." Over the next few sessions, Sal and I continued these discussions and he came to the critical revelation that all of his core worries were ultimately tied to fears of death, both his own and those of his loved ones. When Sal kept tabs on his wife and children, he was essentially trying to protect them from the direst possibility. This insight helped Sal keep his anxiety in check, since it was a relief in itself for him to have identified the core of his unease even though there was nothing he could do to change it.

Over time, with continued discussion about the *Connections Paradigm* and some encouragement from his wife, Sal began to pray and go to church again. Sal decided to petition God daily to keep him and his family safe, and to thank God once each day for his blessings. These activities came naturally to Sal since he had done them for so much of his life, but they were still challenging since he continued to harbor resentment toward God for taking his parents at such a young age. Nevertheless, they restored more than a rudimentary spiritual sensation for Sal, which he reported to be of substantial benefit. As he put it, "I've been getting this feeling that I haven't had in a long time, like God is really listening. There's this warm sensation that washes over me." Sal started to sustain an awareness of God's presence throughout the day by praying more often, and gradually over time, his resentments subsided, and his fear of death became more manageable. "Sometimes I still have thoughts like, 'Why would God do that? My parents and my family just didn't deserve it.' But I do have this gut feeling that there is a heaven and that everything works out in the end according to God's plan, even though I don't understand what that plan is."

Interestingly, according to Rabbi Wolbe, the uncertainty in which we live is by God's design. God wants to draw us into a spiritual relationship, and our lack of knowledge and control engenders a sense of needing to be close to God, which is exactly what the *Connections Paradigm* recommends is necessary for optimal mental and emotional health. In modern psychological terms, independence is not nearly as adaptive and healthy as interdependence. All relationships thrive when we realize our interdependence on each other, and recognizing our reliance on God is part and parcel of a spiritual relationship. Furthermore, once we have accepted that we are vulnerable and God is in control, we can open up a new vista of *Spiritual Connection* and start to see God's design, order, and purpose in the world. The transformative experience of recognizing that beauty, including the meaning of suffering, is discussed in the next chapter.

Exercise 12: Recognizing Our Limited Scope of Control

To do this exercise, first gird yourself for a difficult experience.

Now, ponder a current situation in your life that you tend to worry about. Think about what would happen if the situation were to go badly—very badly. What consequences would that have for you and those whom you love?

Now, think about all the ways that you could potentially prevent such an occurrence, and then contemplate the ways that each of your efforts could fail. Imagine your crisis growing deeper, spiraling completely out of your control.

Now, try to accept the reality that no matter how healthy, wealthy, strong, or prepared you may be, misfortune could befall you at any given time. Recognize and accept the inherent vulnerability in being human.

Now, after envisioning the worst that could happen, pray to God for help and protection. Imagine that God can ultimately prevent this negative occurrence.

This final step will likely be very challenging to do: Try to imagine that it's possible for the worst to come true, but that this *could* be part of God's plan. Try to contemplate that seemingly bad outcomes could ultimately be good and could turn out to be positive in the end.

CHAPTER 13

Spiritual Connection Part II: Recognizing God's Order and Design in the World

Recognizing divine control over our fate is just a first step in developing a healthy relationship with God, and it won't do us much good unless we take further action. In fact, recognizing our limited scope of control without also nurturing trust and love for God is potentially harmful from a psychological vantage point. As Sal experienced in chapter 12, when we accept that God is in control but do not feel God's love, we can become panic-stricken waiting for the next calamity. We can also develop feelings of resentment toward God for burdening us with such an existence. Thus, the goal of recognizing God's control over the world (and our lack of control) is to come to a sense that God ultimately wants what is best for us. Recognizing the blessings that we have been allotted in life and achieving greater understanding and acceptance of suffering are therefore critical parts of our relationship with God.

When it comes to interpersonal relationships, perhaps the easiest way to muster up affection for others is to consider the ways in which they address our needs and feel gratitude toward them in our hearts. A similar phenomenon occurs in our relationship with God. By contemplating God's blessings and attendance to our needs, we can conjure up a sense of gratitude and feel a greater sense of *Spiritual Connection*. However, the nature of our incorporeal Creator is to be hidden, which creates a greater challenge on our part to recognize where our blessings come from. To make this contrast clearer: even though God provides for so many human needs, giving God proper credit requires much more abstract thinking than feeling thankful to another person. We can directly observe another person's kindness toward us, and their gift might even come with a card attached to remind us who it came from. When it comes to divine gifts, however, it is very easy to take them for granted or ascribe them to sources other than God.

The main factor that mediates gratitude is a sense that what we've received was provided intentionally for our benefit by someone who cares about us. For example, imagine finding a twenty-dollar bill on the street. Do you feel grateful to the person who dropped it? Probably not, unless you have reason to believe that they intentionally placed it there for you to find. The reason for this is simple: without a sense that the person cares about us and intentionally gave us the money, there is no reason to feel grateful to them. The same goes for our gifts from God. If we perceive that our blessings were intentionally *given* to us for our benefit—deliberately and out of a place of love—the natural, immediate emotional reaction that follows is one of gratitude. However, if we feel that the benefits in our life are happenstance, there is little reason or cause to feel grateful since we lack a perception of intentionality and love. Thus, in order to perceive our day-to-day benefits as divine blessings, we need to look for God's hand in the design and ordering of our reality as manifestations of God's love. There are two domains in which observing God's design in the world is relevant to *Spiritual Connection*: (1) natural systems and (2) life events. Each of these is discussed below.

Seeing God's Design in Nature

Seeing God's design in nature is pretty simple. It involves perceiving the beauty and utility in the natural world of minerals, plants, animals, human beings, the laws of physics (e.g., gravity), and the cosmos as meaningful and intentional works of God. The profound order of the natural world is clearly and readily apparent, but it is up to us whether we give God credit. Sometimes we instead ascribe the intricate structures within the universe to coincidence, which inhibits *Spiritual Connection* since it interferes with our appreciation of God's gifts. Such a perspective is truly frightening if one also accepts the limited scope of their control; without a benevolent steward watching over us, the entropy of the universe is constantly threatening harm. Conversely, seeing the sacred beauty of even the simplest natural systems can do much to bolster our faith and reduce our fear (figure 13).

Rabbi Avigdor Miller, a prominent twentieth-century Jewish thinker, discussed the divine intentions behind the design of the orange tree. As he noted, the immature orange fruit remains green and difficult to discern from the leaves until it is ready to be enjoyed. Once it is ripe, it turns orange and contrasts starkly with all of its green leafy surroundings, such that its appealing color can be seen at a distance by the human eye. When the orange is ready to be picked, it is the perfect size to fit in the hand of a human adult. It gives off a pleasing scent as it is peeled, and its rind, which is impenetrable by most insects, is easily opened and removed by human fingers. On the inside surface of the peel there is a protective skin that keeps the pungent acidic flavor of the rind from impacting the sweet taste of the fruit. Once the peel is removed, we find bite-size, individually wrapped segments that are appealing to look at, smell, and taste. Inside each of the segments are hundreds of juice pockets containing delicious sugars, surrounded

FIGURE 13 **Recognizing Order and Design in the World**

Recognizing our limited scope of control builds a foundation for *Spiritual Connection*, but to develop intimacy, closeness, and love for God, one must recognize order and design (in nature and life events). This in turn generates gratitude, which we can use to enhance our *Spiritual Connection* (continued below).

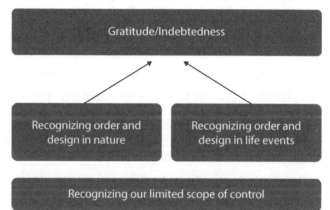

However, one who experiences gratitude will also feel indebtedness: an uncomfortable emotion that emerges from a desire to repay what one has received. Indebtedness can be used to propel oneself forth in *Spiritual Connection* (i.e., by committing to do something for the benefactor in return). However, some individuals back out of *Spiritual Connection* when they feel indebted (e.g., by discounting the gifts they have received). This, of course, is disconnection.

by a healthy fiber. The seeds, which are colorless, odorless, and bitter, are clearly not fit for human consumption. This prompts us to throw the seeds on the ground so new orange trees can grow, all for our benefit out of God's love and care.

Unfortunately, many people conflate such spiritual perspectives with antiscientific views. Appreciating the design in nature is *not* inconsistent with the evolutionary concept of natural selection. Recognizing order and design in nature is not incompatible with a developmental model of nature in which flora, fauna, and the cosmos changed over time into their present state. However, *Spiritual Connection* does require considering that the process of natural development was intentionally guided by God, and not the product of random forces. *Spiritual Connection* similarly requires the belief that God created the universe out of love, in order to engage us in a relationship. Perhaps for these reasons, modern Western culture has a pervasive inability to fully appreciate the blessings in life. By historical standards, many in North America are extraordinarily wealthy and have unprecedented freedom to follow their dreams, choose a source of livelihood, travel the world, and more. Yet our generation is more likely than any in human history to feel lonely and unsatisfied, even when we have all or most of what we've ever wanted. It is as if everything we've ever wanted turns to ash in our mouths and we are totally clueless as to why. We simply cannot seem to find value in the things that we have always expected to enjoy. Our tendency is to assume we are not happy because we still don't have enough, or that we had been following the wrong dreams all along, so we set out on futile missions to accumulate more or suddenly change course. But the *Connections Paradigm* suggests that this unrest occurs because we do not experience the loving gratitude toward God that is necessary to fully appreciate our existence.

My former patient Javier, a brilliant and extremely hardworking Mexican American married man, was on the cusp of achieving all his dreams, but he was less content than ever and ready to throw it all away. A subtle but persistent anhedonia had finally motivated him to come to therapy when he was in the midst of what seemed like the most positive and successful period in his life. He and his wife, Amber, were parents to two healthy young children and the co-owners of a highly successful Brooklyn restaurant. "I'm not really depressed. Most of the time I'm just unhappy. The best way I can describe how I feel is frightened at how unmoved I am by all of this. I've wanted it since I was a teenager," he told me, "and I have been working towards it ever since. Now I'm at a point where I have the opportunity to take it to the next level and I'm not sure it's what I really want."

Javier had opened the restaurant when he was just twenty-seven years old with Amber, whom he married one year later. In addition to being the co-owner, Javier was initially the head chef. He had designed a menu inspired by traditional Mexican recipes his grandmother had taught him, combined with flavors and methods he had mastered while attending a top French culinary school. The restaurant was successful even in its first year, receiving positive reviews in the *New York Times*'s Metro Section and several local and online newspapers during its first month in business. Several years later, it was consistently busy and locally famous in an up-and-coming neighborhood. Javier and his wife were on the verge of opening two more locations, including one in Manhattan that had the potential to dramatically increase their notoriety and income. A lot of work still needed to be done, but many parts were falling into place. He had found perfect spots for the new restaurant locations (albeit at high Manhattan rent prices), and Javier's inbox was full of inquiries from promising young chefs who wanted to work with him and help his business expand. He and Amber had saved a comfortable cash reserve that allowed him to make the big jump without feeling too much financial pressure. Yet, Javier was feeling as though he wanted to give it all up.

"I've dreamt about this, not just the restaurant but all of it, since I was a teenager. I grew up in poverty in Mexico and always wanted to come to New York to have a family and a business. Yet now, I've started thinking that it's even worse to be unhappy than to not fulfill your dreams. The problem is that I can't figure out why I'm unhappy. I have everything, but it all feels so meaningless to me." Over the course of a few sessions, it dawned on me that Javier was out of sync in all three areas of connection. In terms of *Inner Connection*, he was pushing his body very hard and not providing adequately for his physical and spiritual needs. "I often don't get much more than three to four hours of sleep. And ironically, my diet is terrible. I don't sit down for meals and just scarf down whatever is cooking at the restaurant *after* I get hungry, so I usually overeat. And once the day is done I almost always hit the restaurant bar for a few drinks before heading home. It's a stressful life, running a food service business!" he told me. Interpersonally, Javier and Amber had a good relationship but were starting to feel disconnected from one another. "We don't spend nearly enough time together anymore. She is so busy with the kids, and I'm always at the restaurant," he shared. And spiritually, Javier was raised Catholic, but his busy New York lifestyle made it virtually impossible to engage with his religion. "I haven't been to church in years," he told me at our first appointment. Amber was more religiously inclined, and since having their children she had made a point to go to church each Sunday morning. But Javier felt compelled to be at the restaurant early on Sunday in order to clean up from Saturday night and to prepare for the rush that typically came in from midday through the evening.

From this vantage point, the reason for Javier's lack of happiness was very clear to me. As he came closer to his dreams of growing his business, he became more distant from the sources of connection in his life. His body and soul were growing apart, his relationship with his beloved wife was on the back burner, and his sense of spirituality had all but disappeared. "How can I achieve my dreams and also have connection?" Javier asked. "That is exactly the question to focus on!" I answered. And so we worked through several modules from the *Connections Paradigm*. Javier started out by practicing yoga. He hired a teacher to meet him at the restaurant four days a week at 7:00 a.m. to start his day. He also went to a nutritionist who put him on a clear meal plan and asked his employees to help keep him on track at work. Javier also started to spend more time with Amber. After dropping the kids off at daycare around 9:00 a.m. each day, she would come to the restaurant to work for a few hours, and then the two would go for a daily walk just before noon, at which point they would sit down for lunch together. All of these changes made a big difference for Javier, but none as much as working on his *Spiritual Connection.*

Javier really resonated with the idea of seeing God's hand in nature. "I remember when I was a child. My grandmother was very religious. She had a picture of Mother Mary by her bedside, and used to pray morning, noon, and night. One day, we were walking together in a field near our home in Mexico. The sun was shining, the sky was a beautiful blue color, the birds were chirping, it was heaven. And my grandmother said to me, 'Javier, isn't God's world wonderful?' with a big smile across her face. She never achieved any financial or business success in life! But she was happy, because she saw God's hand. I was also happy back then, and I wish I could get it back." I encouraged Javier to not only notice God's blessings in nature but also feel a greater sense of God's love for him each day. Javier added a terrific exercise to his morning routine: after his yoga practice, he would go to the kitchen in the restaurant and take inventory of all the produce, meat, fish, and other food supplies. As he went through each item, he envisioned that God had bestowed it on him, for his benefit and the enjoyment of his customers, as a divine gift out of pure love. After a few weeks of this practice, Javier was able to conjure up at will a sense of gratitude and connection with God. His mood dramatically improved—as did his connection with his wife—and he was able to not only achieve his dreams but remain connected.

Seeing God's Design in Life Events

As mentioned above, the second domain of observing God's design relates to life events. Generally speaking, this is much harder than seeing God's role in nature, since the occurrences of world history sometimes seem unfair, or even unjust. In some cases, people have ample reason to feel that God has forgotten them, abandoned them, or even condemned them to a life of suffering. As a psychotherapist, I routinely meet with patients who have suffered intolerably through accidents, medical illnesses, financial setbacks, losses, or horrifically traumatic events. It is obviously much more challenging to see God's love and experience gratitude from these perspectives. Yet, in most cases it is not impossible to remain spiritually connected. In fact, achieving *Spiritual Connection* from a place of suffering is potentially the greatest catalyst to change, since it can enable us to gain at least some insight into the most fundamental questions that human beings can face (figure 14).

Selma was going through hell when I first met her. When I asked about her faith, she was very clear about how she felt. "I believe completely," she said, "it's just that everything that's happened to me in life tells me that God doesn't like me very much." I didn't dare offer a counterargument. Selma was in a severe depression, having just lost her twenty-one-year-old son to an opiate overdose, less than two months after the death of her husband to pancreatic cancer that was diagnosed just six weeks prior. She was also financially strained, since her husband was the primary breadwinner and his life insurance policy was inadequate to provide for her needs. As Selma described these circumstances to me, I cringed at the idea of trying to help her recognize blessings in her life—to do so would have felt so deeply invalidating of Selma's truly intolerable pain and anguish. And so I just listened

FIGURE 14 Recognizing Order and Design When Life Seems Unfair

According to the *Connections Paradigm*, human beings are incapable of fully understanding why bad things happen to good people, and why good things happen to bad people. Nevertheless, it is worthwhile to attempt to understand these fundamental questions, even partially.

When bad people experience good fortune, it could be . . .

An opportunity for others to demonstrate/build patience and good character	An opportunity for others to demonstrate/build faith and trust in God

A divine reward for good deeds	A divine reward for the good deeds of an ancestor

Because God is being patient	In order for others to benefit	A curse in disguise

When good people experience bad fortune, it could be . . .

An opportunity to demonstrate/build patience and good character	An opportunity to demonstrate/build faith in God	A direct consequence of one's actions

A divine punishment for misdeeds	A blessing in disguise

to her. The conversation naturally veered to the topic of her son. "I'm pretty sure the first drugs he tried came from my medicine cabinet, about a year ago. I hadn't seen him for a long time since I was in prison from the time he was about eighteen, so I had just gotten him back. I noticed he took the drugs but tried not to make a big deal out of the fact that we hadn't spent time together in over three years. I guess I was trying to make up for lost time. Also, I would have felt like a hypocrite because of the things I have done. But my boy loved me, and now I have to spend my whole life wondering if it's because of me that he died. I should have said something!" Over the course of the next hour, between bouts of sobbing, Selma recounted a lifetime of unimaginable pain. Her childhood was scarred by her father's absence, her stepfather's abuse, and her mother's alcoholism. She herself had her own bouts of problematic drug and alcohol usage, which temporarily alleviated her distress but magnified her problems over time. The list of sad events in Selma's life went on and on.

Save for a handful of state-assigned social workers, she had not seen a therapist since she was seventeen. "Things were actually going really well before my husband got sick," she said. "I've been working as a doorperson for two years. It's the first time I've held down a job for that long and I'm getting good benefits and all of my kids were on them. Me and my youngest are in a nice neighborhood now and she's doing really well at school. But Matthew was living on his own since he was eighteen, and he was having problems, getting into trouble. I tried to do what I could, but the truth is I wasn't always there for him, especially when he was young and needed me the most." Selma went on to describe how the worst part of her pain was that things finally seemed to be on track and now she had to pick up the pieces and start over again. "I just don't know if I have the strength," Selma conveyed, adding "I feel like I'm cursed!"

During our sessions, in between copious amounts of reflective listening, I told Selma about the *Connections Paradigm* and we intermittently discussed its principles and practices. Selma initially lacked the required fortitude to engage in any exercises consistently, but we had engaging discussions regarding many aspects of connection. When *Spiritual Connection* became our topic, I struggled to articulate the importance of seeing God's design in life events, considering she had suffered in ways I could never imagine. In fact, I thought she might feel outright offended at the concept that a key to equanimity is trusting in God that things will ultimately work out, considering that so much in her life had not worked out at all and there didn't seem to be much hope on the horizon. As it turned out, Selma took to this idea more easily than almost anyone I have discussed the *Connections Paradigm* with. "When you've really been down—I mean without any glimmer of happiness or hope at all—the good things start to become even more obvious. It's almost like they are shining," Selma said. Initially, I was thoroughly confused and then Selma explained. "In the days after my husband died, I felt so sad but also a rare sense of calm. And then, when I lost Matthew, I was in the gutter, especially right after his death. But ever since then, I've felt so much closer to my daughter. I would be alone in my bedroom in tears, not knowing if I could go on, and she would walk in, crying too, and suddenly all of my worst feelings dissipated." I was fascinated to hear that despite having such a horrific history of trauma, losses, and other life problems, and also despite having essentially no hope or plan for the future, Selma was comforted by a sense of renewed connection with her daughter. Selma went on to describe more, "I've also been much more aware of my senses. When you realize that the sun is still shining, the flowers are growing, and many people are still out there doing beautiful things for each other every day. Then everything kind of has a halo. I can't see it of course, but I know deep down that life is really worth it."

From working with Selma and many other patients, I've learned that it's not *despite* challenging life circumstances that people hold on to their trust in God—in many cases it's *because* of challenging life circumstances that people remain spiritually connected. I have not studied this systematically, but it seems to me that the phenomenology of suffering may be a catalyst to develop a sense that God is eminently present and kind. Perhaps this occurs since people tend to reach out to spirituality in times of crisis, but I think there is something more profound that occurs. When people have hit what seems to be rock bottom, they realize the strength of the human spirit—even in the most challenging, difficult situations, and even without a hope in the world, human beings can choose to be resilient, survive, and rebuild and go on to thrive and flourish. From this vantage point, life challenges provide unparalleled opportunities to dig deep and recognize the God-given strength that lies within us, and to thereby enhance our faith and trust in God. As Rabbi Kelemen once put it, under this lens the age-old question "Why do bad things happen to good people?" should be flipped around into "Why don't more bad things happen to good people?"

Selma did eventually pull out of her depression, which in retrospect was more of a period of mourning than a mental disorder. We have kept in touch over the years, and despite the many life stressors and tribulations that Selma has continued to struggle through, she has remained faithful and drawn deeply on her sense that, ultimately, she is in God's capable and loving hands. With regards to her loss, she has drawn steadily on the concept of the afterlife, and she remains connected to her husband and son. In fact, she recently shared with me that in some ways she feels even more connected to them now than she was during their lifetimes. As for her sense of guilt that she could have saved her son, she still carries around a lot of regret and sadness. However, she believes that ultimately the events of human history—especially matters of life and death—are in God's capable hands, even if she cannot understand God's mysterious ways.

Exercise 13: Tasting the Blessing

This exercise pertains to seeing God's design in nature. As discussed in this chapter, *Spiritual Connection* goes beyond simply developing the perspective that God is in charge, which we discussed in chapter 12. Here, we are aiming to feel that God loves us and acts in our best interest. To accomplish this, we need to develop a palpable recognition of God's blessings.

While there are myriad areas of life we can have gratitude for, one that we experience virtually every day is food. Like Javier, we can learn to appreciate the sacred gift that God provides us in the form of what we eat. This can set us on a path to experiencing the beauty of God's plan in other ways. When we eat, we have a tremendous opportunity to draw close to God if we envision that God packaged nutrition and enjoyment in our food, just for us. This goes beyond simply enjoying food or concentrating while we are eating; it means perceiving that God is nourishing us in a pleasant way when we eat.

So, once per day, do the following exercise: Choose a single bite to focus on, preferably something that is both healthy and tasty. As you put it in your mouth, imagine all the things that happened in order for that food to come to you. Think about the rain, the sun, the plants, the animals, the farmers, and the modern packing and/or distribution processes that were coordinated in order for you to receive that morsel of food from God. As you enjoy its flavor, ponder its nutritional value and consider all of the other blessings you are able to enjoy because you have access to such nutrition. Then, either verbally or mentally, thank God for this tremendous gift, in order to have a greater sense of *Spiritual Connection* to God.

CHAPTER 14

Spiritual Connection Part III:
Developing a Godly Vision

L ike every other aspect of connection, *Spiritual Connection* involves both giving and receiving. In chapters 12 and 13 we discussed the receiving aspects of our relationship with God. By recognizing our limited scope of control and God's order/design in the world (nature and life events), we *receive* from God as humble and appreciative subjects. In chapters 14 and 15 we turn our attention to how we can *give* to God by playing our unique and important roles in the universe. When I discussed these aspects of the *Connections Paradigm* with Rabbi Kelemen, he explained to me that in truth God is infinite and does not need anything from us. However, God created the universe in such a way that human beings play an integral role, and the choices that we make have a real impact—even on God. Why did God choose this path? One reason is that God wanted to give human beings the godlike ability to truly impact the course of history. As the verse in Genesis says, "Man was created in the image of God" (1:27). As we will see in the coming two chapters, human beings can have godly visions for themselves and, through the course of life, bring those visions into reality.

The first aspect that the *Connections Paradigm* teaches us about giving to God (so to speak) is to develop a godly vision. This includes two complementary and equally important elements: developing a godly vision *of* ourselves, and developing a godly vision *for* ourselves. The former arises from recognizing the immense innate potential that every human being has to bring godliness into the world. The latter involves contemplating and honing a clear vision of our unique divine capacity. Even though, as we learned in chapter 12, nothing is possible without God's favor and direct assistance, the following chapters will make it clear that God allows and enables human beings to partner with God as creators, within our limited scope of power and control (figure 15).

FIGURE 15 **Developing a Godly Vision**

Developing a godly vision can be broken into two parts: (1) developing a godly vision *of* ourselves and (2) developing a godly vision *for* ourselves. The former involves recognizing the human capacity for greatness, recognizing that each human being has unique talents and strengths, and believing that our capacity for greatness is within reach. The latter involves determining how to use our specific gifts to serve God, and can be divided into two parts: (1) generic visions for ourselves (i.e., activities that most or all people can do to fulfill God's will), and (2) individual visions for ourselves (i.e., activities that are part of our unique divine service).

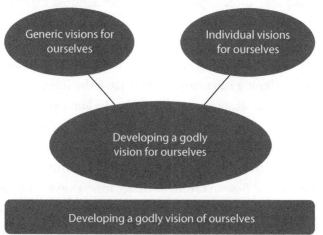

Developing a Godly Vision of Ourselves

The first step in developing a godly vision of ourselves is to recognize the inherent spiritual value of a human being. We routinely see media images and videos of violence perpetrated against human beings. In fact, it is no longer uncommon for mainstream news outlets to depict graphic images of dead bodies for all to see, and certainly not uncommon to hear reports about murder, accidents, and suicide. One unintended but nevertheless important subconscious effect of this background is that we have been desensitized to the greatness of a human. In the Jewish tradition, animals also have value and deserve to be treated with respect. But human beings are infinitely more integral to the goals of the universe, and therefore have more inherent worth and value. As the Talmud teaches, "Whoever destroys a soul is considered to have destroyed an entire world. And whoever saves a life is considered to have saved an entire world" (Sanhedrin 37a).

What makes human beings so special? The immense capabilities of the human race might be most clearly apparent when we ponder amazing human achievements within our society. Some of us have incredible capabilities—whether gifted naturally, attained through refinement, or perhaps both—such as amazing athletic abilities that seem physically impossible. Some have the capacity to perform complex multistep mathematical equations in seconds, without a calculator. Others have the incredible ability to memorize names, places, or people, by the hundreds. Even more impressive, many human beings put their unique and sophisticated skills to work to dramatically improve the lives of others at a seemingly exponential pace. For example, about a century ago, chemists first learned how to create fertilizer from thin air, putting us well on our way to relegating hunger to the dark annals of our past within the developed world. As well, medical scientists have now tamed or exterminated many illnesses that ravaged our ancestors' communities for millennia. Such developments continue into the present day, perhaps to a greater degree and at a faster pace than ever.

But looking at the achievements of outliers misses an important point. On an individual level, as members of Western society, we seldom pause to consider how integral even the most ordinary person is to the functioning of the world. This is because we value the achievement of fame and fortune by individuals much more than the contributions of many individuals to our collective whole. However, it would not be difficult to argue that manual laborers such as plumbers and sanitation workers have more important jobs than pop singers, politicians, or even psychologists. We couldn't last a week without indoor plumbing or garbage collection. Similarly, consider the Apollo space mission program. The climax of landing on the moon, which was undoubtedly one of the greatest achievements of mankind, is typically ascribed to a single man: Neil Armstrong. However, we must recognize that NASA employed over four hundred thousand individuals and relied on over twenty thousand industrial firms to accomplish this feat. This is not intended to detract from Mr. Armstrong's courage and skill, but we must recognize that just like virtually all other great feats of humanity, landing on the moon was not accomplished by a lone individual. In these regards, ordinary human beings who walk around and do their thing play a critical role, even if they occupy the least valued and coveted positions within our society.

In fact, looking at any human achievements misses an important point. Even basic human abilities to see, hear, taste, touch, smell, speak, comprehend, walk, or turn a doorknob with our opposable thumb are nothing short of remarkable. As we discussed in chapter 12, unfathomable complexity is involved in the most basic human behaviors, but we seldom stop to appreciate those gifts. Our limited recognition of the inherent spiritual value of a human being has plummeted in recent decades, in part because our culture has promoted standardized testing within the academic system. The IQ test in particular has robbed a large portion of the population of their confidence and led millions to the erroneous belief that only a handful of metrics effectively judge a person's value. Our focus on certain discrete forms of ability and productivity fails to recognize our inherent value. It has also made it more challenging to recognize the importance of creativity and unique talents, despite the fact that the most impactful people in history have all relied copiously on such abilities. More importantly, our economy is not mission driven, aside from the simple and typically nonspiritual goal of increasing productivity and making money. By contrast, throughout the first half of the twentieth century, American industrial workers took satisfaction and pride in building the economic backbone of their country. Along these same lines, developing a godly vision of ourselves involves recognizing our innate spiritual value, our unique gifts, and the mission and value behind what we do every day. As Rabbi Kelemen taught me, *all* human beings have a sacred role to play in this universe—all we need to do is believe that fact and find ways to hone it and bring it into reality.

Several years ago, I treated an elementary school teacher who was deeply stuck in her professional life. Katie had been teaching fourth-graders how to read for close to three decades, often facilitating dramatic improvements in their skills. She liked her work but had intermittently suffered from depression inspired by persistent doubts about her talents and the relative value of her work. I wasted no time discussing this aspect of *Spiritual Connection* with Katie.

"Do you realize how different our civilization would be if we did not maintain near-universal literacy skills? You just said that you're good at your job and have seen some students in your class go from reading the alphabet to full-length books," I shared.

"Yes, but a lot of them still won't pick up a book unless I assign it to them. They'd rather be playing video games or watching YouTube videos on their iPads. And if my job is really so important, why doesn't anyone else care? The reality is that anybody can do it!" Katie retorted, and I realized that I had my work cut out for me.

Like many of us, Katie evaluated her value in comparison with other people. She considered her sister who was a doctor, for instance, and she often regretted not having worked toward a similarly respected and well-paying profession. But part of the reason that Katie had not chosen a similar path was that she had become a mother at a young age, and by the time she began working it would have been impossible for her to balance her household needs with medical school. Her sister, on the other hand, had no children, so she was able to devote all her energy to her career.

Over the following weeks, I discussed the *Connections Paradigm* with Katie. She was not particularly religious or spiritual, but ironically the *Spiritual Connection* concept of developing a godly vision resonated with her. "I suppose you're right, Dr. Rosmarin," she said at our fourth session. "I brought my daughter into the world, which is a unique job that only I could do. And you're also right that teaching is a lot harder than many people appreciate. Why do I get into these patterns of negative thinking about myself, and how can I stop them?" I was pleasantly surprised with Katie's progress, and so I ventured an educated guess about her technology use. In the ensuing discussion, Katie and I exchanged ideas regarding social media, and it seemed that we were on the exact same page. In the current era, we not only have celebrities to compare ourselves with, but also have everyone we went to high school with, our distant cousins, and people around the world

208 | The Connections Paradigm

whose achievements we see daily in pictures on Facebook, Instagram, and LinkedIn. Katie acknowledged that her most recent depressive episode began when she was perusing social media pages of her old friends and became filled with negative ideas about her chosen profession.

"What did you see online?" I asked.

"Oh, the usual. I noticed that I was the *only* teacher of all my friends, and that everyone else's career is so much more interesting and important than what I do," Katie responded with a sigh.

"But what's the meaning behind their accomplishments?" I asked.

Katie sat and thought for a minute before reverting back, "I know what you're going to say. There is inherent value in teaching, and I should be happy with what I do. Is that right?"

"Partially," I responded as my mind raced to find words to help Katie over this important hurdle. "I was going to add that there is also inherent value in being a mom, and that you are uniquely good at your job, and that your students love you for a reason, and that you're too hard on yourself."

Katie smiled and replied, "Well, that is all true. So, how can I stop getting into these states? Should I just drop the social media?"

"That might help," I responded, "but I think there is something more. I know you're not particularly religious, but have you ever thought about your job in spiritual terms? Like the idea that you have a godly role to play in the world through teaching children to read?"

Katie started to cry. "Can you please tell me that again? I need to hear that again."

I took my time responding since Katie seemed not only receptive but truly interested in learning more. "Katie, you are a gifted teacher. The *Connections Paradigm* would say that is no accident. You have a God-given talent to teach and uplift students so that they can go on to do all sorts of things. Consider that you have a part in *any* accomplishment that *any* of your students does that requires reading, throughout their entire lifetimes! Even more importantly, by using your abilities as a teacher to help your students, you're playing a special role in God's world."

Katie took in the message. In the weeks that followed, her mood was significantly better and her spirits clearly uplifted. At our final session a few weeks later, Katie conveyed to me that it was truly helpful to consider her profession in spiritual terms. "I never thought of teaching as having transcendent meaning before," she shared. Katie and I have kept in touch over the past few years. To our mutual surprise, she has not had any significant relapses in depression since her treatment, and when her mood dips from time to time she finds much solace in the idea that her job is part of a greater spiritual plan.

Developing a Godly Vision for Ourselves

In other cases, however, the main issue is not simply having a godly vision *of* ourselves, which involves the conviction that we *can* spiritually connect to God in a fundamental and profound way through our day-to-day lives. Rather, the struggle is to have a godly vision *for* ourselves, which involves identifying specific roles for ourselves to play in the world that create a sense of *Spiritual Connection* day to day. Of course, without having a godly vision *of* ourselves, it is impossible to have a godly vision *for* ourselves. But even if we see the inherent spiritual value in ourselves, it can be challenging to find avenues to express ourselves in the world and apply our gifts in the service of the divine. More specifically, developing a godly vision *for* ourselves has two parts: developing *generic* visions for us as members of the human race, and developing *individual* visions for our unique skills and circumstances.

Regarding the former, it is clear that God wants certain things to be done by everyone, such as eating healthfully, exercising regularly, sleeping adequately, and having regular social contact. God also imbued each of us with fundamental spiritual needs that can be fulfilled by prayer, other spiritual practices, and spiritual study and discussion. As we discussed in the chapters of this book discussing *Inner Connection*, engaging in behaviors to fulfill these basic needs can foster body-soul connection. However, doing so can also potentially facilitate *Spiritual Connection* if one keeps in mind that they are doing it because it is the will of God. This is because doing *any* activity that one believes is God's will elevates our intentions to the realm of *Spiritual Connection*. To that end, one can potentially build *Spiritual Connection* doing almost anything, such as taking out the garbage, tidying one's desk, doing coursework, paying bills, taking a shower, or going to sleep, as long as we view it as reasonable to believe that it's something God wants us to do. The other side of the coin is that, even though God wants all of us to do these things to take care of ourselves, performing them without God in mind will not bolster our *Spiritual Connection*.

In contrast with generic godly visions for ourselves, individual godly visions involve identifying unique ways that only we can fulfill God's will. Each human being is a once-in- history occurrence, born into a time and place with specific challenges and social needs. If our faith is strong, it thus stands to reason that each person has a unique once-in-world-history job to do. There are certain things that you and only you can accomplish—things that no one has been or ever will be assigned, because they are unique to your cognitive, behavioral, emotional, physical, and spiritual profile. A major challenge to developing an individual godly vision for ourselves is our tendency to eschew our own paths and follow others from a lack of courage. This is tragically a common yet major mistake, since God set up the world in a way that each person has a specific role to play. Thus, *if we don't take the charge and fulfill our unique (not just generic) potential, the world will be incomplete.* God set up the world in a way that God depends on each of us to do our individual jobs, and each of us can be a star in God's divine plan if we do our unique job to the best of our ability. Of course, it takes patience, perseverance, faith, courage, and immense effort (which we will discuss in the next chapter), but if we pursue our path with diligence, we can be guaranteed that we will succeed in an utterly unique way. Those who copy others are, by definition, not on their own path, and they emerge perpetually frustrated when they don't see the success or satisfaction that they hoped for.

I believe that our modern, service-based economy has made it particularly difficult for a large number of us to envision a unique path for ourselves. Typically, productivity is quantified with metrics as opposed to qualitative assessments, and our sense of accomplishment is decreasingly personalized and abstract. As well, many young people struggle to choose a satisfying career path because there is so much opportunity in the modern economy that they do not wish to take risks that are inherent in finding their own, unique path. The reality of developing a godly vision *for* ourselves is such that it often takes many months, years, even decades of trial and error until we can spread our wings and get some air. This was the case with Jacob, whom we discussed in chapter 2. Jacob had complacently chosen to stay in an easy and comfortable job for years, even though it was unfulfilling and left him depressed. This was largely because Jacob was afraid to choose a path that was more specific to his unique talents and skills, since he could not muster up the courage to potentially fail. Yet, the more time Jacob wasted in his current job, the more his sense of unfulfillment grew and the harder it became for him to break free.

Regretfully, Jacob and I terminated treatment before we could discuss this facet of *Spiritual Connection*. However, I was able to help a different young man in a somewhat similar circumstance.

At his first session, Justin told me, "A year ago I was excited and full of hope, now I feel like I'm already washed up." I resisted my urge to chuckle seeing that Justin was only twenty-two years old. Also, in truth, Justin had genuinely been struggling lately. His last year in college had not been what he, and especially not his parents, had hoped for. After three relatively productive years of college, his senior year was marred by a series of mistakes that had severely damaged his prospects after graduation. Academic probation followed his involvement in multiple incidents of on-campus misconduct, and he finished his final semester with two failing grades and an incomplete course. He needed to complete a full load of four courses in order to graduate, but he could not do any more coursework until his academic probation expired at the end of the calendar year. His father, a successful businessman with a spotless personal and professional record, was livid.

"I feel like he kind of set me up for this," Justin told me, referring to his father. "He has always been so hard on me. He never let me out at night on the weekends with friends when I was in high school, and he kept such close tabs on me in college that I was never really able to socialize much until I started doing my own thing. There was never any balance. I think if he had given me more freedom to act out a little, I would have made better decisions. But I sort of started panicking at the beginning of this year because I realized that I was going to graduate soon and then I'd need to get a job and start working for my entire life. I don't know myself well enough to decide what I'm going to do forever! But I know that I don't want to work at Costco." Justin fell into what he described as a "deep depression" and started partying very hard. One of his misconduct incidents involved a clash with campus police when Justin was under the influence of cocaine. The other was an accusation of sexual assault, which Justin had no recollection of since he was so inebriated at the time of the alleged incident.

The psychometric assessment that Justin completed before his first session indicated that he was not as depressed as he believed; in fact, his depression scores were subclinical. But he was clearly deeply discontented with his life circumstances, and he was floundering with very low self-esteem. "My dad basically threatened to cut me off financially if I didn't take the first job I could get. One of my friend's moms works at Costco, so I asked him if she could get me an interview. I went there the next day and I had my name-tag printed and laminated by the following Monday." Justin's compensation was not terrible by many people's standards, but that did nothing to assuage his dissatisfaction. He described feeling "incredibly bored" during his work shifts and spent most of his time daydreaming about the ways that his work could be completed even more efficiently by machine. "I sit there with a clipboard and wait for trucks to come in, then I make sure the stuff in the trucks is the same as what's written on the paper. You almost couldn't imagine a more boring job." To make matters worse, Justin had moved back to his parents' home, and within just a few days they were micromanaging his affairs by demanding that he take weekend shifts that prevented him from socializing with friends. When he resisted, they threatened to reduce their financial support in various ways such as taking away his car. During one particularly heated exchange, Justin's father threatened to tell his grandparents, whom he respected deeply, about his campus misconduct.

Generally speaking, if a patient or anyone solicits my advice about a job they dislike, I often encourage them to look for a better opportunity. But Justin's situation seemed stagnant since he was in a holding pattern. As he put it, he was "killing time" until he could take his final courses and graduate. However, it seemed a waste not to encourage Justin to think about his longer-term plans. And so during one of our early sessions I casually asked him, "What would you want to do if you *did* have the opportunity?" Justin quipped back, "Do you mean now? Or after graduation?" I clarified that at the current time Justin did not seem to have many options, so I was referring to his path after finishing college. "I usually say that I want to be a lawyer when people ask," he said, "but to be honest I never really had any interest in law. It was just one of two options that people like to hear these days, and I definitely am not going to be a doctor." I peppered Justin with nonjudgmental open-ended questions about what he wanted in life professionally and otherwise, and in the end most of his hesitations about himself boiled down to one thing: his father's expectations. "I just can't imagine doing what my dad thinks I should do—finding a job right after graduation, or going to law school and then finding a job after finishing that degree—and staying in my career for thirty years. I know that's what he did and it worked out okay for him, but it's just not that common anymore. I just feel so much pressure from him to produce that I don't even know what I want to do!" Justin went on to say that many of his friends got desk jobs after graduation and they "crunch numbers all day" in order to make money for their corporations. "What's really the point?" Justin asked, rhetorically.

Psychologically speaking, Justin had clearly not found his passion. In *Spiritual Connection* terms, though, the problem was much more profound: he had yet to find a mission-driven godly path for himself that would feel rewarding and also leave him with adequate and respectable compensation for his time and efforts. I tried to get Justin to be open to other ideas by asking if he had any hobbies or other nonprofessional interests that he was passionate about. I shared with him that "work is not the only way we can do something meaningful. Volunteering or honing an art form, even as an amateur, and especially if we can help other people while doing it, can be deeply satisfying." In this discussion, Justin told me he had once been very serious about playing basketball, but he lost interest toward the end of high school when it became clear that he was not going to go pro.

Over the ensuing weeks, I continued to engage Justin in discussions about his interests and professional goals. I kept emphasizing that all people have an important role to play in the world, and this idea seemed to resonate with Justin. I also encouraged Justin to think more carefully about the importance of his current position. At one of our sessions, I said to him as follows: "In the meantime, why not make the best of what you're currently doing?" Justin initially insisted that his job was far too tedious to be worthy of any passion. But I challenged him to think about the systemic consequences that would plague Costco as a company, or its customers, if it did not have adequate shipping and receiving clerks.

I conveyed as follows, "The corporation would certainly lose money and maybe they would go out of business. And customers would not be able to find what they need. Do you realize how many people rely on stores like yours for food and essentials? I'm not saying you should stay in your current job forever; it may not be your ultimate mission in life. But I am certain that your work is very important. And since you're stuck where you are for now anyway, why not figure out why?"

"I was always conditioned by my environment to think that menial jobs like the one I'm doing are certainly not important, and if anything a bit shameful," he told me, "but the more I think about it, the more I realize how important it really is. Also, frankly it has its challenges and I'm pretty good at it."

The following week, Justin approached his supervisors to share some feedback about how his job could be done more effectively and efficiently. He even offered some suggestions about other employees, and his supervisors praised his initiative. Justin seemed to be moving in the right direction.

At a subsequent session, I broached the topic of *Spiritual Connection* with Justin more directly. Justin conveyed to me that he was not religious at all, and that he didn't pray or even have specific beliefs in God, but he did believe there was *something out there running the universe*. When I probed further, Justin shared that he saw spiritual meaning in helping others, and that he started to feel a bit more uplifted spiritually since having his conversation with his supervisors a few weeks earlier. "I just want to add value, I guess," Justin said, and I validated this need as a natural human tendency that was worthy of nurturing and attending to. Over the following weeks and months, Justin really cleaned up his act. He stopped all forms of drug use—without us addressing the topic directly—and his low mood was significantly improved. Notably, Justin started to attend more to his body's needs in regards to diet, exercise, sleep, and social activity. But Justin's most impactful weeks of therapy were yet to come.

"Justin, I'm going to ask my question again to you—the one I asked a few weeks ago. What would you want to do if you *did* have the opportunity?"

Justin knew I was referring to *after* his graduation, but surprisingly he responded in the present. "Well," he said, "I've been looking into technology. There is a firm that developed an application by which truckers can connect with warehouses to find loads to take with them on return routes. It's potentially disruptive, because it will help the truckers make more money directly without their dispatchers, but that could create a great opportunity for them and the app developers, and also for the companies that pay for trucking services."

I encouraged Justin to reach out to the app company to make a connection, which he did. He ended up landing an interview for a position that was not even posted, and within a few weeks Justin was offered a job.

"I decided that I need to see the current process through first. I want to graduate and be done with college. But, I think the company will be interested in speaking after I finish my degree," Justin shared, with a smile on his face.

As we will learn in the next chapter, *Spiritual Connection* involves not only developing a godly vision but devoting our available efforts toward fulfilling it. Just sitting with a vision will leave us unfulfilled. However, before wrapping up this section, one final point must be emphasized: developing a godly vision of/for ourselves extends well beyond the professional spheres of life. Building *Spiritual Connection* extends to any arena of serving God, such as artwork, music, volunteering, and certainly through raising a family and taking care of our loved ones. Even self-care, as described above, can be an integral and holy aspect of life and opportunity to connect with God. This is an especially important point for those without formal employment who need to manifest a godly vision in their uncompensated day-to-day actions. Stay-at-home parents have an unfortunate tendency to undervalue their importance. This has long been true for moms, who have seen society's valuation of full-time child rearing sink as more women join the workforce, but it is often even more problematic for full-time dads, who struggle to reconcile their practical need to take care of their children with conventional paternal roles. To clarify, not all lifestyles aim toward a spiritually connected mindset, and our trajectory at any given time may not generally agree with our true spiritual purpose when we sit and think about it. However, it is possible for any and all domains of life to be dense with opportunities for *Spiritual Connection*.

Exercise 14: Dreaming Big

Sometimes we need a reality check when we are striving toward implausible goals, but most of the time we need just the opposite. For this exercise, spend sixty seconds dreaming about a potential central purpose in life that aligns with your specific passions and skills. This may involve reflecting on your past successes and considering what you truly want to do with your time. As you contemplate your dream, also consider if your vision is something that you think God would want for the world. Once you find something that you love and that is consistent with what you think God wants, dream big by focusing on the vision.

CHAPTER 15

Spiritual Connection Part IV:
Exerting Heroic Efforts for God

In chapter 14, we discussed developing a godly vision in which we take a mission-focused approach to life and dream big about what we would like to accomplish. This can be in any domain, such as health, fitness, finances, our professions, our character, and interpersonal relationships. Having clear dreams is itself spiritually powerful since it can enhance our faith in God, in ourselves, and in others. Furthermore, according to the *Connections Paradigm*, taking time to deliberately hone our dreams and develop visions with high-definition clarity is part of giving back to God, so to speak. However, dreaming without spending the time, energy, and resources to bring our visions into reality effectively shortchanges us from *Spiritual Connection*. The result of not backing up our visions with real investment is that our dreams tend to either wither away, which is tragic, or, worse, come into fruition without our efforts and we lose out on the opportunity to *work* toward a relationship with God.

To these ends, the present chapter—which caps our discussion of *Spiritual Connection*—is about exerting heroic efforts for God. This can be summed up as doing everything possible to see our godly visions come to fruition (figure 16). Constantly exerting heroic efforts for God may seem to be an unachievable ideal. Many people I introduce this concept to are afraid that "heroic efforts" requires exhausting all mental and physical energy for our spiritual

FIGURE 16 Exerting Heroic Efforts for God

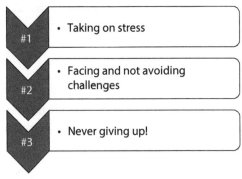

Exerting heroic efforts for God involves digging deep and doing whatever we can to see our dreams turn into reality. This is very difficult to do because it necessitates the following:

#1 • Taking on stress

#2 • Facing and not avoiding challenges

#3 • Never giving up!

missions in life. However, this misconception is based on fundamental misunderstandings about *Inner Connection* and *Interpersonal Connection*. As we discussed in chapters 1 through 5 of this book, *Inner Connection* involves not only pushing our bodies past our comfort zones (chapter 2) but also loving the body, providing for all its needs (chapter 3), and tolerating our idiosyncrasies and shortcomings with love and patience (chapter 5). The ideas discussed in the present chapter assume that one has a loving, caring, supportive, and compassionate body-soul relationship, such that the soul would *never* exhaust all of the body's mental and physical energies for the sake of spiritual growth. Further, as discussed in chapters 6 through 10 of this book, interpersonal relationships are a critical aspect of connection. Thus, we can thrive only when we spend the necessary time and energy to notice and provide for other people's needs and develop emotionally secure attachments. Most importantly, as stated throughout this entire book, *Inner Connection* and *Interpersonal Connection* are therefore necessary though insufficient conditions for *Spiritual Connection*. Regarding exerting heroic efforts for God in particular, at times our efforts may create temporary stress and strain on our relationships internally and with others, but the contents of this chapter assume that people do not sacrifice earlier approaches to connection in the service of spirituality.

The basic concept of exerting heroic efforts for God is that *Spiritual Connection* requires us to push ourselves to achieve our goals and dreams. Devoting time, energy, strength, money, emotions, attention, and more to our cause—to pursue our dreams— is a spiritual value of the *Connections Paradigm*. Understandably, people who push themselves for their dreams will feel stress. However, in contrast to Western culture, which values comfort and happiness, the view of the *Connections Paradigm* is that we can achieve *Spiritual Connection* only under some degree of stress.

In fact, according to the *Connections Paradigm*, stress and struggle are a good indication that someone is on a path toward growth. While in pursuit of our dreams, we must expect to feel stuck, lack inspiration, and even be terrified, for following our dreams tends to come with substantial risks of financial loss, failure, embarrassment, and even injury. These risks are particularly difficult to withstand when one is mentally/physically exhausted from these efforts. Thus, it is perfectly normal and should be expected that if one is truly exerting heroic efforts, they will doubt their own abilities along the way.

Feeling despair about our abilities, however, is not a bad thing from a *Spiritual Connection* standpoint, since it can help us to have better recognition of the limits of our scope of control (chapter 12). By pushing ourselves to capacity to realize our dreams, we become palpably aware that our best efforts are truly not enough to achieve our aspirations, and we need to rely on God for assistance. However, if we balk and pull back from our efforts by giving up, we miss the point and lose out on the opportunity for *Spiritual Connection.*

It is for these reasons that many people struggle to exert heroic efforts for God. "It sounds like a nice idea, but I think only a monk could actually do it," Matteo, a landscaper in his mid-fifties, said at one of our sessions. Matteo had no trouble conceiving of his daily labor as spiritually significant. He had a decent relationship with himself, was beloved by his family, and had a clear vision for his landscaping business. He even viewed his honest and challenging day-to-day work as having a godly component. "Sure, I think God is happy that I'm working!" he said without batting an eyelid when I asked. "However, I'm happy with my work as it is and don't want to push the limits. Things are stable, why would I rock the boat? I have my truck and my equipment and I work on my own, sometimes with 1–2 other guys. It's a simple, happy life."

Every once in a while, Matteo thought about expanding his business. He loved working with his hands and thankfully was in good health and spirits, but he realized that at some point down the line he would not be able to continue. "It's scary, you know? A good friend of mine—also a landscaper—strong guy also around 55 like me. Last year he got injured with a mower. He was feeling sick and went to work anyways and tripped, and now he's all laid up. Had to sell a lot of his equipment just to stay afloat because the insurance company put up a fight. I really don't want to end up like him, but I also don't want to make things harder for myself. I want to spend time with my new grandson." Furthermore, on the surface Matteo was choosing a spiritual path. As a deeply religious churchgoer, Matteo reported significant revelations and increased satisfaction as a result of our connections work, but he did not find that exerting heroic efforts for God, at least the way that I defined it, was a path to greater spiritual awareness. "Believe me, I know my work is holy, Dr. Rosmarin," he said. "You've helped me realize that beautifying the neighbor-hoods is really a beautiful thing to do for God. But I think it's enough for me to pray at home to remind myself. I don't need to push beyond what I'm already doing."

I heard Matteo's predicament loud and clear. He was approach-ing retirement age and starting to feel more connected with his family and God, and he didn't want to rock the boat. But beneath the surface were undertones of fear and doubt in himself, and also doubt in God. I myself didn't know whether Matteo could or would be successful if he tried to grow his landscaping operation. And his concerns were valid ones that I could not and would not refute. But it seemed to me that his true reasons for not wanting to pursue the expansion route indicated a lack of *Spiritual Con-nection*, in some regard. I chose not to push Matteo to exert he-roic efforts to pursue his dream of growing his business, until he got hurt on the job one sunny day in June. Thankfully his injury did not involve a lawnmower, and he did not suffer permanent damage, but he did lose the rest of his landscaping season, save for general maintenance and mowing that his part-time crew could attend to. At that point, I decided to address the issue di-rectly, but before I could, Matteo had already intuited the direc-tion I was going in. "I know, I know," he said, "I'm going to do it. God clearly wants me to build the business." And he didn't waste any time. Matteo had a good relationship with his bank manager, and his first step was to secure a line of credit against his family home. He then invested heavily in a website and marketing mate-rials in preparation for the fall cleanup season, snow-removal sea-son, and the following spring and summer. He also invested in staff, starting with an administrative assistant who could help with bookings and running of day-to-day operations.

And then Matteo hit a wall. "I can't go on like this. I've used up half my line of credit. I can't sleep because I'm so anxious. What have I done?!" Matteo felt that he was in over his head, but my sense was that he just needed to stick it out. "You've taken bold steps to grow your business. You're hitting a wall and that's to be expected. Nothing has changed from last week—nothing at all! You're on course. Just stay the course and it will be okay," I said, privately hoping and praying to God that I was correct. Matteo started to pray as well—literally, while in my office, he held his head in his hands and started speaking to God. I couldn't make out exactly what he was saying; all I could hear was "please, please, please," but I realized what was happening. Matteo was exerting heroic efforts for God and had come to a point that his personal efforts were simply not enough to achieve his goals, so he was turning to God for additional support. As I sat and looked at Matteo, it dawned on me that an outsider viewing this scene may see him as a depressed and disheveled human being crying in a therapist's office because he is overly stressed from work. However, through the lens of the *Connections Paradigm*, all I saw was Matteo's greatness: he had a godly vision, he was exerting heroic efforts for a godly mission, and he was recognizing the limits of his control to strengthen his *Spiritual Connection*.

Thankfully (thank God!), Matteo was successful in expanding his business. His path to success was not linear—he had ups and downs, typically in the pattern of two steps forward and one step backward—but within two years he was employing a dozen workers. During the two years it took to build up to that level, he had less time with his grandson, he missed church once in a while, and his self-care decreased to some degree. But he never went more than a month without church, and all along the way I encouraged him to stick with a reasonable schedule for diet, exercise, sleep, and time with his loved ones. In the end, Matteo seemed not only happier and more connected across all three domains but also more secure. This was not because he now had a thriving business, but rather because he had a deep internalized faith that God would be there for him.

In other cases, however, a lack in preceding levels of connection can undermine our heroic efforts for God. Ingrid, a Catholic hospital nurse I treated for anxiety, had a job that was perfectly conducive to *Spiritual Connection* since she worked 36 plus-hour shifts and gave her all for her patients. She had wonderful *Interpersonal Connection*, in that she routinely noticed and provided for the needs of others in her personal as well as professional life. But throughout her incredibly busy workday, particularly when she was under stress, Ingrid found herself feeling unfulfilled. "Are you feeling overwhelmed?" I asked. "Not really," Ingrid responded. "I just don't feel energized by what I'm doing. I know in my mind that it's important, but my heart just isn't into it. If it were just a lull, I wouldn't be concerned, but it's been years since I felt spiritually connected at work."

Ingrid and I spoke about the matter at length. "God is simply too much to focus on at work," she told me. "After a good night's sleep and early morning meditation, I remember my godly vision and how meaningful my work is until around lunchtime. But after that, the best I can do is focus on my body and doing my best to take care of my patients' needs with love. Recently, when I've been trying to devote my actions to God, nothing about my mind-set has felt connected." I was confused, since it seemed that Ingrid was doing everything right. She had a meaningful mission-driven job, she was exerting herself in a serious way, and she was not neglecting the needs of her individual body; she was not feeling resentful or self-critical in any way I could detect. And so I asked again about Ingrid's relationships with others, just in case I had missed something. Lo and behold, Ingrid disclosed to me that she had a few recent relapses in *Interpersonal Connection*. For several years—before coming to me for treatment—Ingrid had suffered from bitterness and anger toward her coworkers. At one point she was even known as the "nasty nurse" on her unit, a title she was ashamed of and embarrassed by. As we discussed her situation more, I realized that Ingrid was pursuing *Spiritual Connection* at the expense of *Interpersonal Connection*, and the result was a lack of both.

"You actually called your boss a b*@)^ in front of the entire team?!" I asked, with a smile on my face. Ingrid responded, "It was after a long shift and I'd been pushing myself too hard for a long time. I really want to do what's right by God, you know? My patients need me, and I love helping them. But she just doesn't appreciate me, and she undermines me. I just lost it. It was not a good moment, and ever since I've felt terrible at work." "But that was nearly six months ago!" I remarked, with a warm and compassionate look. "I know, it wasn't good. I'm in a bad place," she said. Ingrid and I worked on a plan to clear the interpersonal disconnection by approaching her boss with an apology. It was not an easy plan for Ingrid; she was still very angry inside. And so I encouraged her to write a letter that offered an apology along with an explanation of what she was upset about and what continues to upset her in the workplace. It took two weeks for Ingrid to write the letter and another week for her to give it to her boss. But eventually the message was delivered, and fortunately it was well received.

Reflecting on the situation, Ingrid shared, "I should have known by the fact that I was devoting so much time to work that something was wrong." I disagreed with her assessment. "There is nothing wrong with hard work, Ingrid," I shared. "The only problem was that you were pushing yourself as a way of not dealing with an interpersonal issue, as opposed to doing so in order to connect with God and others." Ingrid seemed sad that she had slipped, and so I comforted her. "Listen, if connection was easy, it wouldn't be worthwhile. Nothing in life that's worthwhile is easy! Keep pushing yourself in all three domains of connection and you will continue to grow. The goal isn't to arrive; it's to perpetually strive toward higher levels of connection at all three levels. *All* human beings struggle with disconnection from time to time. It's a hard balance to get it all right! And life is never static, but rather a dynamic and interactive process. If you're struggling to maintain connection, it's actually an indication that you are on the right path. So, keep it up!"

During our next session, Ingrid reported two interesting discoveries. The first was that over the past six months she had not been doing nearly enough to meet her body's needs. And ironically, her *Spiritual Connection* was also lacking since she had stopped praying and recognizing from her heart that, ultimately, God is in control. "In some regards, I think I was working extra hard because I felt that God was unable to care for the patients," she shared with me. "There is such subtlety between exerting heroic efforts for God and doing so without a God consciousness!" she added. I concurred but clarified that I thought Ingrid's hard work was a manifestation of her *Spiritual Connection* since she was exerting heroic efforts for God. However, I postulated that she was unable to close the loop from exerting efforts to recognizing the limits of her control, due to a lack of *Inner* and *Interpersonal Connection.* I shared with her that "when we exert ourselves to the max, it makes it impossible to recognize the limits of our control. In that context, we are more likely to feel irritated and show anger toward others who get in our way or put us down. And all of that makes it impossible to truly rely on God and feel like we are being carried spiritually through life." Ingrid chimed in, "I know that you're right, Dr. Rosmarin. When I focus on taking care of myself by not taking on responsibilities to the point of visceral stress, everything else gets easier. I have more energy to remember the important things, and I feel closer to God." After that discussion, Ingrid naturally returned to exerting heroic efforts for God, but she did so at a slower pace that enabled her to also recognize the limits of her control.

There are a few additional aspects of *Spiritual Connection* that require discussion with regard to exerting heroic efforts for God. As emphasized above, stress is not something we should shy away from entirely if we wish to live a connected spiritual life. Bringing forth our unique potential in the world inherently involves some level of stress. However, the *Connections Paradigm* takes this one step further by encouraging us to never give up on our dreams. Human dreams are not simply artifacts of random neural activity. They are a window on our unique physical, emotional, and spiritual profile in this world and offer a glimpse into our spiritual role in the universe. Giving up on a dream is tragic since each human being is unique, and if we don't take the opportunity to bring our dreams into reality, the world will be missing our contribution. As the Jewish sages taught in Ethics of the Fathers: If not now, when? (1:14). If we don't take the opportunity to pursue our dreams during our lifetimes—with all our heart and soul— when will we be able to try to bring them into reality? And when we consider that any aspect of our lives can constitute divine service—when we consider the *Spiritual Connection* concept that our ultimate goal is the service of God—the stakes are high.

However, it is crucial not to fall into a common trap experienced by many who aspire to serve God heroically: getting caught up in outcomes as opposed to the process of exerting ourselves. According to the *Connections Paradigm*, being successful in ushering our dreams into reality is not the point, since ultimately all outcomes are within God's hands and out of human control. Rather, "success" in *Spiritual Connection* is entirely measured by how much sincere effort one expends, *not* whether one attains one's goals. As we discussed in earlier chapters, human beings have a limited scope of control, and God is ultimately in charge. This means that God determines whether we achieve what we set out to do with our small capacity to influence change. For these reasons, *Spiritual Connection* involves simply exerting heroic efforts in order to bring our dreams into reality. Actual achievement—even of deep, wonderful, spiritual, meaningful visions—is not the goal. Our only duty is to try, and God will decide whether we are successful. This cannot be emphasized enough. Even though making heroic efforts for God orients toward certain objectives, achieving these objectives will *not* strengthen our bond with God in and of itself. Exerting effort to do that which we believe is most agreeable to God at every moment—whether or not we'll be successful—is the source of our highest spiritual satisfaction and the ultimate goal we are striving for.

Last year I met the director of a prominent nonprofit organization who truly had learned the importance of sincere hard work versus success in her tireless efforts to help some of the most vulnerable and disadvantaged people in the world. Virginia grew up in a Mennonite community where serving the least fortunate was held in high regard. Though she became largely secular as a young adult, a commitment to serving others remained her personal and deeply spiritual focus throughout her life. After volunteering for two summers as an English teacher in Ghana during college, Virginia embarked on a work/study program in which she earned a master's degree while working with a nongovernmental organization that educated children and young people across central and West Africa. Her first year of fieldwork helped her clarify her sacred life mission, though she didn't consider it as such at the time. "Almost all of them were farmers' kids. We were teaching them math and English so that they could move to cities and get decent jobs, but they couldn't come to school half of the time because their parents needed them to work. It was obvious that we needed to help the parents before we could do anything meaningful for the children." Virginia's poignant realization was even more apparent when a punishing drought severely stressed local agriculture in the early 2000s. "The school was almost empty because the kids were either helping their parents desperately try to save their crops, or out in town scrounging for food. The ones who came in were so hungry that they could barely stay awake, let alone learn. All we could do was watch and dole out as much of our own pantry as we could afford, which was never enough."

Ultimately, the drought made it impossible to continue her mission, and Virginia returned home to the United States, downcast and defeated. She ended up in my office after a severe three-week depressive episode left her virtually bedridden, and she was literally dragged into her first session by her two closest friends. I remember the session vividly since Virginia could barely speak and one of her friends attended the intake meeting. As we spoke, I realized that Virginia was officially depressed, but the root of her condition was feeling stuck in the realm of *Spiritual Connection*. "Of course you feel terrible! You've spent years abroad trying to teach English in order to help the world, and you've come to the realization that it's not enough. I'm so glad you came here, Virginia." She already looked a lot brighter with that validation, though she had a long way to go. Over the next several weeks and months, Virginia and I spoke about the *Connections Paradigm* in general, and *Spiritual Connection* in particular. The ideas resonated with her immediately, and she recognized that she had been dreaming big and exerting heroic efforts for God in a beautiful way for many years. "What should I do now, though?" Virginia asked. I didn't have any answers, but I was confident that if Virginia did not give up on her dreams—even though they seemed impossible—a light would shine again. I shared with Virginia that she had made one simple error: "The goal of *Spiritual Connection* is not to achieve," I said. "Rather, it's to try. Don't conflate the outcome with the process—the process is much more important! My suggestion is to simply start searching for other opportunities to volunteer in Africa. Something will turn around, just give it time. Maybe God is putting you on a different path so you can have even more impact than you think?"

Virginia had earned her degree and had several years of great experience. She was also clear that she did not wish to continue with an educational organization, since it was insufficient to achieving her ultimate goal of helping African children and families. With that in mind, and some improvement in her spirits, Virginia began searching for new opportunities. She started out slowly (at my encouragement) and ultimately identified several other not-for-profit organizations focused on improving economic resources to African families. One of them in particular caught her attention, since its mission was to provide access to clean water and teach efficient and sustainable agricultural methods to farmers. The organization seemed a natural fit for Virginia given her extensive teaching experience; however, it had no vacancies posted for employment. "Why not contact them anyway?" I suggested. "Worst-case scenario, they won't return your call? What do you have to lose?" My intention was to refocus Virginia on the process, not the outcome. By calling and applying for a job—even if it was not available—she was continuing to pursue her dream. To our mutual surprise, Virginia received a call back from her inquiry followed by an invitation for an in-person interview in the organization's Washington, DC, office.

Within two months, Virginia was back in Africa in a leadership position with substantial responsibilities. She was even given a small staff of other like-minded young people who came as volunteers from around the world, and she was granted a sizable budget. Virginia studied innovative agricultural methods being used across the developing world, and she immediately started making heroic efforts to implement them. Our sessions could not continue with her move to Africa, but we kept in touch by email and did the occasional session via video chat. "I had heard about a project in Liberia in which they imported guinea pigs because they breed fast and can thrive on almost any vegetation. So, we're now preparing to bring them to Ghana and teach people recipes of dishes from Peru where they're considered a delicacy," Virginia told me. Virginia's team also imported freshwater species of tilapia and catfish, which breed and grow easily in small ponds and poor water quality. They also distributed peanuts to farmers and taught them to interplant them with the most popular local crops, cassava and millet, because they not only provide an additional edible crop but also enrich the soil. All of these ideas were promising, and Virginia and her team worked to implement them relentlessly. But problems arose sooner than expected.

"Apparently the climate in Ghana isn't suitable for guinea pigs, and our entire colony died in a matter of weeks. The peanuts grew much slower than we expected because there wasn't enough phosphorous or calcium in the soil. The tilapia and catfish did okay, but only a few of the farmers either had ponds already or were able to dig them. Our first season was basically a complete failure," she shared with me a few months into the project. However, Virginia drew on her knowledge of the *Connections Paradigm* and did not slip back into a depression. She understood that the task in front of her was simply to try, not to succeed. And she got right back to work, researching other options for her staff to implement for the betterment of the farmers of Ghana. Virginia found many approaches—some of which worked, and others of which did not. Later, she became the director of one of the largest not-for-profit agencies in the region, one that has been lauded by the international press for improving hundreds of thousands of lives. In a recent email exchange, I asked Virginia if things are easier than before. "Not a chance," she shared with me. "I have more doubts and fires to put out than ever. But I'm happy because I constantly try to refocus myself onto what I *can* do, and accept the reality of that which I cannot change. I also look back and see God's hand throughout this whole process. Circumstances beyond my control brought me to my current position, and it would have been a much greater failure if I had given up."

The *Connections Paradigm* teaches that each step we make toward carrying out our godly vision is important in its own right, even if it does not bring us closer to our goal. Thinking about all the incremental steps involved in any goal, and all the vicissitudes and setbacks that are bound to happen along the way, can be intimidating and overwhelming. However, refocusing ourselves on the process of bringing our big dreams into reality can keep us oriented toward God. Another perspective is to try to remember that every challenge we face on the road to bring spiritual goals to fruition is a divinely orchestrated opportunity for growth. This is because, according to the *Connections Paradigm*, we can and will be successful if we pursue our true paths in life. When we hit setbacks, they are typically tests of faith for us to push through, and/or divine attempts to redirect us onto another road. Either way, by continuing to exert heroic efforts and never giving up on our dreams, we can remain spiritually connected. Along the way, all the highest virtues, including dedication, courage, bravery, perseverance, leadership, humility, prudence, hope, and faith, are more deeply forged in the face of difficulty.

Exercise 15: Exerting Heroic Effort for God

For our final exercise, we will identify a simple activity that we believe God wants us to do, and exert ourselves to complete it, for the sake of fulfilling God's will. The action could be a distillation of a dream that we have, or something simple that we believe God wants us to do, such as a basic act of self-care. The latter is typically an easier target and therefore recommended for individuals who are not used to exerting heroic efforts for God.

As you do the activity—big or small—try to envision that you are doing it simply for God. Envision that God wants you to do this activity, and that exerting effort to accomplish it is a divine act and a way to connect to God. Also, envision that completion of the act is beyond your capability, since ultimately God is in charge. Along these lines, as you perform the activity, try to do so with a prayerful mind-set by asking God to help you achieve the aims of the task.

Conclusion

This book is meant to serve as a concise introduction to the *Connections Paradigm* and its basic methods for establishing and maintaining mental health. As mentioned in the introduction, virtually all other written materials about the *Connections Paradigm* are in the Hebrew language, so for most readers there is no other textual source with which to develop an understanding and nurture sustained practice of connection. Readers are therefore encouraged to review the text on a regular basis (particularly areas they are struggling with) in order to stay inspired by its insights and proficient in its practices. Keeping just a few of the paradigm's most central tenets in mind each day and incorporating even some of the exercises we've practiced into our routines can be of great benefit. To help readers keep the *Connections Paradigm* in mind, this concluding chapter seeks to briefly review the entire paradigm.

At the beginning of the book, we learned four core concepts of the *Connections Paradigm*. First, at any given moment, each human being dwells in either the *World of Connection* or the *World of Disconnection*. These worlds are characterized as follows: connection involves compassion, generosity, bravery, and love, whereas disconnection involves separation, isolation, resentment, fear, and anxiety. Second, we learned that connection involves the coming together of two complementary and opposite entities—(1) the body and soul (*Inner Connection*), (2) disparate human beings

235

(*Interpersonal Connection*), and (3) human beings with God (*Spiritual Connection*)—whereas disconnection involves estrangement of these entities. Third, we learned that these areas of connection are hierarchical. The relationship between our body and our soul is the foundation for our relationships with others, which in turn is the foundation for our connection with God. Attempting to jump into *Spiritual Connection* in an isolated state or seeking to love others without responsibility and self-compassion are approaches that will fail in the long run. Finally, we learned that in each domain of connection there is a giver and a receiver. The soul gives to the body, which receives its guidance and kindness and responds by following diligently while providing feedback along the way. We connect with others when we can put others' needs first while being true to ourselves by sharing our inner worlds with them, and when we remain connected despite the natural ebbs and flows of social conduct. And spiritually, we can choose to receive by recognizing God's greatness and influence, while giving back (so to speak) in the form of pursuing our innermost hopes and dreams with wisdom, dedication, and passion.

Addressing Setbacks

In working on connection, perhaps the most important thing to remember is not to be discouraged by setbacks. As we learned in chapter 5, human beings are by nature imperfect and *will* struggle from time to time—wrestling to stay connected is par for the course. Furthermore, even if we abandon our efforts for an extended period of time and fall deeply into disconnection, previous heights can be reestablished relatively quickly if we return to diligent review and practice. As in any area of human behavior, relapses can even offer opportunities for new growth by revealing points of structural weakness in our earlier progress.

I have found that the most common reason for setbacks is when people push themselves too far too fast. As stated above, *Inner Connection* is the foundation of *Interpersonal Connection*, which is the foundation of *Spiritual Connection*. When we are tired, hungry, physically exhausted, or emotionally strained, it is generally not reasonable to expect ourselves to give unconditionally to others, tolerate pain that others are causing us, or exert ourselves heroically for God. Thus, when we hit setbacks in connection, it is generally best to address connection hierarchically, starting by reviewing *Inner Connection*.

It is worth noting, though, that when we experience setbacks due to a lack of *Inner Connection*, it's possible that we can still experience *Interpersonal Connection* by expressing our needs to others and providing them with opportunities to give us support. We can also have *Spiritual Connection* when we are stressed by contemplating God's role in nature and in our lives, and by having faith that we are spiritual beings with unique and special jobs that we can accomplish over time.

The Need for All Three Domains of Connection

Most forms of psychotherapy focus exclusively on only one of the domains of the *Connections Paradigm*. Grossly speaking, cognitive behavioral therapy attempts to help individuals master their inner worlds through maintaining awareness and control over their thoughts (self-talk) and behaviors. By contrast, marriage therapies such as emotionally focused therapy help couples notice and provide for each other's emotional needs, in the service of deepening their bond. Few forms of psychotherapy focus on God, but there is an emerging literature of approaches to help individuals create greater *Spiritual Connection* in order to bring about greater mental health. The *Connections Paradigm*, however, is unique in that it brings all these domains together. Attending only to our inner worlds without our interpersonal connection, or even deepening both of these domains without attending to spirituality, short-changes the process and the person.

Many will find that certain sections of our discussion were more engaging and seemed more relevant than others, based on personal predilections, challenges, aptitudes, and interests. Among my more religious patients, for instance, *Spiritual Connection* is often where they demonstrate the strongest enthusiasm. By contrast, I've found that spiritually inclined but irreligious patients are more likely to be especially intrigued by *Inner Connection*, and those who are naturally more social are often particularly inspired by *Interpersonal Connection*.

It is perfectly natural to take special interest in certain aspects of the *Connections Paradigm*, but because humans are complex beings composed of body and soul, and who live in a social context with great spiritual potential, I cannot stress enough the importance of cultivating *all* domains of connection, even while prioritizing whichever domain is most in need of attention at any given time.

Several years ago, I worked extensively with a young man who had recently returned to treatment for what he termed a "connections tune-up." Eric had initially come to treatment for depression and found significant relief through our work with the *Connections Paradigm*. But a sudden rough patch set him back, just when he felt as though his connection was reaching a climax. "It completely snuck up on me," he said. "One month I was sailing. Everything was going great with my marriage, my work, and my godly vision. I really felt at peace for the first time in my life. And then one day I realized that my body and soul were not in sync, I wasn't really making an effort to notice other people's needs, and I was barely ever giving any thought to my godly vision." As we discussed his predicament, subtle causes for Eric's relapse became apparent.

"What happened during the week when you first started feeling disconnected?" I asked.

"A lot," he said. "My wife and I were arguing over nothing. But that was because I was feeling really grouchy. She's been consistently supportive and it wasn't her fault. I had too much on my plate. My son's baseball team had three games and I was the coach, but my heart wasn't in it. I had just finished three night shifts in a row at work."

"It sounds like you weren't taking care of yourself."

"Not as much as I needed to, I guess. But the next week I was well rested and I still didn't feel much better."

"What was going on then?" I asked.

"Come to think of it, that was also the week that I stopped doing my *Interpersonal Connection* exercises for three days. I haven't really been doing them as much since then, and I've been really stressed out with a coworker," Eric responded.

"And then what happened?" I asked.

"I tried to right the ship by focusing on my spirituality, but that just made things worse."

As we spoke further, it was clear to both Eric and me that he was displaying a valiant effort to maintain connection in all three domains. But he would invariably push ahead in higher levels before attending to lower levels, and he let the latter fall off his radar in the process. It turned out that his decline could be traced to seemingly minor neglects in *Inner* and *Interpersonal Connection*, almost entirely across the board.

At the risk of being redundant, *Inner Connection* is the most important of all, since it is the foundation of the entire hierarchical structure of connection. Yet for many people it is the least popular domain. Newcomers may find the idea of engaging with their inner dynamics to be too abstract, and those who have a sense of body and soul typically want to ascend to higher levels very quickly. Similarly, *Interpersonal Connection* is the next most fundamental, since our relationships with others are a context for our relationship with God, and interpersonal relationships provide key skills that are needed to connect spiritually. But as powerful as *Inner* and *Interpersonal Connection* are, the vast growth opportunities of *Spiritual Connection* are simply not possible without efforts to deliberately draw close to God.

Inner Connection

Inner Connection (figure 17) is characterized by a mutual loving relationship between body and soul. In order for each party to accede to this pact, *both* body and soul must be trained to connect

FIGURE 17 **Review of *Inner Connection***

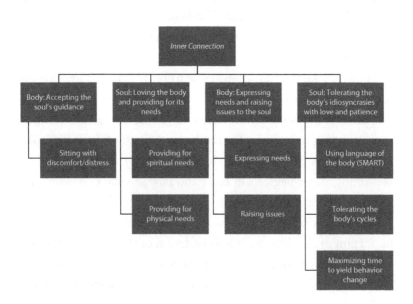

with one another in a giving and caring manner. To that end, in this book we discussed four areas of *Inner Connection*. Two of these areas focused on the body receiving from the soul, and two focused on the soul providing for the body. We encouraged the body to tolerate distress in accepting the soul's guidance, and to express its needs and raise issues to the soul. We also encouraged the soul to provide for the body's spiritual and physical needs, and to tolerate the body's idiosyncrasies with love and patience. More broadly, by entering the world of *Inner Connection*, the body learns to get outside of its own experience and confer with its soul in decision-making, even when under stress, while simultaneously remaining true to its limitations and communicating effectively when issues arise. Conversely, the soul learns to get outside of *its* own experience and to become a quintessential giver to the body, as well as providing specific and reasonable guidelines and practicing self-compassion when the body falls short of the mark. By distilling lofty visions into tangible, practical, and inspiring guidance for the body without being overly demanding, the soul becomes a godlike giver who is never harsh or critical toward its partner. Corresponding to each of these concepts, we had a series of exercises. These included having verbal conversations between body and soul, habituating our bodies to distress by doing activities that are uncomfortable, bestowing gifts (e.g., of food) to the body for enjoyment out of love, encouraging the body to raise issues and express needs to the soul, and speaking words of encouragement and love to the body when it is struggling.

Interpersonal Connection

Interpersonal Connection (figure 18) involves deepening our love for other people through giving and receiving. In this book, we discussed four aspects of *Interpersonal Connection*. Two focused on

FIGURE 18 Review of *Interpersonal Connection*

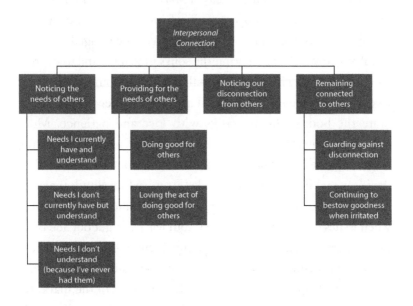

building connection with others, and two focused on decreasing disconnection from others. First, we increased our awareness of others' needs at three levels: those needs we currently have, those needs we have had before but don't presently experience, and those needs we have never experienced. Corresponding to this, we had a daily exercise of noticing others' needs. All of this is connection, because by noticing the needs of others, one gets outside of one's own experience and enters another person's world. Second, we put our increased awareness of others' needs into action by actually providing for the needs of others. More importantly, we strove to make a hobby of taking care of others by feeling excited about doing acts of kindness for others. This is also connection, because by providing for others and doing loving acts of kindness, one can enter the world of another person and connect with them. Third, we *increased* our sensitivity to disconnection from other people by noticing minor behavioral manifestations of irritability and anger that we may exhibit. Our corresponding activity was to count the number of times each day that we display or exhibit any disconnection. This is essential to connection because Western standards of disconnection are very low compared with those of the *Connections Paradigm*. And finally, we strove to remain connected to others by guarding against disconnection and readying ourselves for irritation when others cause us irritation/anger. To this end, we visualized ourselves bestowing goodness on another person who recently irritated us. This too is connection, because without tolerance and kindness in the face of irritation, our relationships cannot be sustained over time.

Spiritual Connection

Spiritual Connection (figure 19) involves our relationship with God. In this book, we turned our attention to four aspects of this domain of connection: two focused on experiencing God's presence in our lives (receiving from God), and two focused on fulfilling God's will (giving to God). First, we worked on recognizing our limited scope of control and relying on God during simple activities on a daily basis. This is connection, because it helped us recognize our dependence on God for help and protection, which is critical for having a relationship with God. Second, we increased our awareness of order and design in the world, in order to generate gratitude toward God. Our corresponding activity was to contemplate the nutrition and enjoyment that God places in one piece of food each day. This is connection, because gratitude creates a sense of being loved by God. Third, we harnessed our feelings of gratitude to propel ourselves forward in our *Spiritual*

FIGURE 19 Review of *Spiritual Connection*

Connection by developing a godly vision *of* ourselves and *for* ourselves. That is, we recognized our capacity for greatness and contemplated the generic and individual ways in which we can contribute to God's world. Our corresponding activity involved dreaming about our divine purpose in life. This is connection, because God created each human being to succeed in a unique mission, and dreaming is a necessary first step to achieving our divine purpose. And finally, we discussed the importance of exerting heroic efforts for God and stopping at nothing to achieve our dreams. This too is connection, because by pushing ourselves to capacity to realize our dreams, we become palpably aware that our best efforts are not enough to achieve our aspirations without divine assistance, and we must turn to God for help.

FIGURE 20 Exercises to Facilitate Connection

Inner Connection

Exercise #1, Building Body-Soul Communication:
Communication is essential to facilitate connection in any relationship. *Inner Connection* is no different: our souls and bodies need to communicate with each other in order to build connection. Our first exercise, therefore, is to have a written dialogue every day between your body and your soul that lasts for at least three volleys. There are no rules regarding the content of the conversation; it can be about anything.

Exercise #2, Sitting with Discomfort/Distress:
Once per day, (a) engage in an activity that your body avoids because of discomfort/distress, although your soul recognizes that it poses no real threat to your well-being, or (b) refrain from engaging in an activity that your body does excessively to escape discomfort/distress although your soul recognizes that the behavior is not truly necessary for your well-being, and (c) reward yourself after completing the exercise. The purpose of this exercise is for your body to build connection by tolerating and accepting distress and discomfort.

Exercise #3, Providing for the Body's Physical Needs:
Once per day, have your soul select a gift of food for the body, initiate a conversation with the body about the

gift, and bestow the gift to the body. Imagine that your soul is giving food to your body, and encourage your body to feel grateful to the soul for the gift.

Exercise #4, Expressing Needs: A critical facet of *Inner Connection* is for the soul to listen to the body. To this end, it's important for the body to open up and connect by describing its needs and speaking to the soul even if it feels uncomfortable, and for the soul to patiently listen to what the body has to say. Therefore, our fourth exercise is for your body to freely describe a need or raise an issue to your soul, in as much detail as possible, once per day. Have your body connect to your soul by speaking freely and without constraints; don't hold anything back.

Exercise #5, Tolerating the Body's Idiosyncrasies with Love and Patience: This exercise involves the soul tolerating the body, once per day. Conjure up a recent event in which your body fell short of a goal, and have your soul speak words of encouragement and love to your body. It's recommended that you take three minutes to do this exercise each day (ninety seconds of conjuring the past, and ninety seconds of speaking words of encouragement). The goal is for your soul to remain lovingly connected to your body when the body doesn't fulfill your expectations.

Interpersonal Connection

Exercise #6, Noticing Others' Needs (Part 1): This exercise is to notice others' needs, once per day. You can noticing any need, physical or spiritual, that another human being has at any point during the day. The point of the exercise is to leave our own internal world for a moment and actively delve into the experience of another person. At this point, we are not involved in providing for others' needs. The goal here is simply to notice: To perceive and understand what others lack.

Exercise #7, Noticing Others' Needs (Part 2): Once per day, notice a need that another person has, when you do <u>not</u> currently have the same need. For example, you could notice that someone else is cold, when you yourself are feeling warm. The goal is to break out a little bit more from our internal world, and delve into the unique experiences of others. Just as with exercise #6, this exercise could be done with any need, physical or spiritual, that any other human being has, as long as it's something you are not concurrently experiencing as well.

Exercise #8, Providing for the Needs of Others: Once per day, after noticing a need of another person, provide for that need (by giving to them or receiving from them). It's a big bonus if you can conjure up an internal sense of love for the other person, while you're doing it.

Exercise #9, Noticing Our Disconnection from Others: Each day, count the number of times that you engage in a behavioral manifestation of anger or irritation, regardless of how small, toward other people. The goal of this activity is to sensitize ourselves to our *Interpersonal Connection* by lowering the threshold for disconnection in our lives.

Exercise #10, Remaining Connected to Others: Once each day, complete the following visualization: Remember a time when someone triggered anger, irritation, or resentment inside of you, and you responded with disconnection. Recall the event vividly in your mind. What did they do? What effects did it have on your life? Now, recall how you responded to the event. What did you do to disconnect from the person? As you remember the event and your response, imagine what would have happened had you not disconnected. Picture them acting just as they did, without any changes, but this time, imagine yourself guarding against the disconnection and continuing to bestow goodness on them.

Spiritual Connection

Exercise #11, Feeling God's Presence: Once each day, try to feel a sense of reliance on God while you engage in a simple activity. As you do an everyday activity (e.g., turning on a light, standing up from your chair, or writing with a pen), cultivate some awareness that God must be involved in order for you to be successful in the activity.

The goal of this exercise is to facilitate greater awareness that God is present in our lives, and we are responsible to be active players in God's world.

Exercise #12, Recognizing Our Limited Scope of Control: Once each day, spend sixty seconds recognizing the limits of our scope of control by contemplating a situation in life in which you are vulnerable. Imagine a scenario or situation in your life that could go badly—very badly—and picture in great detail the terrible consequences that would occur if the worst-case scenario were to materialize.

Exercise #13, Tasting the Blessing: Once each day, when you eat or drink something, try to feel that God placed nutrition and good taste into the food or drink, just for you to enjoy, and express thanks to God (verbally or mentally).

Exercise #14, Dreaming Big: Once each day, spend sixty seconds dreaming about one of your specific and unique divine purposes in life. While you are contemplating your dream, consider whether your vision is consistent with what you perceive to be God's vision for you and the world (i.e., whether you think God would like your dreams to come true).

Exercise #15, Exerting Heroic Effort for God: Once each day, exert heroic effort for God. Identify an activity that you believe God wants you to do, and exert yourself to complete it.

Acknowledgments

As a midcareer clinician-scientist who studies spirituality/religion and mental health, I was excited when Susan Arellano and Angelina Horst from the John Templeton Foundation called me about a potential project. My feelings quickly turned to trepidation, however, when I learned that Nick Gibson had suggested my name as an author for a book about Jewish perspectives on mental health. On the one hand, I have been blessed to contribute to the clinical science of Judaism and mental health together with my esteemed and wonderful colleague Steven Pirutinsky, senior colleague David Pelcovitz, and many others. But on the other hand, I am not a rabbi, nor can I be considered a Torah scholar by any definition of the term. So I felt ill equipped to present an authentic Jewish perspective, especially in the form of a book destined for a broad audience beyond the Jewish world.

However, as Dale Carnegie famously advised, I've surrounded myself with people far cleverer and more knowledgeable than I will ever be. I feel truly blessed to have rabbinic mentors who are not only masters of the Torah but psychologically savvy, and they understand emotional health in ways that never cease to amaze. My wonderful mentor and teacher Rabbi Leib (Lawrence) Kelemen of Jerusalem has been an incredible life guide. His Torah knowledge is surpassed only by his incredible character, both of which I have been most privileged to observe and learn from over the past twenty years. As readers will discern from the very first pages of this book, virtually all of the Torah content within this

251

volume is surmised from my limited understanding of Rabbi Kelemen's teachings. Needless to say, any errors or omissions are due to shortcomings on my part and do not reflect any lacking in my wonderful mentor or his perspectives.

In closer physical proximity to my family home in Boston, I have been privileged to learn from Rabbi Naftoly Bier, his esteemed partner Rabbi Zalman Leff of the Kollel of Greater Boston, and their many students. Their fine institution serves as a small but powerful beacon of Torah light, attracting professionals, scientists, engineers, academics, and students to tens of classes and one-on-one learning sessions each week. I have long said that I could not live in Boston if it weren't for the Kollel. More specifically, Rabbi Bier is an accomplished and sought-after pastoral counselor who provides more hours of clinical care each week than yours truly. His vast and deep Torah wisdom has indelibly shaped my approach to clinical work.

My rabbinic friend-mentors from the International Organization of Mussar Vaadim also deserve special mention. Rabbis Meir Kaniel, Ben Geiger, Yisroel Gelber, Daniel Goldman, and Yosef Weissman (known collectively as the AVL) have been incredibly supportive comrades. They have also provided inspiration and clarification to formulate many of the ideas found within this book. My close friends Dr. Larry Kurz, Omeed Hakimi, Yaakov Nourollah, and Yoni Torgow have also been wonderful companions, and I have learned more from them than they may ever realize.

The John Templeton Foundation has a broad vision: to accelerate discovery, inspire curiosity, and thereby facilitate scientific and spiritual progress. I am most grateful to the foundation for funding this project, for its previous support of my research, and more broadly for its dedication to spirituality and health research around the globe. Along these lines, I'd like to thank my academic

mentors Drs. Ken Pargament and Harold Koenig, for investing countless hours of advice, support, and collaboration into
my training. I shudder to think where the clinical science of
spirituality/religion would be without their dedication to the
field as a whole.

Within the Harvard Medical School, I've been blessed with
several "champions" who have not only encouraged me but enabled my career to flourish. Dr. Phil Levendusky took a risk by
hiring me just over a decade ago, knowing full well about my area
of academic focus on spirituality and mental health. He along with
Drs. Brent Forester, Thröstur Björgvinsson, and Scott Rauch
(president and psychiatrist in chief of McLean Hospital), as well
as Linda Flaherty, have been wonderful academic mentors and
supports each step of the way. I must also thank McLean Hospital's chaplain Rev. Angelika Zollfrank for being a skilled, dedicated, and ever-thoughtful colleague. Without the presence and
encouragement of all these individuals, this book could not have
materialized.

Writing is always a complicated endeavor, and this book is no
exception. I am most grateful to Susan Arellano and Angelina
Horst for spending hours upon hours to review, edit, and consult
on the development of each chapter. Dan Reilly also deserves special mention for his help in promoting the book, as does my assistant Moshe Appel for his help with the copyediting review. Most
of all, though, I must publicly thank Sean (Shalom) Carp, my student and friend of many years, who helped prepare many aspects
of the manuscript with painstaking attention to detail. Sean has
an uncanny ability to synthesize esoteric philosophical concepts
with case material, and he was indispensable throughout the entire project.

This book is dedicated to my parents, Ian and Pam Rosmarin,
from Toronto, Canada, in appreciation for their support of my

Jewish education. Individuals outside the Jewish community may not realize that in most locales outside of Israel (including Toronto), Jewish day schools are not publicly funded, and they also tend to be relatively small in size. This leaves a very significant tuition burden for families in the range of $8,000–$32,000 per child, per year. My parents heroically sacrificed to put me and my two younger siblings through Jewish schooling K–12 and beyond. I am eternally indebted to them for this alone, let alone their broader support, encouragement, advice, and love.

The Talmud teaches that the great sage Rabbi Akiva left his family to study at Yeshiva (an academy of Torah study) for twenty-four years, after which he finally returned home, accompanied by twenty-four thousand disciples. His loyal and dedicated wife, Rachel—who had been living in dire poverty to support his cause—was so excited that she came out to greet him wearing ragged clothing. The students, not recognizing who she was, tried to push her aside. Rabbi Akiva stopped them from restraining her and gave an immediate and clear response: "What's mine and yours, is hers." Rachel's faith in Rabbi Akiva's ability as a scholar was the ultimate cause of his great success, and therefore he credited her with his scholarship. Similarly, anything I have accomplished, whether in my career or otherwise, is solely due to the loyal dedication of my wonderful wife, Miri. She is my most precious gift—my confidant, best friend, and life partner in every way.

Finally, I would like to thank God for bestowing me with more blessing in my life than I could ever deserve or imagine. My ultimate hope and prayer is that I use the resources I've been given to live a life of connection between body and soul, with others, and with God.